The Psychology of Religious Experience
in its Personal and Institutional Dimensions

American University Studies

Series VII
Theology and Religion
Vol. 49

PETER LANG
New York · Bern · Frankfurt am Main · Paris

Bruce T. Riley

The Psychology of Religious Experience in its Personal and Institutional Dimensions

PETER LANG
New York · Bern · Frankfurt am Main · Paris

Library of Congress Cataloging-in-Publication Data

Riley, Bruce T., 1908-1987
    The psychology of religious experience in its
personal and institutional dimensions.

        (American university studies. Series VII,
Theology and religion ; vol. 49)
        1. Experience (Religion)   2. Psychology, Religious.
    I. Title.   II. Series: American university studies.
Series VII, Theology and religion ; v. 49.
BL53.R49   1989   291.4'2'019   88-8818
ISBN 0-8204-0862-X
ISSN 0740-0446

CIP-Titelaufnahme der Deutschen Bibliothek

Riley, Bruce T.:
The psychology of religious experience in its
personal and institutional dimensions / Bruce T.
Riley. – New York; Bern; Frankfurt am Main;
Paris: Lang, 1988.
    (American University Studies: Ser. 7, Theology
    and Religion; Vol. 49)
    ISBN 0-8204-0862-X

NE: American University Studies / 07

© Peter Lang Publishing, Inc., New York 1988

Printed by Weihert-Druck GmbH, Darmstadt, West Germany

Contents

PART 2

The Structure Of Personality

PART 3

Personality Modification In Religious Experience

viii   *Contents*

PART 4

The Institutional Reference

Appendix

Part 1

The Categories of Our Inquiry

I. Difficulties Inherent in the Study of the Psychology of Religious Experiences

The investigation of religious experience involves certain inherent difficulties which must be recognized at the outset, and be overcome or avoided if the study is to have validity. Hence we bring them immediately into review, with such suggestions for their resolution as are appropriate. These factors, structural to the material, which hinder effective research are (A) the essential subjectivity of religious experience, (B) the problem of accurate distinction between religious activity and religious experience, (C) the particularity of the data in the field, so that any generalized conclusion often seems unattainable, (D) the lure of supernaturalism, and (E) the systematic obfuscation of those who are, for whatever reasons, unsympathetic to the inquiry.

A. The Essential Subjectivity of Religious Experience

It is axiomatic that the student of religious experience must depend for his data upon the reports of those to whom such experiences have come, since they are in their essence intimate and personal. This of course, means that the data cannot be reproduced experimentally, and that, since he is getting his information at second hand, the investigator is at a considerable disadvantage: for the subject reporting such experience may be insincere, and not have had the experience he is describing: he may exaggerate, minimize, or falsify an experience he has really had, or he may lack words to describe it, since such experiences are often inchoate, and the symbols are unfamiliar. Then too, since religious experience typically involves paranormal factors, he may be bashful about admitting that he has seen visions or heard voices, and either minimize the occurrence, repress it, or refuse to discuss it.

Yet on the other hand, and over and above a subject's unwillingness to report what he has seen and felt, the greatest difficulty in the interpretation of religious experience may well be found in the seeming *objectivity* of the experience itself: for when it occurs most typically, it takes the form of a personal communication addressed to the subject by some being external to him, and of supernal importance. Since the subject finds the message of enormous significance, he will insist unwaveringly on the objectivity and reality of the being who has thus communicated with him.

However, certain fully objective factors await the observer's attention: *bona fide* physical healings, indisputable recoveries from alcoholism or drug addiction, the regaining of mental health, the restoration of morale after grief or discouragement, the attainment of unusual insights, and the initiation of notable reforms.

Then, too, the extreme importance of any valid religious experience to the one who has it is such that he probably will try to recount it as accurately as he can, to a listener who is sympathetic. Furthermore, there is a degree of similarity in numinous experiences which will enable the investigator to detect insincerity, and, with a background of experience in the area, he will be able to attain enough rapport with the subject to guarantee a veridical account. Thus the subjectivity of our material is no greater than in any other area of psychology.

B. Religious Quest and Religious Experience

A second difficulty, unnoticed until recent years, is the necessity for distinguishing clearly between religious search and religious discovery. Many activities obviously "religious" are not characterized by anything that could be called religious *experience*, e.g., a person attending a religious service simply for form's sake. Again and more vividly, consider the difference between the experience of a person *seeking*, and that of one *receiving* a healing, say, at an Oral Roberts meeting! Since we are interested in the actual moment of religious fulfillment, this involves a fairly neat collection of problems, some of them profound. For instance, what are the criteria of religious experience? Is it a religious experience when a person begins to pray? What prompt him to begin praying? And what, psychologically, has occurred when his prayer is answered? The distinction between these two perspectives on religious phenomena will be implicit to our entire study. Fortunately, simple awareness of the need for making this distinction will save us from obvious instances of confusion, and enable us to analyze whatever perplexities remain in the area.

C. The Particularity of the Investigation

The employment of this subtitle does not mean that our investigation is either trivial or circumstantial, but simply that it is almost impossible to employ universal propositions in expressing our results. Thus, we find it impossible to predict that the same event will always produce religious activity. For instance, what will make a person pray? A bomb scare? A threat to the safety of his family? The fear of death? For one person, at one time, any of these may precipitate the religious quest: but for another person, or the same person at a different time, it may not produce religious activity at all. By the same token, the religious quest may result in religious experience for a given person on one occasion and not on another: and no one else may gain religious fulfillment from such activity at either time. Furthermore, religious experience occurs on many occasions with no antecedent quest at all. Finally, in advance of the event, it is impossible to say what may produce religious fulfillment, i.e., of what such an experience may consist. It will be our task to rise above particularity to as great an extent as possible in dealing with the maze of questions here involved.

D. The Lure of Supernaturalism

All traditions of institutional origins agree in ascribing them to some supernatural source. Also, a religious subject who has had a fully numinous experience is typically so overwhelmed by it that he will refuse to consider or discuss it in any but supernatural terms. Then too, for a long time anyone who cared enough about the psychology of religion to give it serious attention was located within the framework of some institution, and thus imbued with its traditions. Thus, it is not surprising to find early writers in the field concerning themselves with invalid questions, such as how to invite religious experience, i.e., under what conditions a supernatural being might be likely to visit a given subject. Moreover, this theological orientation is by no means extinct, and those working within it are immutably grounded in a conservatism that precludes any approach to the material except that of their own orthodoxy.

Furthermore, there is pressure for supernaturalism from an entirely different quarter—those who are preoccupied with the occult, perhaps as a result of some involvement with psychedelics.

With so much archaic opinion confronting one who would explore the area, and with popular disapproval of anything remotely approaching impiety being what it is, the temptation to make the psychology of religion merely an exercise in learning how to deepen one's own faith, is all too understandable.

Nonetheless, and despite the rather thin line that sometimes separates the paranormal from the supernatural, we shall seek our explanations of religious experience within the natural order.

E. Systematic Obfuscation

Although discussing the circumstances of religious experience in terms of a supernatural referent may be admirable for devotional purposes, and excusable from a promotional standpoint, this perspective does nothing for academic clarity, and yet it is still to be found in the literature to a surprising extent. As indicated in the preceding section, pressures in this direction are considerable, and from one end of the institutional spectrum to the other, we find writers yielding to them, and hedging their statements about religious experience to the point where the reader cannot be sure they realize that the phenomena are indeed subjective.

The discipline within which we are seeking to interpret these phenomena is psychology, and not metaphysics or theology. It is our responsibility to attain clarity at this level, and to make our explanations in these terms: this would seem to be self-evident. However, our task is constantly made more complex by supposedly responsible investigators who confuse these distinctions, surprisingly and inexplicably.

II. Presuppositions of the Study

A. Naturalistic Frame of Reference[1]

While it is altogether likely that we may run across circumstances which we are unable to explain immediately, yet the point of view is that explanation in the naturalistic framework is, in principle, available for any of the phenomena with which we shall be dealing. We are in no sense trying to explain religious experience *away*, or "reduce" it to anything else: we hold firmly to what seems to be an obvious proposition, namely that religious experience is a fact in its own right, just as is radioactivity, orgasm, gravity, ESP or the Republican party. Each of these indubitable factors of human experience exists in its own right, and *investigation* of their nature, causation, relationships and results is recognized without question as permissible and appropriate, within the framework of whatever scientific discipline is fitted to make the analysis. Certainly no apologetic would be expected for avoiding explanations that involved the supernatural if we were investigating radioactiv-

---

[1] For a statement of what is meant here by "Naturalism" the reader may consult Ernest Nagel's fine essay, "Naturalism Reconsidered," which has been reprinted in many anthologies.

ity; and the situation is not otherwise, as regards the study of religious experience.

Nonetheless, there are two important points to which we must call attention here.

The first is, that despite our avowedly naturalistic stance, no reader will find anything in these pages that argues against the validity of any numinous experience he may have had; if he chooses to believe that ultimate reality has broken in upon him, so be it: we are simply describing how it happens. We take it for granted that such an experience is of supreme value to the one who has it, and he will find that he is able to interpret it in his own way without repudiating the explanations that we advance.

The second point is, that we shall, from time to time, use the expression "revelatory experience." This is used in the sense of "revelatory to the subject," or "experience conveying religious certainty," and has no metaphysical overtones.

B. Religious Experience Does Occur

However truistic this expression may seem, it does, in the writer's opinion, need to be made, since he has met repeated expressions of skepticism, particularly from students, as to the actual facticity of the material under consideration. Some of those expressing such dubiety have thought that people claiming religious experiences were faking them all the way; others, evidently sharing the writer's naturalistic point of view, would deny the whole experience, in seeking to dispute its supernatural claims. Still others, unwilling to concede important results to anything so tenuous and perplexing, would deny the connection between religious experience and its effects (e.g., the cure of alcoholism), and insist that the change in personality was due to something else, thus, in effect denying all reality to the religious experience itself.

While we are not trying to promote religious experience, any more than we are trying to explain it away, we do insist upon its factuality, as an important phenomenon of human life. Such experiences of new energy entering consciousness upon a tide of sacredness are at the center of the entire religious syndrome, and are its dynamic. Moreover, while in no way commonplace, they occur more frequently than the merely casual observer would suppose.

C. Religious Experience Is Important

For the most part, religious experience is of the very highest value to its subject, since it is typically the occasion of some profound autistic modification, whereby the personality gains effectiveness. Through this psychic mechanism, innumerable troubled personalities have gained tranquility, integration and purpose. In those rare cases where it has a negative impact, as when a person becomes convinced that he has committed the unpardonable sin, or comes to numinous certainty that the devil has marked him for his own, the experience is of intense *disvalue*, but is beyond question significant.[2] Moreover, as hinted in our preceding paragraph, it is basic to the institutional dimension of religion, since these organizations have come into being as custodians of its insights.

Thus its interpretation is of corresponding importance, which provides the motivation for the present work.

III. Observations on the Nature of Religious Experience

A. Identifiability

Our criterion for the authenticity of religious experience will be the presence of numinosity, or in popular parlance, a sense of the sacred. The term, coined by Rudolph Otto, comes from the Latin word *numen*, meaning spirit, or god. The adjective *numinous* means affected with divinity, or pertaining to the divine. Hence *numinosity* means a situation, or a state of mind, preponderantly affected with divinity. For our purpose we shall consider it to mean *the emotion that a subject feels in the presence of a religious symbol*.

The question might reasonably be asked why we do not take the presence of the symbol itself as the identifying factor, rather

---

[2] See the section on *Efficacy*, III, B, 4, *infra*, pp. 11–12.

than some state of mind which it inspires. The answer is to be found in the stubbornly subjective nature of religious problems, and of the symbolism by which they are solved. Symbols cannot be standardized, however hard institutions may try to accomplish this: it simply is ineffective to show a religious subject a statue, a dogma, an icon, a concept, a legend or anything else, and insist that he has been religiously serviced. On the contrary, since the problem is subjectively experienced, anything at all may have the symbolic effect of solving it for him: if this happens, religious experience is present, however, trivial or obscure the symbol may seem. What is *never* obscure is *the way the subject feels* when this happens—he feels numinous. Hence we take numinosity as the dependable symptom of the experience we are investigating.

Furthermore, by taking the emotion as the criterion, we have moved a little closer to some objectively verifiable evidence of the deeply subjective experience under consideration: and the emotion itself is a part of the experience. If the subject murmurs affirmations, looks ecstatically happy, lifts his hands, kneels down, weeps, or appears suddenly resolute in the midst of profound discouragement, and does these things without regard for their stage effects, we have some grounds for assuming that he is having an important inner experience. Of course we are still admittedly dependent upon the integrity of the one reporting.

Since the function which the symbol must perform, and the personification presented by the unconscious to perform it, have such an infinity of variations, the attendant emotion may be anything from unalloyed beatitude to utter dismay, or even horror. However, upon analysis, the emotion will be seen to be the subject's reaction to the sense of supreme valuation, plus mystery, which is structural in the appearance of any religious symbol.[3] As indicated above, the valuation may be either

[3] Indeed, it is a matter of terminology whether we say that, as an emotion, it *is* the supreme-valuation-plus-mystery, or that it is the response to such an awareness.

positive or negative, but is never less than ultimate, since the symbol solves a religious problem. The mystery, which, when combined with the supreme valuation, constitutes the specific difference of this emotion, rises out of the subject's total inability to understand either the symbol or the sudden rush of energy that it structures and thus liberates. It (the mystery) may be expressed in three questions: (1) What is it? (2) Why do I value it so much? and (3) Why did this happen to me?

Thus when fully and unfeignedly present, the numinous emotion is the invariable concomitant of everything that is essentially constitutive of religious experience. Indeed, we might characterize this entire study as the investigation of the circumstances which produce numinosity.

B. Other General Characteristics

Religious experience has four characteristics which are very important, but of which little has been said or written: (1) it is instrumental, (2) it is involuntary, (3) it is irrational and (4) it is efficacious when it occurs. We shall comment briefly on each one.

1. Religious Experience is Instrumental

Our first observation about the nature of religious experience is that it must be *about* something. Thus, to say "Be religious," is very much like saying, "Have surgery." If a person needs surgery, then obtaining it takes precedence over all else; but one does not undertake surgery merely for its own sake. Similarly, if there is a need for religious experience, i.e., a religious problem, it probably will occur: whereas, to expect valid numinous experience in a vacuum, or without content, is a contradiction in terms. Religion must be *about* something: it must serve a purpose; and what that purpose is will comprise a great part of our study; but it is our most basic premise that religious experience is the organism's autonomous technique for surmounting problems otherwise totally insoluble by science or morality as these are available to the subject.

2. Religious Experience is Involuntary

Although the religious quest may be voluntarily undertaken, as when a person voluntarily engages in prayer or ritual behavior, yet such activity may or may not result in genuine religious experience. Nor is this surprising. Anyone can go to bed at a given hour, but falling asleep is a different matter. While *mariages de convenance* are by no means unknown, it is impossible to fall in love at will. No one ever becomes so highly educated that he can avoid having nightmares, or that he can plan in advance what he will dream. The autonomous quality of numinous experience is precisely analogous to these situations. All of them involve the autistic adjustment of unconscious factors. In short, religious fulfillment comes when it will, and the writer knows of no way that it can be guaranteed at any given time. When Jehovah speaks to Moses from the burning bush, or Ahura Mazda addresses Zoroaster, the experience is totally beyond the control of either man. The same is true of the moment of conversion, however desperate the conflict of the subject may previously have been.

In this connection, it should be noted that voluntary religious behavior is always at second hand. By its very nature, it is always addressed to a previously known deity, about which various formulations have already been made. Thus it is that institutional religion is more directly related to the religious quest than to the religious experience, and since religious experience does not necessarily follow the quest for it, it is in relation to religious institutions that disillusionment occurs.

3. Religious Experience is Irrational

To say that religious experience is irrational does not mean that it makes no sense, nor that it is to be avoided as of no value. What it does mean is that frequently it is beyond logical proof, that it is seldom rationally arrived at, and that it may run contrary to all that the subject has been taught. Furthermore, it originates in the unconscious, which by its nature is other than rational. The fact that religious experience so many times runs directly contrary to the dictates of what we commonly consider reason, justifies our speaking of it as irrational, rather than non-rational or extra-rational.

Thus, when Moses had his great experience, he not only *heard a voice* which claimed divine and even cosmic authority, but he had sensory impressions of a contradiction in terms: a bush that burned, and was not consumed! But what is perhaps the crowning irrationality of the account is most often missed: Moses, who was a fugitive from Egyptian justice, was commanded by this voice, to go back to the place from whence he had fled, and *command the Pharaoh to free his slaves.* The very notion of anyone at all, let alone a wanted criminal, giving orders to the visible deity who occupied the throne of the most ethnic of all ethnic societies, carries the impact of pure phantasy, to say nothing of giving him the preposterous command to dissipate a resource as important as his labor supply! The whole experience was utterly irrational by every standard, yet momentous for all history.

4. Religious Experience is Efficacious

What ever else is said of religious experience, its efficacy must be acknowledged and commented upon. Not the least of the reasons for this need is the almost universal disparagement of such experience, so that "turning to religion" becomes synonymous with "admitting that the situation is hopeless."

Indeed, this is all too often true, in the frame of reference in which this utterance is commonly made, since a radical confusion is involved between "religion," in the sense of the religious quest, and "religious experience," in the sense of religious fulfillment.

Religious solutions are not available like Aladdin's genie, by rubbing a lamp, nor like Ali Baba's cave, which opened to the utterance of a magic phrase. "Not everyone that sayeth unto me, Lord, Lord, shall enter into the Kingdom of Heaven. . . ."

Nonetheless, whenever religious fulfillment has been validly experienced, amazing results have accrued: healings have taken place, social reforms inspired, social acceptability and acceptance achieved, fears externalized and removed, guilt released, and moral clarity attained.

It is of the very nature of religious experience to be efficacious. The numinous moment only occurs when a religious problem is solved, or when such an occasion is recalled. It is the definitive quality of such solutions that makes them numinous, for only when the problem is fully solved is there supreme valuation; and when it is, the completeness of the solution contributes to the mystery which is the other condition of numinosity. Moreover, when a religious problem is solved, there is a transforming quality about the contact the subject has with the archetypal figure who solves it. He remains different thereafter, and his enhancement overshadows all other types of value experience.

In this connection, it may well be pointed out that the only valid distinction between religious experience and psychosis is to be found in a related aspect of this same efficacy. Their similarities tend to accumulate as the investigator compares them; but despite its irrational character, *religious experience always points that subject toward reality*, although it may not be the reality he expects: while *psychosis provides him with an excuse to turn away from it*. All other attempts at distinguishing the two experiences end in failure.

C. Previous Explanations of Religion

As we undertake the analysis of religious experience, it is possible that we may be able to supply a rationale for the entire complex of activities which bears the name of religion.

We do not here take account of the various philosophical interpretations of the human quest for value, which may or may not attach the name "religion" to the undertakings they describe: some of them contain insights of great nobility. We are here speaking of the tangible and obvious phenomenon involving myth, ritual and theology, and manifested in buildings and personnel dedicated to the effort of keeping mankind in proper adjustment with forces held to be supernatural.

Efforts made in the past to account for the religious phenomenon in its totality have ended inconclusively, although a few monumental investigators have shed much light on the field, viz., William James and C. G. Jung; and various lesser scholars must, in fairness, be credited with adding their insights.

These explanatory efforts approach the problem from various perspectives, and have a tendency to interpret religion in terms of whatever other interest has motivated the investigator. Most of them lack clarity at some crucial point. While it is obvious that we cannot review all of them, yet for purposes of illustration, we can cite some of the interpretative approaches made by theology, philosophy, sociology, psychology, and what, for want of a better name, we may call comparative religion.

Theological explanations are the oldest: religion as "belief in the gods," i.e., the acceptance of some system of ideas in the sense of "believing in" it, is an interpretation that goes back to classical antiquity, and of course, explains nothing. Other theories with a supernaturalistic import abound: the dictum of St. Augustine is well-known, who said, "Thou has made us for thyself, and our hearts are restless until they rest in thee." This notion of religion as either the human response to a divine imperative, or as some appetite for the cosmic, is and has been a popular institutional formula.

From the philosophical perspective, religion has been held to be man's attempt to explain the universe, i.e., philosophy in embryo. Other interpretations have held religion to be humanity's quest for the highest attainable value, or, along a similar line, the expression of man's urge for completeness.

Sociologically, Durkheim and his successors, down through E. S. Ames, have equated religion with the quest for social solidarity, making God something like Uncle Sam, and the religious emotion more or less akin to school spirit. Karl Marx, of course, called it the opiate of the people, believing that its essential function was to compensate the masses in phantasy for the deprivations they have to endure in fact.

Psychologically, religion has been held to be the expression of fear, wish fulfillment, sex, guilt, and, in fact, just about every other human motivation. Moreover, the tendency of supposedly reputable scholars right down to the present moment, to seek ways of inviting the supernatural, of stimulating faith, or of determining whether contact has been made with the final level of ultimate reality in religious experience, is surprising, to say the least. And just when they approach some viable account of its origin, they will attribute it to a supernatural alternative, and shy away.

Explanations coming from comparative religion include a development from magic, wherein efforts to control the environment became precatory when compulsion failed. Every student in the field is familiar with Euhemerism, which would make mythology a stylized account of remote historical events, and interprets the gods as deified men and women. Other theories include the spread of an early Aryan sun myth, as well as efforts to increase the food supply, to account for dreams and hallucinations, or to come to terms with the fact of death.

It is probable that the reader will be reminded of other theories advanced to account for the religious phenomenon, whether individual or institutional. The multiplicity of such theories, to say nothing of the absence of agreement among them, is evidence for the need of some cogent and unifying explanation, to which the rest will be seen as ancillary.

IV. A Possible Frame of Reference: Religious Experience as a Response to Insoluble Problems

A thoroughly convincing explanation of religious *experience* would meet this need, for it is in this flooding of the subject's mind with the sense of inexpressible sacredness that every other part of the religious complex has its origin. Such an explanation is to be found in the relation of such experiences to *religious problems*.

Human need, as it appears in various areas, has frequently been cited as the dynmamic of religion, but only in a general way. Even so, there is a great deal of evidence in favor of this view. During the second World War we were told repeatedly, "There are no atheists in foxholes." Any examination of the rituals of primitive religion will show that the religious quest at this level is clearly aimed at the solution of particular problems. The "full gospel" groups that are currently flourishing in such numbers all have healing services, and not only for physical ills: and the enormous popularity of Oral Roberts and Kathryn Kuhlman as faith healers is still a living memory. There is no doubt whatever as to why the adherents of any of the groups follow them. Ever since the 1950's, one of the most powerful religious groups in Japan has been the Soka Gokkai, which title translates into the phrase "Value Producing Society." This tremendously militant organization of more than fifteen million people is dedicated to faith healing, economic prosperity and political power, all promised and produced by massive cooperative efforts to which the members are forcibly enjoined. Bringing our argument closer home, consider the frame of mind of anyone who prays: he prays *for* something, *about* a given problem, or *for* the solution of a given difficulty.

This is exactly the same frame of reference as that of Paul Tillich when he writes.

> God is the answer to the question implied in man's finitude; he is the name for that which concerns man ultimately. This does not mean that first there is a being called God and then the demand that man should be ultimately concerned about him. It means that whatever concerns a man ultimately, becomes a god for him, and, conversely, it means that a man can be concerned ultimately, only about that which is God for him.[4]

Moreover, numinosity, or the emotion of sacredness, occurs when the solution to some particular problem has been reached: the restoration of health, the attainment of social acceptance, the ability to forgive, or the resolution of anxiety regarding some religious doctrine.

This, of course, is where religious experience begins, and, in fact, what it is: the autistic solution of some problem of massive proportions, with which the subject is totally unable to deal, and which is destroying him.

[4] *Systematic Theology*, Vol. I, p. 211.

We now turn to the examination of these problems, and of the solutions they receive in religious experience.

V. Religious Problems

A. Their Characteristics

The basic category in all that we have to say about religious experience is the religious problem. Such problems have certain definite attributes which we now review.

1. *They are Subjectively Experienced*

The problematic dimensions which a given situation will assume for the person experiencing it cannot be objectively determined. Only the individual confronted by frustration or misfortune can tell what its tragic implications are for him: and his total background, both personal and cultural, is involved in this valuation. His threshold of resistance, the concept he holds of his own worth, his aesthetic sensitivity, his prior religious training, and the expectations he has been taught to entertain as to what life should hold for him, are all parts of this experience.

Comparable or identical events thus assume different emotional proportions for different people: consider the death notices in any daily paper. They are so statistical and tedious that many people do not read them at all, yet each of them is a message of final desolation for someone. Intimations of the subject's own demise ordinarily carry profound emotional impact, yet many of us have known persons of philosophic mind who would react to such information with merely a practical interest. Again, consider the difference between the reactions of a laboring man who loses a couple of fingers in an industrial accident, and a violinist who suffers a comparable mutilation. A primitive may believe that his spirit has been stolen away if a tourist takes his picture, and the ringing of a doorbell, which might have brought welcome diversion to a bored housewife, was the occasion of irreparable loss to Coleridge, while writing *Kubla Khan*.

In short, the problematic quality of any situation is totally unpredictable, and is only known subjectively by the one who experiences it.

2. They Are Insoluble

As broadly intimated above, the central characteristic of religious problems is that they are insoluble by science or morality as these are available to the subject. Thus they need not be *totally* insoluble, but at the time they provoke the religious reaction, they are completely beyond the subject's power to solve. The intimate connection between such problems and religious experience is thus central to its interpretation. Not only is the religious quest typically undertaken when a subject is desolated by such a situation, but the augmentation of psychic energy that constitutes religious *fulfillment* never takes place under any other circumstances. It is thus a negative condition of the phenomenon we are investigating. The rush of unconscious energy into conscious availability that is the essence of religious experience, and which is always accompanied by numinosity, never occurs at any other time, although an echo of the numinous emotion can be brought back in ritual recall at the institutional level.

In short, the ultimate dynamic for the religious reflex is the presence of an insoluble problem. When correctly understood, all religious behavior and all religious definitions will be seen to trace back to an origin that is contained in, or is related to, one or more such problems. It is in the autistic response to some trouble with which the subject cannot cope that religious experience *per se* is to be found.

3. They Are Vitally Important

The mere fact of insolubility does not in itself qualify a problem situation as being religiously generative. Some insoluble problems are so essentially trivial that they could not be expected to produce any religious reaction. Thus, if I lost my pencil out of a moving automobile, its recovery might be altogether beyond solution. Yet this is so trivial a deprivation that we would not expect any religious reaction.

However, the subjective nature of religious problems determines how important the circumstances at hand will be to the particular subject who is experiencing any given one. Thus, when our primitive has spasms of anxiety over being photographed, fearing that his soul has been stolen, it is a serious matter to him, however trivial it may seem to one of more sophisticated background. Earlier we referred to the difference between the reaction of a laboring man who might lose a finger or two in an industrial accident, and that of a violinist whose hand was mutilated. While the blue collar worker would not precisely choose such an experience, yet it is without implication for his basic survival or his future well-being; which is to say, it is not vitally important to him. Conversely, the violinist, particularly if he is a performing artist and not gifted at teaching, might well find the mutilation of such desperate importance that he would be moved to deep and serious religious involvement.

Further evidence of the vital importance of the problem out of which religious experiences arise is observable in the non-manipulable quality of the personifications which they inspire. At the magical level, various aches, pains, and panics within the subject, and comparable whirlwinds, thunders and sudden fallings in the external order—such things as might make a horse shy—are personified directly and are exorcised by compulsive techniques, as we all know. However, the gods to which validly precatory behavior is addressed have a certain intransigence about them: they will not be moved, except by compliance with their own conditions, and yet to ignore them is equally out of the question. In Tillich's famous phrase, they are indeed "objects of ultimate concern." Applying our own theory, it is easy to understand that the problems they rise to interpret are of notable importance, whatever be the vagaries of subjectivity.

4. They Are Emotionally Intolerable

Not only are these insoluble problems vitally important; they are also emotionally intolerable. When these two qualities are present, the religious activity may be expected to follow. Indeed, whereas the vital importance of such a problem makes it the necessary condition of religious activity, it is quite likely that the emotional intolerability is the sufficient condition of this reaction. We said earlier that it was hard to predict when religious behavior would occur.[5] Nonetheless, given an insoluble problem of vital importance and emotional intensity, religious activity is overwhelmingly likely to take place. Indeed, it is one of our basic hypotheses that the more emotionally intense an insoluble and vitally important problem is, the more likely religious experience is to follow, and that when the level of intolerability is reached, it may be expected with practical certainty.

The reader may be puzzled as to how anyone can have a problem which is important enough to be called vital, that is, which really affects the core of his personality, yet is not emotionally intense. A moment's thought will show that this is not only possible, but of frequent occurrence. Consider the person who has cancer and does not know it. He has a problem of vital importance but it is not emotionally intense to him. Again, a person may be told that his life expectancy is very short, yet have such a philosophical attitude that he does not go into an emotional state over this. He may regard death as being as natural as life and, as a result, may not move into the realm of religious behavior. This is not to say that this same person may not react very religiously when some other problem comes up. Furthermore, this raises another question which is of far reaching significance. It is whether anyone at all is entirely non-religious. To this question the writer cannot give a definite answer. In principle, he would suppose that everyone had a breaking point somewhere, beyond which his psychic

[5] Cf. *supra*, III, B, 2, p. 10.

patterns would become religious. But this would be a conjecture having no empirical confirmation.

5. *They Are Constantly in Migration*

Religious issues are constantly changing from time to time, from place to place, and from person to person. The commonest migration is from religious to non-religious status. This takes place when science finds solutions to problems which previously had none, or when an individual person gains the ability to cope with a situation which previously was beyond him. It may also take place purely by a change of circumstances, as by a change of climate, an unexpected inheritance, or some stranger offering assistance. Furthermore, one religious problem may well displace another, as when economic insecurity changes to boredom, with the ending of a period of unemployment, and this in turn changes to panic fear if a threat to health is experienced. It is also entirely possible for situations to migrate from the non-religious into the religious area; as, for instance, when the principal medicine man of a primitive group, who has never doubted his social acceptability, must face cultural impact and be regarded as merely one more undesirable primitive by a culturally more advanced society.

This raises the question as to whether science will eventually make religion unnecessary. The efficient earnestness with which institutional religion repudiates the 'need' theory would indicate that its representatives are in some anxiety upon this point. However, when one problem moves out of the religious realm, it is always succeeded by another problem of greater complexity. Thus religion will never become superfluous by running out of material (problems) upon which to work. However, the protective instinct religion displays so plainly in this regard is after all not inappropriate. Each institutional religion is put together in order to meet one particular problem or set of problems, and when such problems migrate into the realm of the non-religious, desuetude is the likely fate of that particular institution. The fact that it is perfectly possible for such an institution merely to shift its focus and deal with whatever constitutes the religious issue in the newer day, unfortunately remains a rather abstract possibility. It takes no account of either the lassitude or the inadequacy of the clergy who constitute the religious establishment. To move from an efficient concern with one problem (or at most, a limited group of them) to the meeting of need in a completely different area is indeed a possibility. But it is rather too much to ask of the caliber of men who feel impelled to pursue religious careers. To summarize: although when we consider the matter abstractly it is in no way necessary for the migration of religious issues to decrease the usefulness of any given institution, yet, in terms of the practical outworkings of the situation, the migration of religious issues does indeed put many religious institutions out of business. Thus exploitation by a religious institution consists in the refusal to let religious issues migrate for any individual person.

B. The Areas of Their Occurrence

1. Nature

Included, here, are all problems which arise when man comes in contact with the natural order. Primarily pertinent to the religious frame of reference are problems connected with the food quest and personal survival, and problems of the organism and its health. The great ethnic religions have sought to control the environment manipulatively in connection with these issues, as well as with the larger contacts of man with nature (weather, tides, storms, *et al.*). Thus they can provide only ostensible solutions to the problems which concern them. That is to say, men may dance and it may rain, but the dancing has obviously not been the cause of the rain. However, questions of health fall into the domain of valid religious experience, as is evidenced by numbers of well documented "faith" healings.

2. Society

Problems of society, insofar as they fall within the scope of a psychology of religion, have to do with the individual's relationship to society. Questions such as "What does our tribe do next?" or "What will become of this social group in the face of disaster?" may constitute religious problems for some leader within the tribe, but they are sociological questions until some individual feels them as problematical in the religious sense. However, the individual's relationship to a person or group whose approval he desires or whose help he needs is beyond question a valid religious problem.[6]

3. Inner-Psychic

Insofar as anything the individual feels within himself constitutes a religious problem for him, we have the content of this area. Thus fear, hate and guilt in all their ramifications—indeed, the full range of problems for which psychiatrists are otherwise consulted—are all potentially religious problems.

One aspect of this requires clarification. Whenever a problem arises in any of the other areas, its impact is felt in the inner-psychic area as well. Thus, if a person with a ruptured appendix fears death, he has the inner-psychic problem of fear, but it is clearly secondary. The care he needs is physical rather than mental. Again, it is obvious that if one who validly feared starvation were given food, he would have received a solution in the realm of nature that obviated his inner-psychic problem.[7] He didn't need a psychiatrist, he needed nourishment! Hence, we recognize the other areas being in no way secondary to this one, although they register their impact obviously enough as inner-psychic problems.[8]

[6] Certain religious problems are, of course, classifiable in more than one category. Thus, a man whose problem in the modern world is that of health, for instance ulcers caused by worry about corporate pressures in a business situation, has both a problem of nature and a problem of society.

[7] Of course, if he continued to worry about privation in the midst of obvious affluence, his problem would fall into the class we are describing.

[8] It seems to the writer that if the work of C. G. Jung has a weakness, it is

What we are talking about is the individual who finds that a lack of integration prevents him from getting anything done, or that a crippling hatred has him so immured that he is ineffective. In short, it is when the inner states themselves become problematical, rather than some other problem registering as an inner state, that the individual has an inner-psychic problem.

4. Failure of Prior Formulations

The final problem area we shall note is found wherever previously made religious formulations prove inadequate to such an extent that their failure constitutes a religious issue in its own right. Such problems arise whenever a subject realizes, with religious intensity, that a previously enunciated doctrine or ritual has failed to function as he has been trained to expect, with relation to his own need. An excellent illustration of such a problem is the plight of the priests of Baal in their famous conflict with Elijah.[9] Even if we suppose that their expectation of being able to ignite a sacrificial pyre magically was based upon some kind of chicanery which Elijah was able to circumvent, nonetheless the disillusionment of their followers must have been complete.

Both Sitting Bull in the Sioux uprising of 1891, and Alice Lenshina, in her revolt against the new Tanzanian government in 1961 provided their shock troops with "ghost shirts," credited with the power to turn bullets. The religious reactions of the casualties are not recorded, but they must have been pitiable.

While these parallel tragedies occurred in connection with a problem of nature (ballistics . . .) an analogous circumstance connected with a problem of *society* occurred when the U. S. Marines took the island of Tarawa in the Second World War.

---

that he is so preoccupied with psychology that he fails to give sufficient weight to this obvious truth.

[9] I Kings 18:20–29

Vast numbers[10] of Japanese civilians committed suicide, by reason of the dismay and terror which they felt at the failure of the Samurai formulations regarding the invincibility of their own troops.

Again, the incredulity and shock which the populace felt at the Mikado's announcement at the end of the war, that (1) the country had surrendered, and (2) he himself was not really divine, were of course the beginning of the end for State Shinto.

Turning again to inner-psychic problems, consider the plight of a follower of Father Divine when this leader died. Such adherents in great numbers had had their own livid sense of inferiority immeasurably relieved by the supposedly cosmic powers of the leader with whom they had merged. At his death, the collapse of their symbolic formulations must have created a new religious problem for hundreds of his followers.

This area assumes particular importance because it is here that all religious change occurs. That is, whenever anyone alters his religious orientation it is because he has experienced a problem of prior formulation. Also, such problems are, in all but a very few instances, connected with *institutional* religion, for all ritual activity, wherein the instrumentality of religion is given overt expression, is institutional in essence, and rests necessarily upon formulations which have already been made. The same considerations apply to all religious instruction. Hence, whenever any decline of faith takes place, it is typically in an institutional frame of reference. This, indeed, (the occurrence of a problem of prior formulation) is the precise focus of theology, which is to be defined as the rationalized expansion of myth, in the interest of ritual efficiency.[11]

---

[10] Their number was officially estimated at 150,000.

[11] These three, *ritual*, the symbolic repetition of successful behavior, *myth*, the explanation of why the ritual is performed, and *theology*, make up the content of any religious institution. See Part Four.

Note on Unconscious Problems

This is probably as good a place as any to insert the statement that religious problems may be present at either the conscious or unconscious level. This might at first glance seem to be merely a question begging device, so that if the individual doesn't feel a conscious problem, we can substantiate our theory by telling him "Oh, well, yours is unconscious!" However, both the unconscious problems and their solutions appear *symbolically* and as such have an even more profound effect than those which are consciously experienced.

To begin with, any problem that is serious enough to have the religious dimension is so painful that it cannot be long endured in consciousness and hence will inevitably be repressed. Once repressed, it is out of touch with the adaptive behavior (the ego) and has no further chance for solution except by fortuitous circumstance, psychiatric help, or religious experience. This last alternative is the channel whereby vast numbers of unconscious problems are brought to solution; partly because it is the only one available to the people having the problems, but more importantly because the essentially symbolic nature of such experiences functions inherently to restore such unconscious problems to consciousness and the adaptive activity of the ego.

Frequently the existence of an unconscious problem is revealed by some circumstance of great beneficence which might be expected to produce rejoicing in the subject, but which, instead, brings a registration of fear or grief. Thus at the successful termination of a period of great danger, he may give way to panic, saying, "I never knew until now how frightened I was!" Many of us have seen someone weep at the recovery of a loved one from illness, with some utterance such as "Just think—I might have lost you!"

The very fact of Thanksgiving festivals, which might at first glance seem to controvert our entire theory, being religious celebrations conducted in the midst of plenty rather than want, is testimony to anxiety that is only admitted to consciousness when its object is so pleasantly contradicted.

VI. The Nature of Religious Solutions

A. External

One type of possible solution to a religious problem is the solving of that problem by some external agency. This may occur altogether by circumstance as when the seagulls ate the locusts who were destroying the Mormon's grain, or when something a subject hears on a television program solves an inner-psychic problem for him. Similarly, an unexpected passer-by may render vital assistance following an automobile wreck in a remote place, his appearance being entirely circumstantial. Again, a surgeon may save the life of a patient who is feeling his illness as a religious problem. The point to be noted with regard to all these solutions is that a religious status may very well be assigned to them, that is, the subject(s) in each case may hold that it was due to God's direct providence that the seagulls came, or that the passer-by happened along, or that the television program contained the particular phrase which resolved his problem. He may say, "I'm so thankful to God for giving skill to the doctor who saved my life." Thus these problem-solving experiences are subsequently classified as religious by an *interpretation* which the subject makes when the experience itself is over. The likelihood that he will assign a religious status to these external solutions is exactly proportional to the vitality of whatever religious belief he has previously adopted.

Before we leave this section, we must comment upon the situation wherein a subject thinks he has an insoluble problem, such as an incurable disease, but subsequently discovers that the situation is not as stringent as he had supposed. The relief that he feels may well be deeply numinous. Must we then suppose that he had had a religious experience in the absence of a religious problem, thus destroying our thesis? Not at all: for his initial anxiety was perfectly genuine, and had all the characteristics of a religious problem, albeit an inner-psychic one, instead of a problem of nature. This is a clear illustration of how essentially subjective such problems are.

However, if he subsequently takes credit for a faith cure, or otherwise seeks to exploit the experience for his own religious prestige, the situation is entirely different, since such a subject is perfectly aware that his claim to supernatural assistance is fraudulent, no matter how successful the deception may be.

B. Autonomous Solution

1. Neuro-muscular

There is a spectrum of numinosity in human experience which begins with religious solutions of a low-grade intensity, and extends all the way to mystic experience of the highest revelatory quality. A common type of religious solution, met for the most part at the lower end of this scale, is the experience of some unusual neuro-muscular ability which comes to the subject's aid in a moment of crisis. Illustrations abound of a small, frail person lifting an automobile off the victim of an accident; or of someone who cannot swim performing a rescue from drowning. Every athlete has had the experience of competing "over his head." Nearly all of us have had the experience of driving an automobile through some impossible traffic situation in a manner that we would not have believed possible. A less common occurrence is that of rescuing oneself from a slipping ladder by some incredible balancing act which no one but a circus acrobat would be expected to perform. A common form of utterance following such experiences is "I would have bet a million dollars that nobody could do that, and I just did!"

Such experiences are probably due for the most part to infusions of adrenalin which are touched off by the autonomic nervous system as a preparation for increased action, at times of emotional stress.[12] Hence it is not unlikely that there is actually a net addition to the total supply of energy when a sudden crisis is surmounted in this way.

[12] Cf. Warren, Howard C. and Carmichael, Leonard, *Elements of Human Psychology*, Boston: Houghton-Mifflin, 1930, pp. 228–232.

Moreover, important and very complex accessions of energy are sometimes experienced in periods of crisis other than physical danger. Just as some of the neuro-muscular solutions mentioned above involved the unprecedented availability of a *skill* (swimming, driving, balancing) rather than the mere presence of physical strength, so the solutions of which we now speak express themselves in a greatly heightened *effectiveness* in performing routine duties under extreme stress. Whereas those mentioned earlier came and went in a few seconds, these may last for whatever time is required for a major crisis to pass. Although definitely higher on the spectrum of numinosity than some of the solutions cited earlier, e.g., having unusual athletic success, or driving a car out of a traffic difficulty, yet like all of the solutions mentioned, those of this class occur quite apart from any visionary appearance, and with little or no supernatural coloration until or unless it is later supplied.

> A theological student in one of our Western states was under somewhat more pressure than he could manage, with final examinations, a temporary organizational crisis in his student Church, some worry over money matters, and the closing week of his wife's pregnancy all coming at the same time.
>
> His frustrations were turned to bitter grief when his wife died in childbirth. However, to his own surprise, he cared for all the painful details which followed, with great efficiency; found the answer to the crisis in his Church (and was able to admit that this might have been due to sympathy for himself); and even took and passed his examinations on schedule.
>
> He had no visionary experiences then or later, but a consciousness of unaccustomed *sustaining*. Once the critical period of stress was surmounted, this consciousness solidified into a positive conviction of divine assistance, so definite that some years later he indignantly repudiated the formulations of a course in the Psychology of Religion, insisting that he had had a veritable contact with supernatural help.[13]

Memorable as solutions of this pattern are, yet when they are critically examined it becomes apparent that they must be

[13] This example is cited from the writer's own counselling experience. Where other examples are not footnoted, the same will be true.

attributed to the same factor which made possible the events of the first group cited—a heightened flow of adrenalin, stimulated by the autonomic nervous system, in response to the stressful situation *per se*.

Now any of the events cited is capable of becoming the focal point for a profoundly religious orientation: the athlete gains acclaim, or perhaps saves his scholarship; an impossible rescue is suddenly and neatly accomplished; a bad auto smash is averted, a fatal accident obviated, or crushing responsibilities met, all seemingly by Divine aid. However, a common aspect of these experiences which is frequently overlooked is that *all neuro-muscular solutions receive their numinous character by a subsequent act of interpretation.*[14] By the same token, it is altogether possible that their religious implications may go entirely unnoticed.

Furthermore, inasmuch as the organism, by its own autonomous response to these problems, can effect their solution, they are thereby removed, at least formally, from the class of religious problems as we have defined them. Hence we must acknowledge that neuro-muscular solutions as a class are more or less on the borderline of the truly religious, although any one of them may assume an intensely numinous coloration when interpreted by a subject with a vivid religious belief.[15]

However, another group of neuro-muscular solutions is inherently a part of the far profounder class of *symbolic* solutions, and is subsumed by it. This group, which is typified by any healing[16] that takes place "by the power of" or "in the name of" any god, under any circumstances, will be discussed further in Part Three, III, C,4, *passim*.

2. Intellectual Solutions

The attainment of noetic certainty that a bad problem which is pressing with religious intensity will turn out favorably is an

---

[14] See discussion of External Solutions, *supra*, p. 26.

[15] Nonetheless, without the access of energy that is later given a religious interpretation, the problem would indeed have been insoluble.

[16] Or the solution of any other neuro-muscular problem, of course.

experience many people have had. Proof that this favorable outcome will indeed prove true is altogether out of the question; there is little or no evidence that such will be the case, but despite all contrary indications, the subject arrives at a religious certainty that a favorable outcome will at last be available to him. He may even come to understand the technique which will, as is later proven, ensure this result.

We must distinguish very carefully between these intellectual solutions to religious problems, and the solutions which are arrived at by *taking thought*. To begin with, reasoned intellectual endeavor is not possible for one who is suffering in the desperate emotional trauma which is an aspect of religious crisis. Furthermore, all the thought in the world will not bring a rationalized answer to a problem which is of religious dimensions. The solutions to these problems flash into the subject's mind entirely apart from his conscious volition. Their commonest characteristic is an altered perspective upon the problem itself, whereby the subject is enabled to see it as non-problematical. Such solutions can be illustrated by (1) the experience of a Jehovah's Witness who, being *in extremis*, comes to the intellectual insight that blood transfusions are not sinful, and (2) the experience of a Catholic matron under comparable pressure, who receives the same numinous assurance regarding birth control.[17] However, intellectual solutions may take the form of a complete system of ideation. All investigators are familiar with the experience of Siddhartha Gotama, who arrived at his system of religious ethics in a single revelatory moment, under the Bodhi Tree. The writer knows a college professor who had a complete system of philosophy revealed to him in a dream. Furthermore, a noetic deposit is a characteristic of many other religious experiences which are not primarily intellectual in their content.

These intellectual solutions may arise in the mind of the subject as random ideas which are numinously and noetically

---

[17] Both of these situations obviously involve Problems of Prior Formulation, which have been discussed above, in B, 4 (pages 23–24).

colored with the unmistakable aura of being solutions to his difficulty, or they may come to him in the full panoply of religious dress, as the utterances of a deity, old or new, who appears to him in an experience of full scale religious revelation.[18] Yet however simply the ideas come, if they have the degree of pertinence which truly solves a religious problem, the probability that they will be *interpreted* as the gift of whatever god the subject believes in, it is directly proportional to the vitality of that belief. However, the characteristics have been delineated, and the content of the ideas which provide intellectual solutions to religious problems is unaffected by the simplicity or the elaborateness of the experience.

3. Symbolic Solutions

References to deity in the preceding section provide us with our point of reference for the present consideration. Indeed, when we think of a completely typical religious experience, we think of a subject making contact with one or another of the gods, since the vast majority of such occurrences, i.e., solutions to religious problems, is found in connection with *symbols* that take the form of the divine figures which comprise the pantheons of the world's religions. Thus it is, that we think of a typically religious utterence as being "God answered my prayer," or "It was only by the mercy of God that we survived." Similarly, the most elementary definition of religion most of us know is that religion is belief in the gods.

These gods appear in many forms. Yet frequently the focal point of a religious experience is something that seems at first glance to be unrelated to any of them. It requires small search to find human beings who, despite heavy adversity, are equipped with great verve, staying power and peace of mind as a result of some experience which has brought their lives to order and brightness from a previous state of chaos, pain and panic, but which is altogether extraneous to any known theology. The experience may be a dream having a revelatory

[18] Cf. Part Three, II, C, for further consideration of such symbolic solutions.

content. It may be the irruption of a startlingly pertinent idea, in the course of ordinary reflection, or it may be an unexpected kindness. It may also take the form of an intense involuntary preoccupation with some fact or factor that has seized upon their imagination: perhaps a book, a prayer, or some other literary formulation of reputed efficacy: it may be a person, a doctrine, an institution, an event, or even a physical object. Whatever be its precise nature, the subject has no doubt of its primary importance to him. Its dynamic quality is such that he structures his activities in terms suggested by this focal point, and within this structure finds the solution to his problem.[19]

These are *religious symbols*, even as are the gods, and their impelling quality carries their numinous coloration with it. Whether or not they are traditional, it is in *their* idiom and on their own terms that significant religious solutions occur. Indeed, all conscious problems may have, and all unconscious problems must have, symbolic solutions. It is to the exposition of the symbolic aspects of religious experience that the rest of this study will be devoted.

A religious symbol may be defined as *a compressed representation made by the unconscious to consciousness, and implying a course of action pertinent to solving the subject's religious problem.* The entire matter of symbolic origins will be discussed later. We shall only allude to it here. But the arresting, irrational, often perplexing, but always dynamic and always numinous character of the gods and other religious symbols makes the question of their origin insistent. Dynamic as they are, we cannot suppose that these entities are the result of any whimsical agreement to believe, any conscious invention, or any bald pretense. The unconscious remains as their probably source.[20]

Furthermore the solution *per se* to any religious problem is to

---

[19] The astuteness of William James's definition of religion comes home to us at this point. Familiar as it is to most investigators, its recitation may be pertinent: "—the feelings, acts, and experiences of individual men in their solitude, so far as they apprehend themselves to stand in relation to *whatever they consider the divine.*" *Varieties*, ML ed., p. 31f. Italics are the writer's.

[20] Their appearance is of course involuntary. Cf. III, B, 2, *supra*, p. 10.

be found in the achievement of an appropriate relationship with the symbol to which that problem has given rise. Thus, when a subject is able to exorcise a demon, bargain successfully with a rain god, or merge with a savior, his relief is obvious and his well-being assured. But if he is forsaken by his culture hero, unable to find a sacrifice the fertility-god will accept, or is possessed by the demon, his condition will range somewhere along a spectrum between lonely desolation, utter despair, and psychotic terror.

It thus becomes apparent that we must examine these symbols closely, inquiring into the phenomenology of their appearance and the manner of their functioning. Included in such an investigation, or ancillary to it, are other questions, already implicit in our discussion: what constitutes a perfectly suitable relationship with one of these symbols? How do symbolic solutions subsume the simpler levels of religious experience? What is the relation of old symbolisms to new? Why and when does a religious subject produce a new religious formulation instead of adopting one that is already in existence? And finally, what is the nature of the involvement between symbol and ritual?

The reason these considerations are important should by now be apparent. The religious symbol is the focal point for the structuring or reconstruction of personality. Religious experience is nothing less than this.

In order to deal with all these questions efficiently, we shall now make a new beginning, and recapitulate the general outlines of personality theory, as these have been delineated by major investigators. A third section will then be devoted to showing what takes place within the personality when religious experience occurs, and our final chapter will undertake to outline the connection between individual religious experience and the religious institution.

Part 2

The Structure of Personality

I. Freud

Any investigator of personality today simply takes the positions reached by Sigmund Freud as his basis for further work. Whether or not he agrees implicitly with them, he assumes a knowledge of these positions on the part of anyone who would have enough interest in his own work to look at it. Hence we present a brief resume of the Freudian formulations.

A. The Unconscious: Repression and Suppression

Probably the most salient thing about the Freudian system is recognition of, and his emphasis upon, the unconscious dimensions of psychic activity. Although this idea is commonplace today, it was for many years a matter of some controversy. It was argued that anything classifiable as mind was *ipso facto* conscious; and if it wasn't conscious, it wasn't mind. However, we now realize on the basis of vast amounts of clinical evidence, as well as by personal introspection, that a great deal of our psychic life is below the level of immediate awareness, and indeed below the level of any recall apart from a therapeutic assistant. Something like three-quarters of all psychic activity occurs below the level of conscious control. References to the "subconscious" are erroneous, for what we have is either consciousness, including the preconscious, from whence such things as a temporarily forgotten name or address may be recovered, or the unconscious proper, from which we are unable to recover any material at all, once it has been relegated to this area of the mind.

The mechanisms of *repression*[1] is central to Freudian doctrine. It is the means whereby ideas enter the unconscious. Repression is basically an unconscious denial of attention. The subject simply slides away from dealing with some object of thought, for the reason that he cannot quite handle it. He doesn't know what to do with it. His perplexity is painful. Hence he dismisses it, non-volitionally, and it becomes part of the unconscious mind. Any idea or proposition which thus exceeds the subject's capacity for structuring it into expression is probably powered by a very definite instinctual affect. Such a failure on the part of the *ego* to deal with an instinctual urge removes it permanently from contact with this organizing principle, the function of which is to provide adaptive behavior, i.e., motor expression, for such instinctual material. Being thus relegated to the unconscious, it maintains its dynamic force, but without any opportunity of discharging it. When this has occurred, the idea can then be recovered only in a therapeutic situation; indeed, if it appears in consciousness in any other context, it will be so unpleasant that it will necessarily be repressed again. This gives rise to a situation that is all too familiar to many people: one item of experience is repressed, and then everything that suggests that item to consciousness must also be repressed, until all the available energy of the subject is devoted to maintaining a complete system of interlocking repressions, which have now become necessary for the avoidance of anxiety. The one exception to this is that the repressed material may appear in some substitute guise which is acceptable to the ego, which is to say *symbolically*. Thus for Freud, a symbol is a symptom of some instinct-laden idea with which the ego has failed to deal adequately, in the past.

At this point we must distinguish *suppression* from repression. Suppression is the *voluntary* denial of attention, and is a perfectly normal technique practiced by every healthy ego for the focussing of thought, in the interest of practical efficiency. Suppressed material is available to consciousness at any time

[1] Cf. *infra*, B, 3, s.v. Defense Mechanisms of the Ego, p. 43.

the subject wants it back again, and indeed, the ability to employ this useful technique effectively is evidence of a strong and adequate subjectivity.

1. *The Id*

Completely within the unconscious, and native to it,[2] is *the id*, which is the great reservior of *libido*, or psychic energy. It has been characterized as the totality of instinctual energy, but this formulation might well be modified so that we speak of it as the totality of energy which assumes or receives instinctual patterning. There are many instincts, but for Freud, they can all be subsumed under two major classifications—sex and hostility.

a. *Sexuality*

Freud's sexual theory holds, in essence, that all energy is sexual energy. Sexuality begins much earlier in childhood than has previously been recognized. In fact, it begins in earliest infancy. Whatever energy the organism exhibits, then, is either a direct, symbolic, or sublimated manifestation of sexual activity. This affirmative flow of life-energy he terms, not surprisingly, the *Eros*.

b. *Hostility or Aggression*

The other great collection of major instinctual drives is known as hostility or aggression. Freud's ideas on this point apparently changed markedly throughout his working life. Although there is a considerable literature relating to a *thanatos* or death instinct, he apparently modified this until it became a destructive instinct, or patterning for aggressive acts, and we will accept this as representative of his teaching. Thus, the id is made up of two opposing drives: sexuality and aggression.

---

[2] Whereas ideas which are *energized* by instinct have to be *repressed* into the unconscious, the energy itself *rises* there, and only achieves conscious expression in terms of some idea which the ego finds acceptable, and hence does not repress.

c. Instinct and the Pleasure Principle

The final aim of an instinct is the removal or satisfaction of a bodily need, or in other words, to eliminate the source of that instinct.[3] Another way of saying this is to say that the goal of every instinct is to obtain access to motor expression.

> The id does not change with the passage of time; it cannot be modified by experience because it is not in contact with the external world . . . it is driven by one consideration only; to obtain satisfaction for instinctual needs in accordance with the pleasure principle.[4]

The pleasure principle is simply the principle that all of psychic life is determined by the tendency of the organism to seek pleasure and avoid pain, whether physical or mental.[5]

d. The Primary Process

The *id* can satisfy the pleasure principle by a technique which Freud called *the primary process.* Reduced to its absolute fundamental, as the writer understands it, this is the visualizing of a source of satisfaction—phantasy. It consists simply in the recall in memory of the image of a perception. The subject entertains memories of past perceptions of something he desires in the present. If he has never experienced the activity leading to the satisfaction he now desires, he may phantasize other activity which, by association, suggests the satisfaction to him. Like the rest of the id, this process is totally irrational. It operates independently of what consciousness thinks of as time and space. This the reader can observe introspectively by recalling whatever phantasies he himself may have had.

2. The Super-Ego

At the opposite pole from the instinctual energies of the id, we have the demands of the social environment. Whereas the id simply wishes to express the urges of the organism with direct sexual activity and overt aggression, both of these drives

---

[3] Cf. Hall, Calvin S., *A Primer of Freudian Psychology,* p. 37.
[4] *Op. Cit.,* p. 26.
[5] Thus it is obviously the dynamic for repression, q.v.

are unacceptable in their unadorned aspect to other members of society. Hence, at a very early age the child must internalize the demands of society as they are relayed to him by his parents, or suffer exceedingly. The process of internalization is known as *introjection*. Hence, we may advance a preliminary definition of the super-ego as the totality of introjected behavior. Or, if it is not too redundant, we may define the super-ego as the totality of internalized social pressures.

This internalization is always a painful process, involving a measure of defeat on the part of a personality. It is always based on fear—basically, the fear of punishment. The mechanism is, in fact, simply that of "if you can't lick them, join them." After repeated and humiliating collisions with the authority, a moment comes when the subject suddenly discovers that he has adopted the perspective of the enforcing agency, and is fully in accord with its requirements and prohibitions: moreover, he is at the same time able to carry them out. Introjection reaches all the way to the unconscious, so that a folkway may be so thoroughly internalized that it cannot be laid aside, even when it has become impractical, as when a person who has left the Jewish faith finds himself nauseated by the smell of pork.

An interesting and little noted aspect of introjection is that it occurs much more readily and completely when accompanied by *identification* with the enforcing agent. When the subject unquestioningly accepts the total value structure of some other person or personification of whom he approves intensely, either because such a figure has rendered him significant assistance in the past, or because he hopes to receive important benefits from him or it in the future,[6] the internalization of

---

[6] Calvin Hall lists four important types of identification: (1) *narcissistic* identification, whereby we identify with persons who resemble ourselves; (2) *goal oriented* identification, whereby we identify with people who are able to obtain the things we desire, but which we have not been able to attain as yet; (3) *object loss* identification, or the assimilation of the standards and values of someone who has either rejected the subject or has been separated from him in some other way, possibly by death; and (4) *aggressor* identification, which

whatever arduous, painful, or irrational demands such a figure may present, is accomplished much more quickly and thoroughly than when such identification is not present.

Another definition of the super-ego is that it is the unconscious part of the conscience. As such, its action is oftentimes merely inhibitory, as in the case of otherwise healthy young people who get married only to find themselves either frigid or impotent. A more representative illustration of the authoritative quality of the super-ego is its complete regulative force in managing excretory matters. The ordinary person would find it entirely impossible to perform an excretory act under any circumstances except those that are socially permissible. Thus, we see that apart from psychotherapy, it is impossible to argue with the super-ego. A person who makes a mistake at some conscious level may be able to rationalize it, but it is impossible even to perform an act that is truly forbidden by the super-ego. If such an act *is* somehow performed, the guilt which results is enormous.

The experience of prolonged and morbid guilt that is to be observed all too frequently is likely to be not so much the result of an overly cruel super-ego, as of a sick one. A super-ego that is healthy simply gets the subject into gear with what he is supposed to do, whereas, if he is able to make deals with his super-ego, this part of his psyche is out of order, and the result will be prolonged guilt. It is as though the subject were told by his super-ego, "I'll let you sleep half an hour longer if you'll feel guilty all day," and then replied, "Okay, we'll do it that way."

The importance of having a coherent and reasonably operational super-ego thus becomes very plain. At its best, a healthy super-ego is a fine thing to have: it simply gets a person into action without the necessity of making fatiguing and time consuming decisions. At its worst, however, it can be a cruel and demanding taskmaster, which sets up impossible demands, and punishes with hideous guilt and failure to com-

---

is the incorporation of prohibitions imposed by an authority figure. See *A Primer of Freudian Psychology*, pp. 75–78.

plete their inordinate requirements. If, as sometimes happens, a child with inconsistent parents develops a super-ego containing violent contradictions, then indeed trouble is in store for him. The writer once knew a young man who was a seriously afflicted alcoholic. His problem was that he had a super-ego requirement to be rich, dinned into him by both his parents throughout his childhood. At the same time, he had introjected a drastic guilt over *working*! This was for the common people, and any constructive economic activity was felt to be demeaning! The results of this internalized contradiction were all too plainly seen in the wreckage of his life.

It should be noted that not only action, but merely the thought of action will produce a heavy protest from a tightly rooted super-ego, so that even the phantasy of some forbidden activity may throw the subject who entertains it into a state of extreme guilt.

We must also note that Freud distinguished between the *ego-ideal*, which was the body of behavior which the subject performed because he was afraid not to, and the super-ego proper, which was the body of behavior the subject avoided because he was afraid to do it. Both, however, occur in the personality as a result of introjection.

We have only mentioned in passing that the super-ego is unconscious. This should be stressed, since in its own area it is as irrational as the id. It may be very aggressive against the ego by falsely presenting to it a picture of what ought to be rather than what is; and it may force the ego into acts of great cruelty on the plea that other people are immoral or unworthy.

B. Consciousness: The Ego

1. Functional Definitions

Various descriptive phrases have been applied to the ego by Freud and his interpreters. Perhaps the one which best serves as an introduction is that the ego is *the resultant of forces between the id and the super-ego*. Suggestive as this formulation may be, it is, of course, incomplete. It gives no indication of the element of rationality which is, after all, the most important aspect of the ego. Indeed, the concepts of the id and the super-ego have long been understood as clinical theories advanced to account for what might be wrong with the obviously conscious elements of personality. It is in the ego that we find the miracle of reason. Here we assign a locus to man's generalizing and deductive abilities. Here the instinctual drives of the id are routed into social acceptability, so that they can gain a modicum of satisfaction. The ego has well been called the executive aspect of the personality. Another very expressive phrase describing it is *the totality of adaptive behavior in the personality.* Although it would be very easy to make a thumbnail presentation of the ego as being identical with consciousness, yet the ego is both conscious and unconscious. It is in contact with the environment at one point of its range, and at the other it is in contact with the blind insurgency of the id, which is, of course, always unconscious.

The basic task of the ego is to provide motor expression for the id drives. Hence it is *the principle of practicality* that keeps questing for success. The lofty reaches of human reason are simply equipment which the ego has evolved to meet the demands of the physical environment without doing violence to those of society.

2. The Secondary Process

While engaged in this task of implementing the id, it is, of course, essential that the ego be not deluded. Hence, it is *the reality principle* of the personality, and perhaps its outstanding characteristic is what Freud called *the secondary process*: which is simply the fact of distinguishing between the reports of perception and the autistic presentations of the personality itself. It will be remembered that the id cannot make this distinction, but will take pleasure from the autistic presentations of the primary process as well as from the perceptual presentations of reality.

The aim of the reality principle is to postpone the discharge of energy until an actual object that will satisfy the need has been discovered or produced . . . the postponement of action means that the ego has to be able to tolerate tension until the tension can be discharged by an appropriate form of behavior. This does not mean that the pleasure principle is forsaken, it is only temporarily suspended in the interest of reality. Eventually the reality principle leads to pleasure, although a person may have to endure some discomfort while he is looking for reality.[7]

The secondary process accomplishes what the primary process is unable to do, namely to separate the subjective world of the mind from the objective world of physical reality.[8] All advances in knowledge consist in making one's mental representations of the world more accurate pictures of the world as it really is.[9] The id cannot satisfy the vital needs of life by phantasy alone, and the secondary process is the tremendously important function of reality testing, whereby our concepts are known to be congruent with external fact before we act upon them. Then and only then, the ego acts in problem solving ways.

3. Some Defense Mechanisms Of The Ego
As the ego develops throughout infancy and childhood, it is frequently challenged beyond its ability, and from such situations rise certain defensive patterns of activity which are much discussed, since they usually characterize whatever abnormal behavior the subject may exhibit, should he fail to develop beyond the point where they serve the normal needs of childhood. These Defense Mechanisms of the Ego are numerous. We shall discuss the major ones which are Repression, Projection, Reaction-Formation, Fixation and Regression.

a. Repression
We have already spoken of repression, characterizing it as the involuntary denial of attention to a situation of circumstance which is beyond the ability of the ego to solve.

[7] Hall, Calvin S., *A Primer of Freudian Psychology*, pp. 28–9.
[8] *Ibid.*
[9] *Op. Cit.*, p. 42.

Actually, there are two types of repression: Primal repression, which is the ego preventing something that is unconscious from entering consciousness, and repression proper, which is the banishing from consciousness of something that is already conscious. It is to the second type that we will devote the present discussion.

The purpose of repression is to eliminate or diminish anxiety. This is done by removing from consciousness, through the denial of attention, some threat, external or internal, which confronts the ego. Apparently, anything at all may be the object of repression. A percept may be repressed so that a person fails to see, hear, or feel something undesirable to him. An instinctual drive which the ego fears may be unacceptable or painful, as a sex stimulus or fright-producing percept (either the fright itself as an emotion, or the thing producing the fright may be repressed). Unwelcome ideation, either in the form of abstract concepts, memories, or of any other type, is all too often familiar to us as something that we have "forgotten."

We must not fail to note that a certain amount of repression on the part of the ego is performed under orders from the super-ego; certain things must not even enter into consciousness if the super-ego is to be satisfied. Typical examples of this are unacceptable ideas about sex, religiously liberative ideas, or hostility. Appearance of these thoughts in consciousness has traditionally been forbidden by society. This prohibition is internalized in the super-ego and hence, such ideas are usually repressed, which is to say denied access to adaptive behavior.

Repressed material is dynamized by instinctual force, and exists in the unconscious with an increasing pressure for expression. By association, anything that suggests the repressed material must also be repressed, until the effort at maintaining repression becomes disproportionately great.

As we said before, repressed material is inaccessible to the subject's recall for the most part. If it does return to consciousness in a non-symbolic way, it is the occasion of anxiety. Hence, the only way to get it back at all is in symbolic form.

Here we have the dynamic for many of the extravagant symbols which appear when a person dreams or phantasizes.

b. *Projection*

Projection is probably the most generally familiar of these mechanisms, since we can so readily observe it in our associates. Thus, the student feels that he is not lazy but the instructor is abstruse; while the instructor is certain that he could not possibly be dull, but that the students are inattentive. Obviously enough, what takes place is that an inner inadequacy or fault is assigned to an external source. Thus the ego is freed from anxiety, whether it be that of fear, hate, or guilt, since an external danger is easier for the ego to handle than those with inner origins, whether in the id or super-ego.[10]

Nor is the elimination of anxiety the only purpose served by projection; if an external threat is confronting the ego, the ego can express some of the hostility which is surging upward from the id, and do it with a sense of appropriateness. Thus, two things happen: the ego feels adequate and the id is able to discharge hostility. Actually, there are three things because the super-ego need not condemn hostile behavior which is undertaken in a necessary cause. One more aspect of projection deserves mention before we turn to our next point. This is that a subject will likely hold the belief that his ideas are more widely shared than actually is the case; he projects, in short, his own ideas to other persons in his environment. The defensive function of this aspect of the mechanism is plain if we consider it but for a moment. The subject feels himself in the majority, hence accepted, probably correct in his estimates, and in short, successful. The opposite of these conclusions would be extremely painful.

---

[10] It seems to the present writer that a great deal of guilt originates at this point. The ego seems to feel obligated to solve the situation before it, whatever that situation is, and whenever the ego lacks the ability to do this, guilt will result. Thus, whatever other elements enter into the anxiety which the ego is seeking to avoid, guilt is a large part of it.

c. Reaction-formation

This defense mechanism might simply be called compensation. Its nature is that when one instinctual impulse makes the subject anxious, the ego stresses its opposite. Thus, one who feels hostility may engage in exaggerated type of love behavior; however, it can be distinguished from basic love or valid love, by its exaggerated and compulsive quality.

In one frame of reference, the entire super-ego may be thought of as a system of reaction-formations which protects the personality from social retaliation for unacceptable id expression.[11] External as well as internal threats may produce reaction-formations; thus, a person who inspires anxiety may receive elaborate politeness, deference, and exaggerated consideration. A situation which inspires fear may be approached with a resoluteness approximating bravado, so that the subject will not be held suspect of feeling any lack of courage with regard to it.

d. Fixation

When a person has either too much or too little satisfaction at a given stage of development, he may remain at that stage abnormally instead of progressing on to the next higher level of personality growth. Thus, the child movie star may remain in a "cute" and saccharine posture toward life long after childhood and its exaggerated successes have gone by. Again, a person who has been denied normal satisfactions at a given state of development seems to be always trying to go back and complete that stage, in what should be the later strata of his psychic growth. In either case, the force operative is fear of moving to a higher level; whether it be due to too much or too little satisfaction at the level which ought to be superseded. A certain number of hobbies which are pursued with unusual avidity by adults would seem to evidence their desire to go back and pick up childhood satisfaction, which presumably was denied them at the time when it might have been appro-

---

[11] Credit must be given to Calvin S. Hall, *Primer of Freudian Psychology*, pp. 92–3, for material used in this section.

priate. Of course, we must take into consideration that the hobby may provide the symbolism for the satisfaction, rather than the satisfaction itself.

Of course, there is one circumstance of which we must take cognizance in connection with fixation which implies no basic inadequacy in the ego, and no fault on the part of the subject; that is, when some external authority forbids him to move upward in the scale of development. Thus, fear of punishment brings about a fixation at a less mature level than he is capable of achieving. Along with this, we find anxiety over fear of ridicule, if success does not immediately attend his efforts at the advanced level, and a more generalized fear of insecurity amid problems with which he is not so familiar as those of the past.

e. Regression

This last of the ego's mechanisms of defense is very similar to fixation, but carries the same procedure farther; for, whereas in fixation the ego remains at a level of development which it ought to leave, in regression, the ego returns to an area of development which it supposedly *has* left. Actually, any departure from controlled and realistic thinking is regressive; hence, many of the activities practiced by what are considered normal people fulfill this definition. Thus, smoking, getting drunk, indulging in fantasy, going to the movies, practicing sex perversions, chewing gum, all fall into this classification of regressive ego defense.

While these mechanisms of defense are useful for the functioning of the infantile ego, they become pernicious if persisted in when the organism has reached maturity. Indeed, under the pressures which characterize mature life, dependence upon any one of these ego mechanisms of defense may produce a complete failure of personality function, with ensuing breakdown. In fact, it is to the liberation of the ego from these inadequate and childish substitutes for valid action that a great deal of psychotherapy is directed. Fortunately, they yield to therapy rather readily.

II. Jungian Formulations

A. Introductory Observations

C. G. Jung, 1875–1961, was the favored associate of Freud from 1907 to 1913, at which time their friendship ended, largely because Jung had refused to accede to Freud's demand that they elevate the sexual theory to a dogma.[12] He is famous for several terms and techniques that have become household expressions, viz.: "complex," "introvert-extrovert," and "collective unconscious," as well as word association tests.

1. Importance of His Work

Carl Jung may very well be remembered as the most significant thinker of the twentieth century. Although some psychologists, apparently without studying him sufficiently, speak of his work as "mystical" instead of scientific, this is not a valid criticism, for he literally spent years investigating phenomena not only perplexing and highly unpopular, but personally forbidding and even frightening—spiritistic and apparently occult events of a religious nature, but the impact of which upon the human psyche Jung rightly regarded as of transcendent importance.

Nonetheless, it must be admitted that much of Jung's work is difficult of comprehension, and in some cases requires a familiarity with the entirety of his writings in order to make a given passage intelligible. This is partly due to the unfamiliarity of the concepts being presented, and partly to the fact that he wrote too fast, so that the content of his thought changed as time went on. Be all this as it may, his insights into the nature of religious experience are valuable in the extreme, and well worth whatever effort is required to understand them.

2. Jung as a Phenomenalist: The Imago

An important introductory point that contributes to understanding Jung is the fact that he was a phenomenalist in the Kantian sense, so that the experienced world was for him a

---

[12] *Memories, Dreams, Reflections*, p. 150. This was in 1910.

construct of the perceiving and understanding mind. In addition to this, Jung depended heavily on his own idea of the *imago*, which was that any perceptual datum was always known in terms of an emotional coloration which the subject himself brought to it. Thus, reality-as-experienced was for him not some simple objective fact, awaiting perceptual recognition, but was rather such a datum plus the totality of all the subject had previously learned about it, correctly or otherwise; of all the prior emotional conditioning he might have had concerning it, and all of the anticipations he might have built up regarding it. Thus the baldest common fact might have widely divergent meanings for two observers, since each of them would have awareness of the object in terms of his own *imago*.

3. Imago and Complex

Indeed, this notion of the *imago* would seem to lead directly to another important Jungian idea: *the complex*. A complex is simply a constellation of ideas with which a subject is notably preoccupied: but the aspect of this popular concept which popular parlance has never come close to grasping is that every complex has an archetypal core and an associational shell.[13] The archetypes will be discussed shortly: associational shell is an *imago* of something the subject has experienced.

4. Jung and Freud

The great difference for our purpose between Jung and Freud is to be found in the fact that Freud regarded religion as a neurosis to be cured,[14] whereas Jung viewed the religious dynamic as the pivotal factor in human experience, whereby each individual might come to terms with the total experience of the race, as he himself could best receive it, and through

[13] Whitmont, Edward C., *The Symbolic Quest*, pp. 68–69. Cf. also Singer, June, *Boundaries of the Soul*, p. 33.

[14] Cf. *The Future of an Illusion*, and *Moses and Monotheism*, passim. Cf. also, and particularly, *Leonardo da Vinci*, (1932), p. 103.

which he might gain access to a source of verve, originality and effectiveness which would make him most truly himself.

Other differences will become apparent as we outline the Jungian system: we may mention in passing, however, that for Jung the libido was a generalized life energy, rooted in biology, but not necessarily predominantly sexual. Jung never abandoned Freud's basic insights regarding the importance of sexuality, but he refused to assign exclusive importance to this one aspect of energy.

B. The Ego and the Self

Jung's notion of the ego is of a far less important aspect of the mind than that envisioned by Freud. Jung sees the psyche as a sphere, with an atomic nucleus at its center[15]: this nucleus he calls the self, and indeed all of the interior of the sphere bears this designation. On the surface of this sphere, there is a small bright area, which he calls consciousness, and at its center, presumably directing consciousness to some extent is the ego. The principal function of this ego seems to be *awareness*; for that of which we are not aware does not exist, according to numerous Jungian statements. However, if the ego becomes too intimately aware of the dynamic contents of the sphere, i.e., the archetypes, it will become what Jung calls *inflated*, that is to say *overenergized*, so that the possessor of such an ego is psychotic, or in a state approximating psychosis. However, unless the ego obtains access to *some* of the libidinal energy through utilization of symbols from the collective unconscious, it will be a puny, rationalistic center of futility, without any real control over the actions of the personality.

Indeed, as the writer understands the Jungian formulation, the ego always remains more or less the center of awareness for the *Self*, a larger entity, within which, at an unconscious level, the basic gradient of the personality is established.

The approved adjustment is for the center of the self to shift to a point midway between the (surface, conscious) ego and the previous (centrally interior, unconscious) center of selfhood.

[15] See *Man and His Symbols*, p. 161.

C. The *Persona*

By the term *persona*, Jung denotes the official side of the personality; the facade which is presented to the world or to society by the subject. This facade, or officially adopted personality is the construct of the ego, and entirely conscious: even so, it is profoundly influenced by the archetypal image held by the subject of what a personality ought to be.[16] The Latin word *persona* means either mask or personage; we are familiar with the term from theatre programs whereon we read the words *dramatis personae*, "characters of the play." The Latin word in turn, came from the words *per sonare*, meaning "to speak through" and had reference to the custom of actors wearing masks as they took part in dramatic presentations. Thus, *persona* is the mask which the personality wears as it meets the public.

This officially adopted character or mask may very well reflect the first economic opportunity which the individual has. However, by "economic" we do not mean merely the making of money; rather the gaining of gratification, prestige, or any other advantage; of course, the traditional sense of the word "economic" is the one which probably obtains in most instances. Be this as it may, the individual who thus gets a start or obtains a foothold, frequently pursues this avenue of success much farther; in so doing he finds reassurance for himself and, in the phrase of the day, "gains an identity." As he progressively gains greater confidence in himself as the representative of a given type or character, he tends either to neglect or repress other aspects of his personality. Thus, if his first beginning is as a business man, he may neglect a very definite ability at writing poetry of which he was aware before his entry into the business world. Moreover, as time passes he will come to regard the writing of poetry as something unworthy of a business man, and in the end will feel no urge whatever to express himself in this direction. Indeed, he will probably be unusually harsh to other embryonic poets, and take a negative

---

[16] Cf. Laszlo, V., ed., *The Basic Writings of C. G. Jung*, p. 138.

attitude toward their efforts. In short, all other aspects of the personality are repressed just to the extent that they interfere with the character which the subject has officially adopted for himself as the one he will present to his public. Of course, this is a socially efficient means of letting people know what to expect from one who follows a given pattern of life. Hence, the subject with an intelligently constructed *persona* will probably succeed much better than one who has neglected the formation of such an "image," if we may be forgiven the jargon of the present day.

However, the urge for efficiency being what it is, the *persona* is likely to become too restrictive in a great many cases. So many alternatives are excluded from it, and efforts to endow those which remain with psychic energy are so great, that frequently the subject experiences a withdrawal of libido from this *persona*, which is to say, he "goes stale" as regards his narrowly intense ambition, and may well suffer a breakdown as a result.

Such crack-ups usually take place at the climacteric, which has nothing to do with menopause in women, but refers, rather, to the point at which youth ends and the aging process begins; it is intended to designate the moment when the anabolic processes of the organism are more than offset by the catabolic processes.

Just as the maintenance of constantly expanding repressions always requires an increasing amount of energy, so the subject finds it necessary to expend increasing amounts of energy in maintaining the *persona* in the face of the various urges to step out of character, and the time finally comes when he cannot longer remain in character at all, no matter how much conscious effort he applies to the task.

He now finds it beyond his strength to continue on any basis in the pattern of life that he followed for so long. The work which previously was so important to him is neglected; unfamiliar and inconsistent behavior patterns appear; he may fall into moral lapses, but his predominant symptom will be the absence of any strong motivation whatever.

A young man of excellent mind began to show great promise during his first years in the ministry. He was married, and struggling to complete his seminary education when a wealthy industrialist undertook to sponsor him, urging him to continue in school at the sponsor's expense as long as he (the student) deemed it worthwhile. This the young man did, discontinuing his educational program just short of doctoral achievement. His ecclesiastical advancement followed with great rapidity until he had achieved the highest preferment attainable in a leading Protestant denomination before he was 45 years of age.

About five years later, he was "threatened with a nervous breakdown." Though an avid student before, he never studied at all now. Gracious and suave in company, the only companionship he now sought was that of a ne'er-do-well family dependent. Formerly enthusiastic in his Church's support of a strongly temperate morality, his family were now only too well aware of his barely clandestine use of liquor. Fluent in the pulpit, and ready of word at all times when in good health, even routine preaching engagements now exhausted him.

He was finally persuaded to take a year off: a full-scale breakdown followed, from which he ostensibly recovered, but after the recovery he made no basic change in his manner of life, and lived only a few years following his return to work.

This illustrates the Jungian principle of the flow of psychic energy. Jung held that energy always tended to find its own level, and this by sort of principle of compensation. Thus, if one facet of the personality experienced a loss of dynamic, it was to be expected that an increasing amount of libido would flow to some other aspect of the psyche. Hence, when the maintenance of the *persona* no longer constitutes a vital challenge for the subject but rather becomes an arduous duty, the psychic energy flows into some other area of his life, from whence he may derive a new dynamic, if only he is able to discover it there.

A few incidental observations must be made before we leave the *persona*. This element of the Jungian personality structure of course corresponds in large part to the Freudian ego. However, in its directive functions it also parallels the super-ego in some respects, but in other ways stands in contrast to it. Thus, the *persona* is altogether conscious, whereas the Freudian super-ego is always unconscious and is universally the result of introjection,[17] based at last upon fear. The *persona* on the contrary, is built up in terms of practicality, as a sort of running answer to the challenge of each successive moment. Insofar as it is wisely constructed, it will endure longer, and work more efficiently; to the extent, however, that the subject yields to excessive ambition, and narrows his life overmuch in its pursuit, the *persona* will become so restrictive that it cannot maintain its dynamic, and the personality structure will collapse at precisely the time when the subject needs it most, namely the moment when he discovers that his youthful energies will no longer serve him.

Conscious though it is, the *persona* is dynamized by libido from the profounder areas of the collective unconscious, and hence is powerless except in its integrated functioning as a part of the total psychic life. Of course, it will be effective and satisfying in direct proportion to the expression it provides for the archetypal symbols which make up the forces of psychic individuation for the subject.

D. The Shadow

The Shadow, as Jung has described it, is very closely akin to the Freudian personal unconscious.[18] In saying this we have of course already intimated that the Shadow is composed very largely of repressed experiences. To a large extent, this is material which has been validly repressed, or ought to have been repressed, such as impulses to murder and incest, impulses to id release on a level markedly beneath that at which the subject habitually lives, and, in short, impulses to all types of markedly antisocial activity. However, in addition to the validly repressed material, the Shadow contains much that has been *invalidly* repressed: our own failures and inadequacies make up a good part of this classification, which is why the

[17] Also, Jung himself has compared the super-ego to the collective unconscious, by reason of its social dimension. Cf. *Collected Works*, IX, 1, p. 3, n. 2.

[18] C. Jung, *Two Essays in Analytical Psychology*, translated by R. F. C. Hull, New York: Meridian Books, 1956, page 76.

Shadow is so likely to include material that we simply cannot abide in the behavior of other people. However, the contents of the Shadow which make it unique and interesting as Jung outlines it, are those things which are contrary to the demands of the *persona*: thus the poetry which the business man found no time to write, and the relaxation which the churchman would not take time to enjoy, come to have an existence as something altogether undesirable because they have been repressed into the personal unconscious, which Jung calls the Shadow.

Jung's doctrines about the Shadow illustrate his principle of compensation clearly; for as the *persona* loses energy the shadow becomes more insurgent. Hence, just at the time when the personality structure falters, with the collapse of the *persona* at the climacteric, the Shadow clamors for attention and becomes increasingly difficult to keep repressed.

This brings us to the most picturesque aspect of the Shadow itself, namely, the form in which it is symbolized. The Shadow is brought to the attention of the frequently horrified subject in the form of either a very attractive animal or a brutal person, or quite possibly something even more startling. This may merit an illustration.[19]

A Swedish woman of Lutheran background was married to a brutalized and inconsiderate husband who gave her a very unenviable life. However her Scandanavian religious background was so rigorous that she was never able even to entertain any purposeful ideas of divorce, let alone act upon them, although her friends tried to suggest such a course to her. At last she broke and became psychotic; she was duly hospitalized, her case was diagnosed as catatonic schizophrenia, and presently she was adjudged incurable. She was lodged on one of the hospital's back wards, and the attention she received thereafter was altogether nominal. Finally, after seven years interval during which the woman had lived in this uninspiring and to a large extent unattended environment, on the incurable ward of a state hospital, the husband died. Word of his death was taken to her in a routine way, which is to

[19] Professor Carroll Wise, later of Northwestern University, advanced this illustration years ago when he was on the faculty at Boston University; it may come from the investigations of Anton Boisen.

say some attendant walked up to her and told her, "We have word your husband has died." She gave no sign of understanding, which surprised no one, as she had given no sign of anything for a long time. The message was repeated in a routine way by various attendants and nurses who made some effort to communicate with her, but she made not the slightest response to any of them. However, after a few days she surprisingly began to show improvement; this continued with remarkable rapidity until at the end of about ten days she was able to talk, take some personal care of herself, and to communicate intelligently. The medical staff at the hospital was of course delighted. They called her in and talked with her, and were told that she had had a dream in which she had shaken hands with the devil. Immediately following this dream her improvement had commenced.

She was discharged from the hospital and never returned.

The relevance of this material to what we were saying about the Shadow is very direct: the figure of the devil, with whom this unfortunate woman saw herself shaking hands, was of course the symbolism of acknowledged wishes for her husband's death. Since she could not think of divorcing him, she obviously could not entertain in consciousness any thought of admitting that she would prefer him dead or would welcome the idea of his decease. However, once she admitted in this symbolic manner her desire for what was now a liberative fact, she recovered from what had long since been judged incurable catatonic schizophrenia.

If, at the time that the *persona* breaks, any permanent cure is to be effected, it will be necessary for the subject to overhaul his personal unconscious, and re-evaluate the material which the Shadow symbolizes. Some of it will, in all likelihood, be found to have a considerable endowment of libido, making its incorporation in the renewed personality not merely clinically advisable, but emotionally attractive.

Jung believed that it was no great task to empty the contents of the personal unconscious; a few hundred hours spent with any capable operator would exhaust this material. Indeed, he speaks at times as though the subject could recall most of this by himself. It was rather the getting down to the symbolisms of the collective unconscious that made analytic therapy difficult, and of course, significant.

E. The Collective Unconscious and its Archetypes

Of all the differences between the outlines of personality structure set up by Freud and by Jung, the Jungian doctrine of the collective unconscious is of course the most obvious and the most striking. By the collective unconscious, Jung would refer to certain symbolic materials which the individual subject could not possibly have experienced in order to repress, and which under no circumstances can be recovered unassisted, except indirectly, and then in terms of dynamic rather than memory. Such material is found in the mythologies of the world's various religions; their pantheons, and the various exploits and adventures of the gods and other supernatural beings make up the content, for the most part, of this area of the psyche. Indeed, it is not incorrect to say that the collective unconscious consists of the archetypes which produce these various mythological figures as their symbolic fulfillments. Hence, as a characterization of the collective unconscious, we can do no better than to undertake some description of the archetypes.

An archetype may be defined as a structural aptitude for thinking in certain terms. Elsewhere, Jung speaks of them as the permanent possibilities for thought. We might modify this by saying that archetypes are structural aptitudes or potentials for producing *symbols*, which in their turn are dynamic and compressed portrayals of how human life can be lived with maximal satisfaction. They release energy for effort, and suggest by implication the ideal structure of activity by which a challenge can be met or a new activity undertaken.

> As we know, there is no human experience, nor would experience be possible at all, without the intervention of a subjective aptitude . . . Ultimately this consists in an innate psychic structure which allows man to have experiences of this kind . . . The form of the world into which (man) is born, is already inborn in him as virtual images, as psychic aptitudes. These *a priori* categories have by nature a collective character; they are images of parents, wife, and children in general, and

are not individual predestinations. We must therefore think of these images as lacking in solid content, hence, as unconscious. They only acquire solidity, influence and eventual consciousness in the encounter with empirical facts which touch the unconscious aptitude and quicken it to life.[20]

Just as a crystalline structure, after being dissolved in water, assumes once more the appropriate shape of its crystals when the water has evaporated, so the mind has a structure that makes it symbolize certain dynamic experiences in characteristic ways. It is not that men inherit pictures in their heads, nor that they transmit acquired characteristics: but they survive best if their structural abilities to *symbolize*—i.e., to portray possible patterns of action, together with the impulse so to act—i.e., if the archetypes of their collective unconscious are functioning well.

These archetypes are not symbols. Let us say it again: symbols are not inherited. Indeed, the symbols to which the archetypes give rise will vary from culture to culture, but there will always be an underlying similarity of function which makes symbols of a given type, such as the culture hero, unmistakable in their relationship. Thus, it requires no effort of genius to classify Dionysus, Osiris, Mithras, Tammuz, Jesus, and Hermes Trismegistus in the same category.

Throughout all that he has written Jung has held that it is of the very highest importance to come to terms with these archetypes in the collective unconscious. While, as we have said, it is impossible for the subject to gain awareness of these simply by taking thought, yet, if he attends carefully to the backgrounds of thought, and if, particularly, he accepts will-

[20] Jung, *Anima and Animus,"* in *Two Essays*, p. 200. Somewhere the writer has read the statement by Jung himself to the effect that there are two crosses which he bears: the first is that people ask him how he came to reject the Freudian sexual theory, which in point of fact he never rejected, and has repeatedly so stated; the second is, "How is it possible that you think people can inherit pictures in their heads?" To this he protests not angrily, not impatiently, but with real pathos that he never did argue that people inherited such pictures, but only that they inherited the capacity to produce them. This has been explained in the above.

ingly and examines intelligently everything that comes to him with symbolic force, that is, which provides him with verve and joy in living, he can gain a great deal of information about the collective unconscious, for it is the source of his life energy.

Of course, the principal avenue to knowledge of the collective unconscious is psychotherapy. This requires a longer continuance than it takes merely to empty the personal unconscious, and also requires a certain specialized insight on the part of the analyst. However, quite apart from the analytic situation, the individual subject can attain a certain amount of insight into the nature of his own collective unconscious, simply by adopting the correct attitude toward it, which is one of understanding acceptance. The observation of dreams, a careful attention to the subject matter of fantasies, and what Jung calls "active imagination," which consists in attentively regarding the backgrounds of consciousness, together with a watchful attitude for whatever the unconscious seems to be doing to create or maintain psychic balance in his personality, will enable the individual subject to gain a modicum of knowledge concerning the archetypes.

We will leave further discussion of how the individual may become aware of the archetypes for a section a little later on, and proceed to describe some of them directly.

1. The Anima-Animus

As was the case with the *persona* and the Shadow, several statements of definition are available, each one correct in its own frame of reference, if not exhaustive. At the very outset, we must, of course, state that the *anima* is the archetype of what Jung calls the soul; not in any metaphysical sense, but the unconscious life in its totality. As such, it assumes female form for men; Jung assigns three reasons for this:

1. the influence of women upon men, beginning with the mother, then by whatever succession of women inspire the feeling function in a man;

2. the *anima* is the symbol of whatever feminine components occur in the male personality; and
3. the inherited image of woman in man with the help of which he apprehends the nature of women.

When the *anima* appears in dreams or fantasies it may very well be symbolized by the figure of a woman of mystery; a feminine figure only secondarily sexual, but veiled with an aura of attractiveness and intuitive wisdom. As such, it frequently is a guide to the unconscious. If the subject be sensitized for the examination of his unconscious life, the *anima* frequently may give him extensively revelatory insights. In fact, another way of speaking of the *anima* is a function of the relationship between consciousness and the unconscious.

Whereas the *persona* seems to be the individual's effort to embody rationality, the *animus* provides the subject's basic introduction to feeling. This is another reason why it is symbolized in a feminine way. The *anima* causes moods in men, and the *animus*, (which is the counterpart of the *anima*) experienced by women, makes them opinionated and pseudo-intellectual.

Whereas the masculine *anima* takes the form of one characteristically mysterious woman, the *animus*, as women commonly experience this archetypal symbolism, takes the form of a council of elders, or an assembly of fathers who make *ex cathedra* judgments. These judgments are, as Jung outlines them in *Anima and Animus*,[21] "a compendium of preconceptions which, whenever a conscious and competent judgment is lacking, as not infrequently happens, instantly obliges with an opinion."[22]

A characterization of the *anima*, which has apparently been greatly neglected by all writers, is the fact that this archetype subsumes all of the other archetypes of the collective unconscious. It is the symbol of the unconscious life of the subject in the large. Since a far commoner view of the *anima* is that this

[21] *Two Essays*, pp. 198–223, see particularly pp. 218 and 219.
[22] *Ibid*, p. 219.

archetype is the first to appear when the subject is faced with the need to reconstruct his personality, and that it simply leads to the others, this view, which is expressed in *The Integration of the Personality*, pages 78–80, is of some significance.

If, however, by careful attention to all manifestations of the unconscious, with or without therapy, the individual succeeds in coming to terms with his *anima*, the next symbol which is likely to appear as a result of the archetypal activity, is the culture hero.

2. The Culture-Hero

Jung himself says in *The Integration of the Personality* that "it does not help in any way to learn a list of the archetypes by heart,"[23] and again, in the same volume, he identifies Orpheus, Hermes Trismegistus and Nietzsche's Zarathustra with the archetypal image of the Old Wise Man.[24]

Nonetheless, it seems to the present writer that whether we call it culture-hero, redeemer-god, or savior, this archetype both reflects and dynamizes a unique and significant function of human experience, and so deserves mention in its own right. The figure of the hero, who, at a great price to himself, wins some basic advantage for his fellows, either by the help of the gods or in the face of their opposition, is surely one of humanity's most dynamic symbols.

Thus, whether we speak of Prometheus, Gilgamesh, Moses or King Arthur, we are dealing with a fundamental pattern of human idealism, the appearance of which in symbolism has the power either to dynamize the subject to unprecedented effort, or to engulf him if he merges with it too completely.

Indeed, this is the next danger which confronts the subject who, by patience, luck and courage succeeds in gaining mastery of the *anima*: he may become so inflated with a sense of his own importance that he will identify completely with the hero-symbol, and so become psychotic. Every mental hospital has its back-ward Christ to keep us reminded of this danger,

[23] Page 79.
[24] *Ibid*, Page 88.

and every reform movement its entirely situational Messiah to illustrate our point.

3. The Wise Old Man

In *The Integration of the Personality* Jung speaks of the Old Wise Man as a symbol of meaning;[25] but elsewhere he refers to this presentation of the unconscious as the archetype of spirit;[26] and M. L. von Franz, who understood Jung's thought in every detail, speaks of it as an archetype of the self.[27] Now Jung understood spirit as the symbol-forming function of the psyche, possessing a purposive tendency to hold conscious and unconscious together.[28] It operates as a principle of psychic growth, and points us to meanings not yet realized in consciousness.[29] Hence these statements are in no way inconsistent, and the dynamism of this symbol is seen as describable in any of the terms mentioned.

Also, when the *persona* collapses at the time of the climacteric, the principal symptom is *loss of meaning*, permeating all existence. This situation is remedied only by the expansion of selfhood, through the amalgamation of unconscious material. Hence an augmented self supplies the meaning which life lacks, and this archetypal image is the symbol upon which the solution is based.

> The archetype of spirit . . . always appears in a situation where insight, understanding, good advice, determination, planning, etc., are needed but cannot be mustered on one's own resources. The archetype compensates this state of spiritual deficiency by contents designed to fill the gap.[30]

[25] Pages 82–88.
[26] Cf. *Archetypes and the Collective Unconscious*, p. 216. Cited in Brooks, H. C., "Analytical Psychology and the Image of God," in Andover Newton Quarterly, Nov. 1965, p. 49.
[27] Art., "The Process of Individuation," in *Man and His Symbols*, page 196.
[28] Cf. Jung, "The Transcendent Function," CW 8, pars. 132–148.
[29] M. L. von Franz, *C. G. Jung: His Myth In Our Time*, p. 96.
[30] Cf. note 26.

It is thus apparent that the wise old man, as the archetype of the spirit, which is the intent of the unconscious, is the symbol of exactly how the subject's pattern of individuation should proceed. Of course, the situation as regards mergence with the wise old man is exactly the same as in the case of the hero; identification with this unconscious symbol as though it were a personal possession is a simply psychotic course.[31]

Before leaving the archetype of the old wise man, we must say something about the comparable archetype of the great mother which appears in women at the same stage of exploration of the collective unconscious.

> The figure of the magician has a no less dangerous equivalent in women: a sublime, matriarchal figure, the Great Mother, the All-Merciful, who understands everything, who forgives everything, who always acts for the best, living only for others and never seeking her own interests, the discoverer of the great love, just as the magician is the mouthpiece of the ultimate truth. And just as the great love is never appreciated, so the great wisdom is never understood. Neither of course, can stand the sight of the other.[32]

4. Selfhood or Psychic Balance

The fourth archetype which we shall review is that which produces the various mandala symbols, whereby the "nuclear self" or the organizing center of the subject's own unique psychic structure is presented.[33] The mandala is a circular

[31] This is why Jung recommends that all of his patients who can adjust to such a program, should reunite themselves with one of the major units of the Church. The vast machinery of ecclesiasticism is specifically designed to protect the individual from direct encounter with these symbols, and Jung simply takes it for granted that going back into the sheltering institution is *ipso facto* assurances that the subject will never attain individuation. Cf. *Two Essays*, p. 236.

[32] Jung, *The Mana-Personality, Two Essays*, p. 241. The above reference to "the magician" comes from a context in which the magician-figure is equated with the wise old man; Jung believes that both trace back to the figure of the tribal shaman.

[33] M. L. von Frantz, *Man and His Symbols*, pp. 166, 199, and 213. This is very graphically portrayed in a diagram on page 161 of that book.

diagram of which the name comes from Buddhist usage in Tibet,[34] and which in some way not only portrays but dynamizes this fact of unconscious wholeness. Mandala diagrams are frequently produced by patients who are either seeking or gaining access to a feeling of psychic strength, and favorable orientation around the center of their psychic self. These unconscious drawings may take the form of concentric circles, or concentric rectangles, or combinations of these. Jung holds that roundness generally symbolizes a natural wholeness whereas quadrangular formation represents the realization of this wholeness in consciousness.[35] Although it seems strange, Jung used to encourage his patients to draw these mandala diagrams, believing that they exercised a dynamic effect upon the unconscious as the patient would first construct and later comtemplate them. In the interest of clarifying our reference to the "nuclear self," let us look with some care at the different usages which Jung makes of he term "self," as these are outlined by Frank M. Bockus:

> From one point of view the self is the *total system* of the psyche. It is the superordinate system in relation to which the various structures and subsystems of the mind stand. From a second viewpoint, the self is the *centralizing tendency* of the psyche as a whole. It is the central point and function around which are clustered and integrated all the structure and dynamics. As one moves toward selfhood, one moves toward greater integrity and individuality. One becomes a unique center of one's personal history. From yet another standpoint, *the self is the whole*, within which and in relation to which, progressive differentiation and complexity proceed. The distinct structures of the self must be viewed in relation to the large ground to which all are related. From a fourth vantage point, the self can be understood as *the goal of human development*. But this goal, grounded in a collective base, can be reached from a wide variety of developmental histories. Finally, the self, in yet another aspect, is an *archetypal tendency* which predisposes man toward human development.[36]

[34] The word itself is apparently of Sanskrit origin.
[35] Bockus, Frank M., "The Archetypal Self," in *The Dialogue Between Theology and Psychology*, edited by Peter Homans, Chicago University, 1968, pp. 229–30.
[36] *Ibid.*

This "nuclear center of the self," of which von Franz speaks, is apparently identical with the second of the five usages of the term "self," which Bockus has pointed out in our quotation, namely, the centralizing tendency of the psyche as a whole, or "the central point and function around which are clustered and integrated all the structures and dynamics . . . a unique center of one's personal history."[37] The wise old man symbol apparently refers to the fourth usage of the term self, or the goal of human development.[38]

Another way of expressing the things symbolized by the mandala figure is psychic wholeness; Jung constantly stresses the importance of uniting opposites, so that the self is not deprived of the energizing effect of unconscious forces tied up in whatever archetypes are opposed to any given pattern of action. Another way of saying this might be that *the mandala is the symbol of homeostasis, or of psychic balance.*

Although the process of individuation is never completed, yet the mandala symbolism represents the deepest layer of the collective unconscious, since here the universal patterns of human action are related to the individual subject. Many other archetypes exist, among which Jung lists those of the mother and child, and the animal, or various animal figures in addition to the ones we have mentioned: of course, these are reflected in symbols which are simply innumerable, since the symbolizing function of an archetype must fit the circumstances of the individual subject who is receiving symbolic experience. However, when the subject has gained control of the archetypal symbols we have discussed, by admitting their existence and seeking to learn what they have to say to him, it is within the mandala symbol that his further and final efforts at gaining communication with the collective unconscious will be made.

---

[37] *Ibid*, Cf. "official" mandalas.

[38] An alternative interpretation of the wise old man might be that it symbolizes the *manner* of development, the Platonic notion of wisdom, or knowing what to do next.

F. Individuation and the Transcendent Function

Although we have covered a great deal of the material which properly belongs in this section *en passant*, as it were, yet, some summarizing effort ought to be made, in which we attach the religious labels to the activities to which they properly belong, and in which we unite under one heading the incidental remarks we have previously made about the subject matter of this section.

What has *not* been said before is that the function of individuation is a function of the second half of life. The Jungian religious crisis occurs at the climacteric; and although the *persona* is usually presented in the role of the villian of the drama, we must remember that the framing of a *persona* by which economic adaptation can be gained in the early years of maturity is in itself no small achievement. We should also note here that it is by no means a metaphysical impossibility for a person with a well constructed *persona* to carry on some communication with the collective unconscious, even as he pursues his economic aims: e.g., he may carry on a vital religious life. In this connection a famous and generally misinterpreted dictum of Jung's comes into focus, wherein he says that no one had ever come to him as a patient who had retained an active belief in God past the age of thirty-five.[39]

Nevertheless, the typical situation is for the ambitious person who has had a highly rigid *persona*, to find this mask too restrictive and energy consuming to be maintained any longer when the climacteric overtakes him. At this time, he seeks psychotherapy, and if it is possible, Jung directs him back into the church, as we have seen above. If, however, he is temperamentally unfitted to return to the cloying atmosphere of institutional religion, then he must face the task of getting acquainted with his objective psyche at first hand; for Jung regards the therapeutic problem as being fundamentally the restoration of balance to the personality which has had an over-emphasis upon consciousness at the expense of the col-

---

[39] See *Modern Man in Search of a Soul*, p. 264. *Collected Works*, Vol. II, p. 334.

lective unconscious; he assigns an entirely secondary importance to draining the pressures of the personal unconscious, so much stressed by Freudians. The reason for this is that Jung takes a prospective instead of a retrospective view of psychotherapy; whereas Freud sought to discover what had made the personality this way, Jung seeks to determine where the personality wants to go now, and what forces within it may be unleashed to make this possible.[40]

However, Jung takes a very serious view of the therapeutic quest for a knowledge of the archetypes: in fact, he calls this undertaking "the perils of the soul." Let us look at this process again. The *persona* has ceased to satisfy, and life within it has become unendurable because of a movement of the libido away from this conscious part of the personality. It has now moved into the deeper reaches of the unconscious and the patient must regain contact with this life energy if he is to recover. To this end, he must restore his psychic balance by getting acquainted with the archetypes of the unconscious; and there is always the danger that he may become either so terrorized or so enamored of these primordial forces that he becomes psychotic; or if this does not occur, that the progress of his recovery will be halted and that he will remain in an unsatisfactory state of health. Now, as he contacts these deep forces of the racial unconscious through the symbols which they produce, he is engaging in what is essentially religious activity as Jung sees it, and is pursuing the solution to a religious problem. Each time a subject establishes contact with an archetypal image or symbol, he experiences a profound degree of numinosity, for each of the archetypes carries its own intense charge of energy: it is as if each one was seeking its own fulfillment; and to confront the primordial sources of his own psyche may be more than his ego can manage. In short, these symbols are the stuff of which the gods are made.

The substantiation of this statement should be in no way difficult: for instance, it is easy to identify the shadow as the

---

[40] C. G. Jung, with C. Kerenyi, *Essays on the Science of Mythology*, p. 112.

devil. Jung comments somewhere else that the devil has hooves and horns in every religion in the world. Turning to the *anima* figure, Isis, Ishtar, Demeter, and possibly Aphrodite exemplify it beautifully. Lists of hero gods were cited in our earlier discussion of the archetype of the culture hero; they include Prometheus, Dionysus, Osiris, and Orpheus, just for a start.

"God with a beard" is an archetype deeply rooted in student protests down to the present day, although it has been years since the present writer has found anyone at all who has ever seen such a portrayal in an actual illustration. The unconscious symbolism of the Wise Old Man remains as the source of the idea. The recurrent impact of the Mother-and-Child symbolism is familiar to every reader at Christmas. Again, and finally, we are all more or less familiar with Paul Tillich's dictum that God is the object of ultimate concern. From this point of view, the restructuring of the self, obviously of primary importance to anyone who needs it, becomes clearly understandable as an event of the most deeply numinous significance; and one which, while most intimately personal in its application of the cultural heritage to the individual, is yet symbolized by the impersonal mandala. Only one additional thing remains to be said at this point: it is that anyone who has ever had direct contact with one of these archetypal symbols has no further doubt as to its numinous significance and impact.

This is the process of individuation, of which so much has been written. It is easy to describe, but painful as well as dangerous to pursue, for the subject's most basic energies may be stimulated almost unendurably, and in ways he does not understand; he may be confronted with challenges to his courage that stretch his powers beyond their limits, as symbolic suggestions for deeds he never contemplated come to him, while at the same time he is made agonizingly aware of errors and weaknesses he had hoped to keep permanently repressed.

Moreover, every archetypal image by which he is confronted comes dripping with the raw energy of life itself, which to behold is either inspiration or terror, and which the dismayed beholder has probably spent most of his past life seeking to avoid.

Yet, symbols can be attractive, too. Although they are never understood, yet as the subject tentatively explores the meaning of such a presentation, each part of it that he implements with action implies further pertinent activity, so that, without knowing the outcome, the subject finds an entire pattern of conduct not only programmed for him, but dynamized with pleasure and significance.

Nevertheless, as we have said before, it is of the highest importance that the subject shall not fall into a state of premature mergence with any of these archetypal images. They are, after all, *unconscious*, and although he might well gain an aura of psychic intensity by so doing, (the "mana-personality") he would obtain no real authority, inasmuch as he would not possess this constellation of energy, or pattern of activity, but would rather be possessed by it. The appropriate response of the subject to the appearance of these symbols, as Jung outlines them, is *exploration*; mystery is of their essence, and he cannot hope to understand them, except by patiently accepting their guidance; but if he will, with a certain humility, seek to learn what they are "trying" to communicate without identifying with them, their dynamic effect can be utilized without inflating the subject's consciousness to the point where he is in danger of psychosis.

The goal of the process of individuation is for the subject to become so completely himself, so well acquainted with the symbols of the collective unconscious that their fearsome mystery is dissipated, even as their instinctual energy and ingenuity are utilized in patterning his life according to their implications.

The process itself is the strategic *telos* of a more basic one which Jung calls the *transcendent process*; in simple words this seems to denote a method whereby the subject precipitates the appearance of symbolic material by "Continual conscious realization of unconscious fantasies, together with active participation in the fantastic events,"[41] as well as "active imagination," defined as "a vision perceived by intense concentration on the background of consciousness, a technique that is perfected only after long practice."[42] By this persistent determination to be aware of them, plus a clinical willingness to explore the symbolic revelations which they produce, the subject gradually, and not without psychic danger, becomes aware of the archetypes themselves, and gains access to at least some of their dynamic power.[43] Jung is careful to state that this is not his usual clinical procedure, but that the process does occur in certain cases, "because it springs from inner necessity."[44]

III. Proposed Modifications

Since religious experience is basically an autonomous modification of the personality structure, any writer in the field is obliged to elucidate his own notion of personality, before he begins to theorize upon how it may be autonomously modified. This we now do.

A. Freudian Formulations

The formulations of Sigmund Freud are fundamental to our approach. We depend throughout on his concepts of the id, super-ego and ego. However, his notion of libido as being totally sexual in nature seems to be unnecessarily restrictive. We make this statement in full awareness that some allowance must be made for terminology in Freud's use of the term "sexuality." Nonetheless, our concept of libido is more like that of Jung, namely, a generalized life energy which is both biological and psychic. Again, we have never found Freud's notion of the *thanatos*, or death instinct, very meaningful. Indeed, the concept of an aggressive instinct just for its own sake, leaves something to be desired.

[41] *Two Essays*, p. 231.
[42] *Ibid*, p. 234.
[43] Cf. *Supra*, s. v. The Collective Unconscious and Its Archetypes, *ad fin*, pp. 73–85.
[44] *Two Essays*, p. 236.

With the concepts of libido and hostility both giving rise to some discontent, we have sought to reformulate these ideas.

1. *Love as Environment Embracing Behavior*

The libido, or life energy, is most clearly discernible in the manifestations of love, of which it is the dynamic, and with which it can, in fact, be identified. It becomes fully understandable if we think of love in the sense of *environment embracing behavior*: so that the emotional drive of the healthy organism, in addition to being that of the lover for the beloved, is also that of a mother for her child, a teacher for his classroom, a doctor for his practice, a scientist for his laboratory, or a farmer for his farmstead. We might add to these the way an artist feels about his work, including the materials he works with. These examples should suffice. It is not a question of aggressively dominating the environment on the one hand, or of trying to account for all aspects of creative enthusiasm in terms of a draining off of some biological sex drive, on the other, but rather the outgoing life energy of an organism which accepts and affirms all phases of its environmental contact insofar as these are successful.[45] The guidance of the ego is of course implicit in every circumstance cited.

2. *Hostility as Obstacle Removing Behavior*

The same energy, when employed in the removal of obstacles to the embracing of the environment, is hostility, which is thus to be understood as *obstacle removing behavior*.

If the reader will introspect only slightly, he will discover that the emotional attitude that is called upon in starting a hard job of work is identical with that in starting a fight. It is a matter of summoning up energy, getting a charge of adrenalin, taking sudden and direct action, and then relaxing if and when success comes. It may also be noted that the pleasure accruing from making progress with work is very comparable to that

---

[45] This idea was suggested to the writer by an article entitled "What Shall I Teach My Children," by Priscilla Robinson, in Harper's Magazine, August 1952.

attained in winning an athletic contest or a fight. Moreover, no subject will embrace an environment that is filled with obstacles, since it is an emotional impossibility for him to do this. However, once the obstacles are removed, he will find it perfectly possible to feel at home in the environment, and gain a sense of adjustment to it. Observe an infant crawling across the floor; he runs into a dog lying there asleep. His immediate reaction is anger, and he will strike the dog and make outcry, until the unfortunate pet gets up and moves. At this point his anger evaporates instantly, and he proceeds on his way happily: the obstacle has been eliminated.

We have inadvertently stressed the next point that we wish to make; love is more profound than hostility. Once the obstacles to embracing any environment have been removed, the Eros or libido will flow, uniting the subject constructively with his surroundings, and enduring them with an aura of lovability. However, prior to such removal, he will be unable to curb his hostility, because it will be building up in him constantly as the libido continues to flow. He may be persuaded not to express it, but he has no control over the fact of its generation.

A further observation relating to hostility as obstacle removing behavior must be made. It is that any structuring at all that such behavior exhibits must be credited to *the ego*. From one perspective, this is self evident, since the ego *is* the structuring agent of the personality; but there is more, and our experience comes from the world of psychedelics: for users of LSD experience obvious, if temporary ego cancellation, and concurrently find their obstacle removing abilities deleted.[46]

At the other end of the scale, this structuring is illustrated by the activity of any closely organized and highly motivated executive: his work is a perpetual series of obstacle removing acts, dynamized by the id, but structured by his intelligence, which ranges through its entire field of knowledge to bring

---

[46] Braden, Wm., *The Private Sea*, Pps. 11–20, 163. Cf. also, Cohen, Sidney, *The Beyond Within*, Pps. 85, 110, and 259.

appropriate technologies to bear. Indeed, this obstacle removing activity, in which the ego utilizes the aggressive energy of the id in constructive ways, constitutes *the adaptive behavior*, the central function of the ego, whereby the Principle of Practicality is implemented.

The relationship between the ego and hostility, which is simply the removal of obstacles, is thus seen to be closer than has been generally recognized; for as it structures such activity, the ego stands revealed as not merely the *awareness* of reality and practicality, but as both efficient cause and sufficient condition, whereby the life energy is utilized in *shaping* the environing reality into patterns of feasibility.

Finally, we must remember that the *telos* of all this adaptation is to make it possible for the subject *to embrace the environment*: that is, to create a situation in which the personality can carry out the various functions of life without impediment, and interact with the environment in whatever ways are appropriate and meaningful.

3. *Hate as Frustrated Hostility*

Carrying our discussion of hostility a step farther, we come to *hate*. Hate is frustrated hostility, or the strongly emotionalized wish to destroy. As long as the obstacle removing behavior has worked successfully, there is no reason for hate to build up, and it will not be present. It is only when the obstacles are too great to be removed, or the ego is too weak to remove them, that we find the mounting of hate within the subject. At this point, the subject is overcome with helpless anger or rage, and the effort to destroy the obstacle totally, supersedes that of removing it: thus the goal to which it was originally an obstacle is lost sight of, and the subject's behavior is without structure. Furthermore, this emotion of hate may turn against an inadequate ego, i.e., one that cannot structure the hostility efficiently. Hate is an obviously cankering emotion, as destructive to subject as to object, and abandonment of selfhood in the cultic sense is, as a result, not infrequent among those who fall victim to its ravages.

B. Jungian Formulations

Turning now to the Jungian formulations, the writer is in practical agreement with all of them. The notion of the collective unconscious, composed of archetypes which provide the patterns for all types of human activity by giving rise to symbols that dynamize the personality of the subject to whom they appear, is one of the great discoveries of psychology, ranking with Freud's doctrine of the personal unconscious. There are however, a couple of points which would seem to need modification.

1. The Ego

The first is the Jungian concept of the ego. The Freudian ego as a rugged and changing, indeed a turbulent agency of implementation, in which conscious and unconscious forces are commingled, and in which the unconscious frequently comes to consciousness, seems a more operational concept than the Jungian notion of a mere center of awareness, quite outside the profound forces that comprise the core of personality.

Jung's central thesis is the imperative importance of an appropriate balance being achieved between the collective unconscious and the ego: this mutual totality is what he calls the Self, and its attainment is the goal of the process of individuation.

This is excellent: but while we hasten to affirm the dynamic power of archetypal energies, and acknowledge the barrenness of a personality whose ego is divorced from them, yet that same ego must somehow direct and interpret these forces, by the exercise of its principles of reality and practicality: and more than this, it must utilize the energy they provide, in its capacity of an agency of adaption. Finally, the ego is the organizing principle of the entire personality, by whose activity the enormous complexity of the intrapsychic processes is reduced to order.

What remains is perhaps our most crucial point. Our emphasis is upon the ego since *all we can know of the personality happens here*. That there is an unconscious, and that it does influence conscious behavior, are axiomatic statements; but the way that influence comes about is what we are seeking to describe, and the ego is where it must be observed.

2. Limitation of Religious Problems to the Inner-Psychic

The other Jungian formulation with which the writer differs is that which locates the origin of the religious cycle in the breakup of the *persona*. As nearly as he can see, this makes the only religious problem a lack of communication or interplay between the *persona* and the objective psyche or collective unconscious. Hence, if this maladjustment did not occur, Jung would have no need for religious experience. The point of view to be implemented herein is quite different, namely, that many religious problems occur which are not the fault of the personality itself. These may be, as we have said above, either conscious or unconscious. And while it is indeed true that the application of unconscious resources to any problem may contribute to its solution, yet, as we have previously observed, it would seem that Jung had so stressed the type of religious problem that we have called the inner-psychic that he ignores the existence of the other types, and gives no account of what goes on in the personality when they occur. This lack we shall try to remedy.

In the ensuing discussion, we shall seek to correlate Jung's positions with those of Freud, modifying both in the ways indicated. We shall then utilize the resultant synthesis in the analysis of how religious problems give rise to religious experiences. It is our hope that the system of insights thus made possible may constitute an account of religious experience more lucid and coherent than hitherto attained.

Part 3

Personality Modification in Religious Experience

I. The Basic Mechanism:
Personification and Relationship

A. The Nature of Personification

The basic mechanism in religious experience is the personification of some aspect of a problem in such a way that the subject is able to form an advantageous relationship with the resultant personified figure. When such a relationship has been formed, the subject will have solved his religious problem. The activity leading to this relationship is implicit in the personification itself. Such personification is autistic and involuntary, i.e., unconsciously produced; but the formation of the relationship, while reflexive, and dictated by the character of the personification, may also be conscious. These two aspects of the mechanism, while formally distinguishable, are inseparable in actuality.

This personifying process is not to be confused with anthropomorphization, which is the ascription of human characteristics to things not human. A child, who stands at a window chanting "Rain, rain, go away, Come again some other day," need not imagine the rain to be an old woman with long gray hair, yet he is surely personifying. Again, the golfer who beseechingly says "Get in there!" to his ball when a putt is about to go astray, is not invoking anything beyond the ball, in his unfeigned supplication! And if these instances seem trivial and non-religious, it may be pointed out that both are thoroughly precatory. The following further illustrations may be adduced.

A prominent psychotherapist related to the writer how one of his clients, in a directed phantasy, conducted an extended two way conversation with a *tree*: the colloquy was crucial to the therapy.

A trusted associate of the writer reported dreaming, with strongly numinous affect, of a *horse* he had known in childhood. In the dream, he spoke not *to*, but *with* the animal, which turned out to be, after considerable association, a surrogate for the dreamer's father.

Although the examples cited may seem trivial, comparable personifications are to be found throughout the Ethnic religions; and in addition to showing the distinction between personification and anthropomorphism, they provide an introduction to the relation between personification and religious symbolism, which will be discussed presently. Obviously, the clearest instances of this process are the big archetypal personifications that make up the pantheons of the world's religions.

The entity that is personified has symbolic force for the subject in that it portrays, or promises, or suggests, a way of dealing with his problem. Once personified, the subject can relate to it most effectively, and it is in the relating that the problem is solved. The personifying process is unconscious, and when the subject is confronted by what he sees as a personal entity, he experiences numinosity. The revelatory experience is thus an experience of personification. It is here that new energy enters consciousness, but it is only structured in the relationship, which is where the solution takes place.

The mechanism in its entirety may thus be understood as a subject autistically relating himself to any entity wherein he finds symbolic force, as though it were capable of rational understanding and sentient response. The rise of personifications will be discussed in Section II, and the outworking of the relationships which are integrally a part of this religious mechanism, in Section III.

B. Personification and Infancy

That personification does, in fact, take an anthropomorphic form, is not hard to explain. The very early memories of any child are bound to reflect the personal nature of whatever assistance he received when in distress. The relief and immediate transition from panic to total reassurance that he experiences when parental help and comfort are given are the very prototype of numinosity. As a result, the portrayal of assistance-as-such that his unconscious produces in later life takes personal form. The universal character of this experience is entirely sufficient to account for the archetypal and collective quality of the personifying process.

C. The I-Thou Relationship

Nor is the collective memory of personal consolation in infancy the whole story. When a problem arises, of any sort, it is deeply satisfying to gain access to whatever personal sources can set it straight. Even when the problem is basically impersonal, the archetypal pattern of reaction is to personify, for in this way of approaching the world there is some chance of getting a response to command or entreaty. H. A. Frankfort has aptly commented,

> The fundamental difference between the attitudes of modern and ancient man as regards the surrounding world is this: for modern, scientific man the phenomenal world is primarily an "It"; for ancient— and also for primitive man, it is a "Thou."[1]

We might amend Frankfort's statement by pointing out that modern man still carries this approach to the universe in his unconscious mind. William James takes cognizance of this distinctly religious way of approaching the universe which science is at such pains to depersonalize:

> Religious thought is carried on in terms of personality, this being, in the world of religion, the one fundamental fact. Today, quite as much as at

[1] Frankfort, H. A., *et al., Before Philosophy*. Baltimore: Penguin Books, 1968, p. 12.

any previous age, the religious individual tells you that the divine meets him on the basis of his personal concerns.[2]

Thus, whether or not a given personification is anthropomorphic, the important thing is that the subject gets the problem into a personal focus as he personifies it. He has now come to grips with it on a personal basis, which makes it vastly more manageable for him, and gives his deepest and most hopeless distress an aspect of controllability.

D.　All Religious Symbols are Personifications

Before going farther in our discussion of personification, it is necessary that we connect our present train of thought with what was said earlier in Part One about religious symbols and their agency in solving religious problems.

It is obvious that personifications, as we have been viewing them in the paragraphs immediately preceding, are symbolic: but if personification is the basic mechanism of religious experience, then what of the symbols that are not personifications?

This question troubled the writer for some years, until he finally concluded, after prolonged investigation, that *all religious symbols are either themselves personifications, or are ancillary to them.*

Consider the most impersonally symbolic facts, or objects, or entities, that can be found: a mandala, the syllable *OM*, the word Hallelujah and the steeple of a Church. The mandala turns out, under systematic association, to symbolize the *subject's own selfhood*: indeed, Jung cites a case history in which Edward Maitland, introspecting on a mandala, found that it contained God, in the Christian frame of reference, but as a union of opposites. The "vision" was deeply numinous, and was accompanied by an intense heightening of consciousness.[3]

In a recent conversation the writer was presented with the argument that insofar as the mandala refers to the subject's

---

[2] *Varieties*, ML ed., p. 481.

[3] Jung, C. G., *The Secret of the Golden Flower*, in *Psyche and Symbol*, Anchor, 1958, p. 322 ff. Cf. 324.

selfhood, it is a non-personal symbol of something entirely personal, and hence *not a personification.* However, the "self" to which the mandala refers, and to which it is ancillary, *does not yet exist.* Rather, it is a portrayal of an ideal self, toward which the process of individuation may hopefully lead, and so is, in the fullest sense, a personification—of what the subject hopes to become. It is this personification to which the mandala is ancillary.

The syllable *OM,* seeming at first to be merely a nonsense sound employed by Hindu devotees to produce auto-hypnosis, turns out under examination to be a name designating either Brahm the creator (Taittriya Upanishad, i, 8), the entire Trimurti of Brahm, Vishnu and Shiva (its commonest signification), or Krishna "as the universe and the Brahman." (Bhagavadgita).[4]

Again, the word Hallelujah means "praise to Jah (Jehovah)", and while it is within itself undeniably symbolic, it carries this impact by reason of its being an invocation of deity.

The steeple *of* a Church has its symbolic effect because the Church is the Church *of Christ,* or of some clearly personified deity.

Similarly, *the Bible* is the word *of God:* another sacred book, the *I Chang,* is itself so vividly personified that Jung would not pose the same divinatory question to it the second time, since to do so would be impolite![5]

These illustrations should establish our contention, so let us summarize the qualifications to our general statement that all symbols are personifications:

1. The major divinities are, of course, everywhere directly personified, and intensely symbolic.
2. Some symbols are *ancillary* to known personifications

[4] Keith, A. B., Art. *OM,* E. R. E., ix, 490–92. In addition to its substantive meanings, OM is also an expression of assent, or surrender; a saying "Yes" to the gods.

[5] Jung, C. G., *Preface to the Secret of the Golden Flower,* in *Psyche and Symbol* (Anchor, 1958), p. 230 ff.

having symbolic force, as, the cross *of Christ*, the blood *of the Lamb*.

3. Some symbols, seeming non-personal in themselves, designate the psyche of the subject.
4. In some cases, a non-personal symbol will be ancillary to a personification which remains concealed in the unconscious, but can be brought to consciousness subsequently.
5. A final qualification may be added. If and when a non-personal symbol produces remarkable effects for good in solving a religious problem, its appearance and action will eventually be interpreted as due to God. Thus at last even this kind of symbol, if such there be, becomes ancillary to a major personification.

E. The Utilization of Existing Personifications

Obviously, not all of the personifications that are made when religious problems occur are original and new. Existing deities are for the most part the deities to which men turn when their religious consciousness is activated. Indeed, the formulation of a new deity is an event of historic importance, and even the adoption of new views about an old one by an "ordinary" man, i.e., one who is not a religious thinker by profession, is a matter for serious comment among his friends.

Nonetheless, the mechanism is exactly the same, as regards personification, *per se*, whether the subject *finds* the personification he needs, or whether his own unconscious makes it for him. Something archetypal is presented to his consciousness at the suitable moment[6] and he accepts its symbolic impact for his problem. The mechanism has already been traced in part, and will be spelled out in full, presently. The present point is, that wherever the archetypal figure comes from, that mechanism is the same. When the personification is already in existence, the relationship is never as precisely suited to the subject as when the symbolic figure is autonomously produced: but symbolic impact is symbolic impact, wherever the symbol comes from. It is a solution to the problem, brought about by the structuring

---

[6] Cf. Section II, The Rise of the Personification, *Infra*, pp. 83–102.

of energy that results from seeking and attaining the correct relationship with the personification which the latter implies.

II. The Rise of the Personification

The sequence of events involved in the appearance of a personification can be delineated far more precisely than has hitherto been done. Since such an experience is nothing less than a total reconstruction of personality for the subject, it is a matter of considerable interest, both to professional investigators of religious phenomena, and to those having a philosophical interest in the dynamics of psychotherapy. We shall, in the present section, try to do some justice to this delineation.

At this point, the attention of the reader is called again to the essential characteristics of religious experience, which is *instrumental, involuntary, irrational* and *efficacious*. These characteristics are discussed in Part One, Section III.

A. Presence of a Religious Problem

The *sine qua non* of religious experience is the presence of a religious problem. Such problems have been discussed in Part One, Section V. Apart from the presence of such a personality crisis, religious experience simply does not occur. This does not mean that any given problem can predictably give rise to paranormal experience, but simply that religious experience *when it does take place* is a function of human crisis.[7]

This is of course not difficult of interpretation. When the subject finds that a problem which is vitally important and emotionally intolerable is completely beyond his ability to solve, he experiences a tremendous concentration of blocked energy at the point of the problem:

> In a situation such as this, relief is frequently sought in violent, uncontrolled movements and even in self-inflicted pain. A discharge of the pent-up energy is thus effected. Is not this what happens in great

[7] The apparent exception created by a problem-free individual who seems to delight in worship for its own sake, and does in fact arrive at numinous emotion, will be discussed in Part Four, Section I, A, *infra*, p. 203.

sorrow, when, under the shock and the pain of a disaster, one behaves like a raving maniac? No purposive action appropriate to the circumstances being at hand, the energy released by the distressing situation is spent in violent, irrational behavior.[8]

However, it is when even these conventional expressions of rage, indignation, sorrow or despair, whether motor or verbal, have ceased to give any relief at all, that this dammed-up energy at last creates its own outlet, in the mechanisms of religious experience. Nothing less than a problem of these dimensions could dynamize the momentous changes of orientation which this experience entails.

The writer has recently encountered a conservatively-voiced dictum to the effect that 'God sometimes breaks into human life at His own good pleasure.' Assuming, as we must, that this position is taken sincerely, rather than being an instance of the systematic obfuscation discussed as one of the difficulties in the field, the reply he would make is that when, if indeed ever, a *bona fide* religious experience occurs with no religious problem discernible, we have an unconscious problem somewhere near at hand, and that careful analysis of the solution which appears will presently reveal what the problem is.

However eager a supernaturally oriented religionist may be to ascribe impressive or favorable events to the direct intervention of a personification which is important to him, we cannot grant this contention at all, since apart from its origin in the religious problem as here defined, religious experience simply does not yield to investigation. We repeat—the *sine qua non* of religious experience is the presence of a religious problem.

B. Exhaustion of the Ego

A second condition of religious experience is the exhaustion of the ego. Until the subject has validly striven to the absolute limit of his strength and ingenuity, he cannot say the problem is insoluble, which is to say in our terms, in the religious realm; and it is only at this point that the religious mechanism may be

[8] Leuba, *Psychology of Religious Mysticism*, p. 161.

expected to become active. Furthermore, until exhaustion has produced the quiescence of the Principle of Practicality, the relaxation and passivity which James noted with such perspicacity as the immediate precedents of numinous experience[9] will not be present. And whereas James did indeed cite the repeated incidence of this passivity just before the onset of inspiration, he did so in the manner of noting an important coincidence,[10] whereas it is actually a necessary condition of the experience. For note: with the final exhaustion and collapse of effort, as well as the desire to *make* any effort to solve the problem, *the entire Secondary Process has become inactive*, so that the troublesome distinction between inner and outer reality is removed!

Father Divine's favorite slogans were "When you become as a leaf in the wind I can use you," and in later years, "The intellect is a bar." Both reflect his practical awareness of the point we are making. On the current scene, the scalp-lock worn by the Hari-Krishna adherent is the sign of his having ceased all questioning. In cultic usage this is taken as equivalent to enlightenment!

Every evangelist who ever urged his tutored audience to Surrender! and who eroded their resistance with verse after verse of hyper-suggestive hymns, has been aware of this

[9] Cf. the case of Stephen Bradley, *Varieties*, p. 188; of David Brainerd, p. 209; of "T. W. B.," p. 211; and of Henry Alline, p. 214. Other examples appear on p. 205. Cf. also pp. 245 and 249.

[10] On p. 207 of the *Varieties*, M.L. ed., James acknowledges the centrality of self-surrender in the history of Christianity. He then goes on to point out, very correctly, that it is preposterous to ask a man with a religious problem (he happens to be discussing *guilt*, just here—) to surrender to some higher power on the plea that all will then be well with him. His discussion continues with the assertion that there are just two ways of getting rid of undesirable emotions: (1) the overwhelming onset of some opposite emotion, and (2) getting so exhausted that we cease to care about *anything*. He then gives us his crucial comment: "Now there is documentary proof that this state of temporary exhaustion *not infrequently forms part of the conversion crisis*." *Op. Cit.*, p. 208. All italics are the writer's. He then goes on to cite the experience of David Brainerd as a prime example of ego exhaustion, which it certainly is.

principle, if only pragmatically; but only a few theorists have noted it, and they with no clarity. However, it is absolutely central to the rise of the Personification, for here is the Suspension of Disbelief of which Coleridge and Tolkien have spoken—here is the cradle in which the True Believer is born.

Now blind capitulation to mass pressure is more piteous than admirable: but in autonomous personality adjustment, the exhaustion of the ego is central to the occurrence of the phenomenon we study. Unless the critical faculties are rendered inoperative, the symbolic presentations of the unconscious will never be accepted, since they are in their very essence irrational: yet it is in terms of these that the personality must restructure itself if it is to surmount the problem which is destroying it.

C. The Primary Process: A Solution Phantasy

When the exhaustion produced by prolonged yet unavailing struggle, carried on under intolerable psychic pain, has thus rendered the ego inoperative, both adaptively and critically, the primary process takes over, with a phantasy of the desired situation. At this juncture we may note that the subject is in exactly the same situation as he was in infancy, when he had no resource available for dealing with insecurity. That his reaction should now be similar is most logical. Calvin Hall has stated the matter succinctly:

> However, should the ego fail in its task of satisfying the demands of the id, ego-cathexes are reconverted into instinctual object-cathexes, and infantile wish-fulfillment reigns again. This is what happens during sleep. Because the ego cannot function efficiently during sleep, the primary process is invoked, and produces hallucinatory images. Even during waking life, the primary process may be reactivated when the ego does not produce results directly. This is known as *autistic* or *wishful thinking*.[11]

This presentation of the primary process may be simply a forlorn and wistful mental picture of what the desired state

[11] *Primer of Freudian Psychology*, p. 44.

would be like, or it may become so intense that the subject actually is hallucinated, and has sensory impressions of the situation for which he yearns. We find these exemplified in the experience of the desert wanderer with hallucinations of water (as distinct from the experience of mirage); in those of starving men with visions of food;[12] and in that of the exploratory mystic,[13] who, under the pressure of intense desire, has a vision of God. It is also frequently illustrated in the experiences of the recently bereaved, who catch hallucinatory glimpses of their beloved dead. In all these circumstances, the exhaustion of the ego is an obvious precondition of the autistic experience. Speaking of the vision of the person seeking to gain mystic enlightenment, Leuba says,

> There is no or little external perception to contradict the hallucinations, neither is there enough independent mental activity to cause their rejection.[14]

Two more observations are pertinent. First, this phantasy is of the end, not the means. Obviously, the id, *per se*, can depict no instrumental activity more effective than that which the ego has been carrying on, and which has ended in failure. Second, this id-drive toward solution, unstructured though it is, is powered by the basic energy of the personality, and supplies the dynamic for everything that follows. To this we now proceed.

D. Archetypal Structuring: The Personification Proper

It is at this point that the most central and significant fact of religious experience takes place: the rise of the personification, which we have been adumbrating from time to time, throughout the foregoing material.

---

[12] Such autistic experiences are feelingly and convincingly portrayed by McKinley Kantor in his book *Andersonville*. That the accounts are fictitious does not detract from their psychological accuracy.

[13] Cf. the section on Mysticism, III, C, 2, a, *infra*, pp. 125–126.

[14] *Psychology of Religious Mysticism*, p. 162.

The subject is traumatized, the ego is helpless, and the only psychic content is infantile phantasy, borne into consciousness on a tide of desolate yearning that will not be put down. This is the religious crisis.

It is here that the religious mechanism goes into action: the collective unconscious provides archetypal structuring for the energy which produced the solution-phantasy of the Primary Process. This archetypal image may structure the content of the id-phantasy implicitly, or it may, so to speak, rather implement the *intent of the id*, and provide a better solution for the problem. Thus, the Primary Process may phantasize the death of an enemy, but the archetype will suggest making him a friend. The id may phantasize *escape* from a bad society, and the archetypal image suggest remaining in the danger zone to effect reform. The id may hallucinate the return of a loved one recently dead, but the collective unconscious will structure a quality of life that permits rejoining the beloved in immortality.

This archetypal structuring of the solution to the problem is accompanied by the Personification of some aspect of the problem. The thing personified may be either the problem itself, a force behind the problem that can either cause or cure it, or the *solution* to the problem. Whatever form the particular personification takes, its function seems to be to provide the subject with a course of action that will relieve the intolerable emotional pain that the subject feels. To fight or to run; to plan better or to try harder; to assume a new perspective, or to hallow defeat; whatever it be, the personified symbol somehow suggests a pattern of behavior which bears the stamp of racial wisdom, fitted to the subject's need with an exactness that will eventually become apparent, although it may at first appear impractical in the extreme.

Sometimes the personification will give the subject explicit instructions as to what he must do, as when Moses was confronted by Yahweh in the burning bush,[15] or when Wovoka had the vision which was the basis of the Ghost Dance

[15] Exodus 3:13

religion.[16] Again, the symbolic figure may only *imply* the appropriate activity by its own affectional nature, so that as the subject fears, or hates, or loves, or covets, or despises the archetypal image, the activity he undertakes in establishing a suitable relationship to it will solve his problem. This *structuring* of the energy which the id cannot otherwise express is apparently the key to getting it admitted to the ego. The entry into consciousness of energy which previously was unconscious constitutes a clear gain in disposable libido, and is the explanation of the enhancement of personality that religious experience brings.

The personification which appears may be so archaic that the subject is at a loss to understand it at all, or so contemporary that part of its mystery may be why *this* particular figure should carry such a weight of importance; but one characteristic it always has, is a perfect applicability in one way or another, to the cultural situation and personal circumstances of the subject to whom it comes.

Currently "charismatic" figures, including the major social reformers, and even the military and athletic heroes of any period may appear as religious symbols; but obviously the personification appearing most often and most numinously will be that of some deity already in existence and receiving vital worship.

As this autonomous experience overtakes the subject, precisely at the moment when his despair has become too great to be borne, it becomes apparent why religious experience universally has the format of an objective intrusion from without. His own abilities, proven inadequate under pressure, have collapsed in failure: yet in the ultimate apathy to which his distress has brought him, he is addressed by a personal entity with a wisdom utterly beyond his own imagining, who, at the very least, restores him to effectiveness, and quite possibly lifts

[16] Mooney, James, *The Ghost Dance Religion and the Sioux Outbreak of 1890* (RBEW, 14, 1896), pp. 771–774.

him to beatitude. The divinity with which this archetypal figure is clothed is what we mean by numinosity.

E. Numinosity

1. Definition and Use of the Term

The defining characteristic of religious experience is *numinosity*, which is the emotion that a subject invariably feels in the presence of a religious symbol, and is his response to the sense of supreme valuation and mystery which such a symbol inspires in him.

In taking this emotion, which is the invariable concomitant of the personification[17] and has traditionally been described as an awareness of the divine, as the identifying factor in religious experience, our usage is closely related to that of James, who defined religion as [all that men did . . .] "*so far as they apprehend themselves to stand in relation to* whatever they may consider the divine."[18] However, James was at pains to extend his understanding of the divine to all manner of vague reverencabilities, whereas for the present study, the meaning of the term "symbolic" is simply "problem solving." Thus, at the same time, we have nailed down the presence of religious symbol, by the emotion it alone generates, even though the symbol itself may not be obvious in the subject's field of consciousness; and we have accounted for the sense of supreme valuation which it always inspires, since the symbol is that which does indeed unlock a previously insoluble problem; and this of course, is what religious experience is.

No one who employs the concept of numinosity in any way can avoid coming to terms with the views of Rudolph Otto, who originated the expression. For him it was the primitive basis[19] of "The Holy" which he regarded as a *category*[20] by

---

[17] Cf. Section I, D. *supra*, p. 80.

[18] *Varieties*, ML ed., p. 31.

[19] Otto, Rudolph, *The Idea Of The Holy*, 2nd ed., translated by John W. Harvey. London, New York, Toronto: Oxford University Press, 1950, pp. 124–25, 133.

[20] *Ibid.*, Chaps. XIV *in toto*, and XVII.

which we apprehend that which is truly divine. His point of view was frankly supernaturalistic,[21] and amounted to an attempt to document the authenticity[22] of the Judaeo-Christian deities in their traditional formulations, as being metaphysically certified![23] Quite apart from the metaphysical intent of his entire study, which the present writer found altogether obvious,[24] it would seem contradictory that anything having the status of a category should have antecedents, or require the progress of civilization to be developed[25] out of some more basic and fundamental emotion. Nonetheless, many of his observations are undeniably penetrating, and his genuine attempt to grapple with the data of religious experience makes him one of the half dozen writers who have actually done this.

By way of summary, then, Otto's position is that numinosity is the primitive emotion which, by a process of refinement,[26] is developed into the category of *The Holy*, whereby the real divinity of an object of worship may be authenticated.

For the present writer, numinosity is understood to be the identifying characteristic of the experience of symbolic encounter; or, in other words, of the experience in which a religious problem, as defined, is being or has been solved. Stated still differently, it is the emotional concomitant of any experience in which the circumstances or abilities of a subject are enhanced so that he is either (a) externally relieved of an insoluble problem, or (b) gains the ability within himself to solve such a problem.

2. Occurrences of Numinosity

What, then, are the occasions when numinosity occurs? We have made the general statement that 'numinosity invariably accompanies the religious symbol.' Within the limits of that statement, certain specifications can be made.

[21] *Ibid.*, pp. 110, 112, 129.
[22] *Ibid.*, p. 145.
[23] *Ibid.*, pp. 110, 142.
[24] *Ibid.*, Cf. pp. 142, 153.
[25] *Ibid.*, Cf. pp. 140, 144.
[26] *Ibid.*, pp. 109–110.

a. Subsequent Interpretation

The first type of numinous occurrence is that in which the symbol is invoked by a subsequent act of interpretation, *after* a problem has been solved, so that the solution is ascribed to a previously known deity. It includes three types of religious solutions—(1) that in which some external force solves the problem adventitiously, (2) neuromuscular solutions of the non-symbolic type, in which the organism itself achieves some seemingly impossible feat, probably because of a sudden infusion of adrenalin, and (3) intellectual solutions in which the subject comes up with the answer to a previously insoluble problem in a sudden insight. All three of these are considered in Part One, pages 26–31, and their discussion there may be reviewed at the reader's option.

Two things are to be noted in the present frame of reference: (1) As we have said before, these three instances are noteworthy in that the subject might have interpreted them otherwise—i.e., they owe their religious status to a belief which the subject has previously held, and the likelihood of their being thus interpreted is directly proportional to its intensity. (2) Contact with the symbol is made when a solution which *actually did occur* is ascribed to the god, and this is when the numinosity is felt: the emotion of sacredness, compounded of supreme valuation and mystery.

b. When the Symbol First Appears

The next type of numinous occurrence that appears for our classification is found *when the symbol appears*, i.e., when the personification described in Section D, above, takes place. Thus, whether the personification exists previously, or is autonomous: whether it is of a problem-, cause-cure-, or solution-type god, when it dawns upon the subject, and his pressured consciousness becomes truly aware of it, there is a moment of recognition in which he says, as it were, "This is the way out, now I can do it," with an eager and literally rapturous acceptance *of the idea*, which is never forgotten by anyone who has ever known it, and which is the very essence of what we mean by 'numinous.'

Of course, if the personification is that of a problem-god, the acceptance is not *of the god*—quite the contrary; but now the subject sees that all he has to do is drive this figure away, i.e., achieve the proper relationship, and things will be better. Such a god, repulsive as he is, and loaded with *negative* numinosity (which we shall presently discuss) is nonetheless a portrayal of whatever needs to be eliminated from the subject's environment or expunged from his life, and this recognition carries clear numinosity with it.

Similarly, when the personification is of the cause-cure variety, the moment when the subject feels its symbolic force for him, and recognizes that his problem can be solved by discovering and meeting this deity's conditions, is always one which is heavily fraught with the emotion we are considering.

And, of course, the moment when a solution god is envisioned is one of numinous rapture for anyone who has ever known it. The awareness of a personal entity, presented with all the power of the subject's own unconscious, whose apparently cosmic function is to assist the subject, is without a parallel—"I am come that ye might have life and have it more abundantly."

c. Establishment of the Appropriate Relationship

The third occasion of numinosity occurs when the appropriate relationship with the symbol is attained. Whereas the initial appearance of the symbol inspires hope, the attainment of the relationship which the symbol suggests brings relief, fulfillment, joy, or bliss.

The religious experience is complete only when the relationship is reached, so that while the sense of restored psychic potency through the structuring of activity is the basis of the numinosity felt at the appearance of the symbol, that which rises when the relationship with it is consummated is more in the nature of relief, normalcy, satisfaction and rightness: a sense of health. This is the "New Dimension of Selfhood" of which James has spoken so convincingly.[27] The precise quality of the emotion which will be felt depends, naturally, upon the type of personification that has been made.

Thus, whether a problem-god has been exorcised, a successful bargain struck with a cause-cure deity, or a state of mergence reached with a solution-god, the resultant numinosity is always strong and distinctive.

We do not mean to imply in any way that there is a "numinosity-gap" or failure of sacredness between the appearance of the symbol and the attainment of *appropriate* relationship with it. Certainly religious experience is unitary, and its two aspects (personification and relationship) may even be chronologically indistinguishable; but there is a different complexion to any experience as it reaches its conclusion: It then has a finality which is unmistakable.

The sequence we are describing begins in the emotional pain of an insoluble problem, and moves autistically toward its solution. This is reached as the appropriate relationship with the symbol is attained: and the aura of hope which informed the numinosity attending the symbol's first appearance is changed to a sense of consummation, as the subject, now safely past his crisis, knows a more complete sacredness, dynamized by fulfillment instead of promise.

3. Negative Numinosity

No discussion of numinosity would be complete without some consideration of its negative aspects. The reader may have noticed that each reference to sacredness in the preceding pages was hedged by some mention of dismay or horror. Although bona fide instances of negative numinosity are scarcer than general impressions might suggest, they still cannot be ignored, since the literature of comparative religion abounds in allusions to the necessity for appeasement or aversion of supernatural beings who are either inherently evil, dangerous, or ill disposed. What, then, are the instances of truly negative numinosity?

[27] *Varieties*, ML ed., p. 506. Cf. 499 *et pre.*

a. Autistic Personification

We must begin with the totally autistic personification of an inner fear. Here the subject sees a ghost, or hallucinates an enemy, an animal, or something else that is frightening. This entire mechanism is discussed in connection with Problem Gods. The point here is two-fold: (a) The subject makes this personification autonomously and with no prototype, and (b) while it lasts, the experience is one of supernatural horror. The subject reacts as aversively as he can, and, if the personification be truly autonomous, he can leave it behind, or cast it off, i.e., externalize it, very shortly, since this is the purpose of the symbol.

b. Possession by a Problem God

Instances of being *possessed by* a figure of evil are, of course, well known. These, however, entail the fact of *prior formulation*, since the supernatural being who takes control of the subject's personality is usually minutely described. Nor are we talking about the Faustian situation, in which a subject seeks out a supernatural source of power for the purpose of bargaining with it, albeit dangerously and disastrously, but rather of an unwilling subject being consciously beset by some apparition of horror, which he cannot shake off. If this malign being is a demon of disease, the symbolism is easy to understand, both for the subject and for the investigator; but the whole experience can assume a more cosmic frame of reference. Compare, for instance, Mary Baker Eddy's M.A.M., or "Malicious Animal Magnetism" with Oral Robert's demons of disease: bad as the illness is, which gives evidence of their troubling the patient, it is after all, just illness: whereas the effects of M.A.M. were far reaching and sinister in many areas far outside that of physical health. Mrs. Eddy referred to it as "The Fiend":[28] and curiously enough, believed in it herself.[29]

[28] Cf. *Science and Health*, 3rd. ed., 1881, s.v. *Malicious Animal Magnetism*.
[29] Cf. Dakin, E. F., *Mrs. Eddy: The Biography of a Virginal Mind*. New York: Scribners, 1930, *passim*. Cf. pages 129–34, and 214, in particular. In point of

Along with possession by the devil, or some other major personification of evil, the phenomenon of bewitchment claims our attention briefly—the situation in which a subject is sure that he has fallen into the power of some lesser being who is still supernatural, or has access to supernatural powers. This can be illustrated conveniently from the lore of the medieval witch-cults, since these have so much in common with all primitive religions. Typically, the subject feels that he is under some kind of spell, because his luck is bad, or he doesn't feel good, or he is beset by strange and frightening impulses. If he insists that he has seen one of these beings, he is probably telling the unvarnished truth, as there were plenty of them around. Also, he may have been missing livestock, stolen to provide the feast at the next Sabbat: and if his physical malaise takes a really alarming turn, he may have been given poison, at the instance of an enemy who has purchased the services of the local herb granny. Hence, if he accepts her ability to cast spells at face value, and becomes deeply alarmed when she mumbles at him, he is not acting altogether without reason! What we are saying, of course, is that a hard core of the bewitchment syndrome may have been and probably was, due to individuals getting hold of secretly held scientific techniques, and using them inimically against those whom they happened to dislike. The pattern recurs throughout primitive religion.

c. Resulting From Interpretation

i. The Uncanny   We now come to several kinds of negative numinosity which are strictly the product of interpretation. They are all very similar: indeed the only distinctions separating them are purely formal, but these distinctions need to be drawn. The first kind is found in connection with the merely uncanny—some event, not in itself greatly alarming, but apparently without an explanation, is attributed to the agency of

---

fact, it was the one thing in her entire theology that she believed unfalteringly.

a problem-god. The resultant negative numinosity which the subject feels—supreme *negative* valuation plus mystery—may linger in his mind for a disproportionately long time.

ii. Misfortune Due to a Problem-God   Another type of negative numinosity, and perhaps the commonest, is that which accompanies the ascription of some misfortune to a problem-god. The problem need not be inordinately great, and might have escaped any numinous coloration, except for the interpretation which is given it. However, once it is interpreted in this way, it becomes the occasion of numinous emotion with a negative value, since it is now held to be indicative of the unwelcome attentions of the problem as thus personified.

iii. Misfortune Interpreted as Due to a Cause-Cure God   This instance of negative numinosity is very close to the preceding one, but distinguishable in that this time the routine misfortune is ascribed to the cause side of a cause-cure-god. We need to remind ourselves constantly that there is indeed a difference between the personification of the *problem itself*, and of a *force behind the problem*, capable of either causing or curing it. Whereas aversion *per se* is the appropriate relationship to be sought with a problem-god, a cause-cure-god must be bargained with. Consider the Vedic Rudra, who is destructiveness, *simpliciter*: he must be flattered, paid, or overcome, all with intent of getting him to leave, as quietly as possible. The Greek Poseidon, on the other hand, as god of the sea, can either arouse or quiet the wind, and so must be dealt with quite differently: an agreement must be reached whereby he will give enough wind to make navigation possible, but not so much that it becomes perilous. When, therefore, misfortune is interpreted as due to the cause side of a cause-cure-god, the ritual response will be one of bargaining.

d. Negative Numinosity Due to the Anger of a God

i. A Cause-Cure God Who Has Been Offended   Once more, the material classified here is so very close to that of the preceding section as to be distinguishable from it for the most part only formally. The writer hopes its inclusion is justified.

First, the idea that a misfortune is due to a cause-cure-god who has been offended, probably by not having received acceptable or sufficient sacrifice, may be due to interpretation, or may arise from directly revelatory experience: the same is true of our next point—that of a solution-god who is angry.

Second, the concept of a cause-cure-god who is destructively angry, and must be placated, is clearly distinct from that of the same personification merely functioning according to one aspect of his nature, without thought of human consequences. The latter is no more alarming than any other view of a natural force, whereas the negative numinosity inherent in a natural disaster which the subject seriously believes has been staged on purpose to do him injury, must be greater than anything we are familiar with at the present time.

ii. A Solution-God Who is Indignant   The final category into which occurrences of negative numinosity are classifiable is that due to the anger of a solution-god who is indignant. The thing rousing his indignation is the failure to observe the new morality which he has revealed and commanded earlier, as instrumental to the establishment of an ideal society. As before, misfortunes may be interpreted as due to his anger, subsequently to their occurrence, or the god may announce them in advance, through a prophet. Such a deity may also claim authorship for them concurrently with their happening, in a similar revelation.

All of the Old Testament prophets proclaimed the wrath of God, to be manifested in an early judgment, which would relentlessly winnow the righteous from the unrighteous: Amos, Jeremiah, and Ezekiel give clearest illustration to the syndrome, which may be termed Theological Prophecy.

4. Numinosity as Supreme Valuation

We now come to the matter of delineating numinosity itself. In various places above, we have spoken of it as the emotion accompanying ideas of supreme valuation, accompanied by mystery. The analysis and exposition of this position will make up the present section, and the one to follow.

a. Religious Experience as Instrumental

It is of some importance to spell out the intimate and necessary connection between sacredness, and the instrumental aspect of religious experience, inasmuch as institutional attempts are constantly being made to produce numinosity in the absence of any real solution. However, it is always at the moment when the subject has been reduced to helpless apathy by his struggles with a problem which is totally insoluble, overweeningly important, and emotionally intolerable, that the symbolic personification appears to him, or, as he would express it, a god comes to his rescue. The access of energy into consciousness, and its meaningful structuring, which such a manifestation typically provides, constitute the most important event that any human being can experience. Thus the numinosity which accompanies and identifies such an occurrence, containing as it does, elements of tender dedication, and instantaneous surrender to an Ultimate Source of Value, is seen upon analysis to be an aspect of the supreme valuation which the subject feels by reason of the instrumental function of the experience, in solving the problem which previously was destroying him.

b. Religious Experience as Efficacious

Another aspect of numinosity as supreme valuation is the *efficacy* of the experience in which that emotion arises. If religious experience occurs at all, i.e., so as to produce numinosity, or, in other words, so as to solve the religious problem, it occurs full scale, so that the personality of the subject is profoundly changed. Spiritual impotence is alleviated and psychic energy enhanced by the appearance of a personified figure, archetypal in nature, of such compellingness that the subject immediately seeks to establish whatever relationship with it is most appropriate. Insight as to what this relationship is to be is given by the symbolic figure itself, either *explicitly*, in some command, or *implicitly*, by the affective quality of its own nature. In the formulation of this relationship, the subject finds his problem solved and his personality reconstituted, by the action undertaken in attaining the appropriate relationship. The exuberance and joy which this experience brings can never be overstated. This is the "new dimension of selfhood" of which James writes (*Varieties*, M. L. ed., p. 506); it is the Kingdom of God that it is within; it is the ineffable moment of which the metaphysical mystics speak; and its bliss is so intense that ecstasy is the only word by which it can be adequately described.

5. Numinosity as Mystery

a. Religious Experience as Involuntary

The feeling of supreme valuation by which a subject is dynamized in the moment of his contact with an archetypal image is inevitably accompanied by a sense of mystery. It can be summarized in three questions, which the subject will always ask, albeit not always in full and verbalized consciousness: (1) What is it? (2) Why do I value it so much? and (3) Why is it happening to me?

It is important to note that if the source of his sudden well-being is something known and recognized, the subject will not experience numinosity, since he will feel valuation, but not mystery. That is to say—he will not have a religious experience! Of course, if he attributes a natural circumstance which has solved his problem (e.g., the seagulls, which ate the locusts for the Mormons), to the agency of an archetypal personification, i.e., a god, the numinosity will follow, and the experience becomes religious: but if the naturalistic interpretation be chosen, as is perfectly possible in such a situation, the religious classification of the occurrence is totally obviated. This whole syndrome was discussed on its own merits under "Occurrences of Numinosity," in Section II, E, 2, a, *supra*, page 91.

When closely examined, an essential characteristic of all

events capable of assuming a numinous coloration is seen to be their *involuntariness*: they cannot under any circumstances be undertaken or produced at will. The appearance of an archetypal symbol is, of course, our premier illustration. It is not a matter of charted and familiar value-experience, such as orgasm, occurring at times autistically; it is *always* autistic. Furthermore, if some value-experience, occurring autistically, and accompanied by numinosity, i.e., having a religious dimension, is so mastered and reduced to routine skills that it can be produced at will, as for example by some meditational technique, *the numinosity departs*! Moreover, when this situation is brought about, the possibility of numinosity occurring as a result of the event being *interpreted* as divinely caused, is also greatly diminished, for the subject is well aware that now it is the result of something he did himself.

b. Religious Experience as Irrational
  The mystery which is an essential component of numinosity is also structurally related to the irrational quality of the experience which inspires the emotion. Not only is religious experience impossible to produce at will, but when it comes, it is totally different from anything the subject has been trained to expect, and is, on its surface, often preposterous: and yet it brings his most desolate affliction under immediate control.
  The archetypal image that makes the experience memorable is unrelated to any logic but its own: it may be so archaic that the subject cannot even identify it, or as commonplace as a barnyard animal; but it comes loaded with an emotion the subject can neither deny nor explain: and the activity that it suggests is by definition other than that which practicality would ordain.
  Yet when it comes, this enigmatic personification relieves the intolerability of the religious problem, and suggests, by implication as often as by direction, a vector for activity which the subject may not understand for a long time, but which he finds satisfying from the first step he takes upon its path. Indeed, as we have seen, his response to the experience as a whole, is one

of supreme valuation. Hence it is altogether unsurprising that he also feels a sense of mystery, inasmuch as the source of this new beatitude completely eludes his comprehension, even while it dominates his awareness.

c. Intensity of Valuation

A definite part of the mystery which the subject feels in the numinous moment arises from the intensity of his own response to the symbolic figure which structures the experience.

Not all archetypal images are of the caliber of the one met by Isaiah in the year that King Uzziah died.[30] Beloved people, appearing in dreams, phantasies, and sudden memories, can assume archetypal proportions which will detonate a subject's emotions uncontrollably: actual parental figures may assume symbolic force as the Old Wise Man or the Earth Mother; the archetype of the Divine Child may assert itself in the memory of a real child, living or dead; a friend may become a Culture Hero, and a lover be seen as Anima or Animus.

Furthermore, material objects may have enormous symbolic impact, when a contemplating subject gains emotional clarity or release through their agency, and thus sees them as having archetypal reference. Baby's shoes, a scholar's hood, the old oaken bucket, a lock of hair—who can calculate their dynamic?

Any one of these homely and familiar entities may, on occasion, assume the symbolic role, in a religious experience; and when such is the case, the emotional response of the subject is shattering to him, and usually a total surprise. This intensity of valuation, in itself, constitutes an element of mystery which makes the moment numinous, and documents the occasion as religious.

III. The Structuring of Relationship: The Solution As Such

As the archetypal personification appears, it brings with it an obvious awareness of the relationship which will be most

---

[30] Cf. Isaiah 6:1–13.

advantageous for the subject to adopt toward it. This has been explained above. Of course simply being aware of this person-ification at all is a relationship of sorts, since the subject is in its presence: but it is the *favorable* relationship with itself that the symbolic figure ennunciates or implies. We must now consider how this quality of relationship is structured, and how and why such relationship to a symbol can solve religious prob-lems.

A. Problem Gods and Their Aversion

The most primitive type of personification is that of Problem Gods in which the problem itself is personified. Thus Marett[31] cites the Kaffirs who gather on a hilltop and shout at an approaching storm, commanding it to pass them by. G. Foucart says, "The personification of the solar or lunar eclipse as a horrible monster is a universal religious phenomenon, and is everywhere of first importance."[32] Fever, Cough and Rash are names assigned to certain of the Rakshases, a particularly malignant group of Vedic demons.[33] The only cause of disease recognized in Babylonia was the entrance of demons into the body of the sufferer.[34] References in the literature to beings of this class commonly speak of them as demons, and it seems usual to refer to them as pre- or sub-religious. The reason for this apparently is that problem personifications carried with them such a weight of primitive horror that presently they themselves were regarded as religious problems, and at some very early time were made subsidiary to other gods which came into being for the precise purpose of controlling the earlier ones.[35] The instantaneous success of Buddhism in Tibet is closely related to the astuteness of its clergy in assuming an exorcistic function toward the problem gods of the earlier Bon

[31] *Threshold of Religion*, p. 14.
[32] E.R.E., ix, 782b.
[33] Moore, G. F., *History of Religion*, I, 259.
[34] *Ibid.*, p. 223.
[35] This illustrates with precision what we mean by "Problems of Prior Formulation."

religion, whereby the latter were reduced to controllability and consequent demonic status.[36]

Be all this as it may, the mechanism is that the problem itself is personified so that it can be driven away. The plausibility of this approach to crisis situations increases with a few moments reflection: for a storm will fall quiet, a fever burn itself out, a flood subside, a prowling animal go away, or darkness yield to dawn, with the passage of time, so that anything done to exorcise personifications of these unpleasant facts or events can eventually claim at least a degree of success. Also many ghosts and goblins represent the hallucinatory productions of inner panic, and the mere fact of giving them identifiable personification externalizes them, thus dissociating the subject from fear which otherwise would have continued to dominate his consciousness.

Then too, the definite symbolic portrayal of what is disaffirmed structures the beginning of a value system by showing the behavior, circumstances and situations to be avoided.

The techniques of aversion are well known, and in themselves of only secondary concern for the moment. Their employment, however, puts the obstacle-removing behavior into focus if the problem is a social one. Furthermore, when these techniques involve communal participation, i.e., dancing, chanting, or collecting ritual objects, the basis of much subsequent cooperation has been established.

Moreover, theories of what will drive a disease-demon away, naive as they are at first, contain the beginnings of science.

Various cautionary observations need to be made. Thus, if the apotropaic rituals are compulsive in themselves, we have descended to the level of magic, and are outside of the psychology of religion: consider the profound difference between the way a pilot would have felt about carrying a stuffed animal as a fetich against gremlins, supposed to cause mechanical problems to aircraft, and his unfeigned and validly religious reaction, in the event of being hit by shrapnel. It is when

---

[36] Noss, John B., *Man's Religions*, 4th ed., p. 182.

truly precatory rituals are conducted, beseeching deities such as Rudra, the Vedic god of destruction, to go away, that we are truly dealing with problem gods as such. Furthermore, when Oral Roberts invokes Jesus Christ, in order to cast out the demons of sickness, whose presence he says he can detect, we are no longer talking about problem gods at all, but about *the invocation of a solution god*, whose function it is to overcome the personified figures of evil.

1. The Devil: Satan

With the returning popularity of "evangelical," i.e., literalistic and fundamentalistic Christianity, a renewed emphasis upon the devil, commonly known as Satan, has come into being. As a personification of whatever impels a subject to antisocial behavior, as this is defined by the religious group, or whatever makes him unhappy, since the believer's euphoria is, by definition, one aspect of his mergence with Christ, the devil is constantly spoken of, and becomes a convenient object upon which to project all social and inner-psychic problems. Most of all, however, the devil is invoked to account for errors of belief, and failures of faith in the major creedal affirmations. Since the benefits promised in these revitalized strongholds of orthodoxy, i.e., healings, forgiveness of sins, financial success, freedom from anxiety and the certainty of immortality, are all contingent upon total acceptance of their doctrines, and absolute faith in the claims made, it is immediately apparent that the devil serves an important apologetic purpose (a) in accounting for ritual failures i.e., the non-appearance of benefits promised, in the lives of adherents, and (b) the elimination of guilt from the consciousness of those persons who are convinced they should obtain the promised benefits of membership, but are not receiving them. It is of course by the agency of the solution-god that the devil is driven away, and the subject strengthened meanwhile to resist his attacks. Such protection is typically gained when needed by simply appealing to the solution god.

The same personification, in a more primitive frame of

reference, is the object of a ritual of exorcism in the Catholic Church, which is described by Montague Summers on pages 207–209 of his *History of Witchcraft*. It is still available upon request, being conducted by clergy who are specially trained for this work, in a monastery somewhere in the Middle East.

The need for such ministration is indicated by illness beyond the skill of available medical practitioners to cure, or for which they find no cause; by psychosis, particularly when accompanied by blasphemous utterance: by the subject's own belief that he is possessed, and most definitely, by his persistent inability to accept required doctrines. The ritual may be requested either by the subject himself, or by those who feel responsible for him.

The ritual proper is to be held in a Church: idle curiosity seekers are not to be allowed to view the performance, although witnesses of devout and stable character are required. The Blessed Sacrament is not to be brought near the body of the "obsessed" during the ritual for fear of irreverence. Holy water and the Crucifix are the sacred objects most used.

After preliminary prayers, the priest wraps the end of his purple stole around the patient's neck, and enjoins the evil spirit to depart, almost constantly making the sign of the cross over various parts of the patient's body with the crucifix, as indicated in the rubrics, as he invokes all members of the Trinity, various saints, and various mysteries of the Church, in each case citing their power over the possessing spirit. This is done three times, with a wealth of imagery. Every known symptom that might be caused by a problem-god is recited, and every possible form and guise that the devil might assume, as well as every possible designation that might be applied to him, is mentioned. The rubric at the end says that if by this time the possessed person is not set free, the exorcism shall be repeated. It is interesting to note that the three long exorcisms are not directed to the patient, but to the devil who is troubling him.

2. *The Telos of Aversion*

Of course our basic interest here, is in the telos of the religious experience, when the correct relationship has been established, and the problem thus solved. The symbol, here a personification of the undesired element, has shown the subject what to do: and the activity thus structured has laid the ghost, compelled the storm-god to go elsewhere, or cast out the demon of disease. The negative numinosity which the subject has been feeling now turns to positive, and he feels relief, escape, and thankfulness.

But is it numinosity? All we can say is that if it is, it is. This ambiguous comment is made necessary by the fact that frequently the exorcism of a problem-personification explains it entirely out of existence. The resultant sense of freedom, gained by the migration of a religious issue, is a tremendous experience, though all too soon forgotten. Indeed, the only emotion as powerful as numinosity is the discovery that none is necessary! The clear and pleasant light of reason, illuminating some area of previously uneasy superstition, carries an emotional impact fully equal to that generated by an occasion of successful contact with the gods.

3. Note on The Complexity of This Area

This area of primitive personifying, where the bare problem itself is addressed as personal, has an odd and perplexing quality, for it is here that many disciplines intersect, or perhaps it would be more accurate to say that here a number of areas shade into one another.

Thus, sociology and psychology meet here, by reason of the fact that techniques for the aversion of problem gods are for the most part socially undertaken. In just this connection we find the religious quest in a close association with religious fulfillment that taxes our power to describe, since ritual and autistic experience almost coincide in these aversive efforts.

Again, science and religion meet in this area, since anything done to problems of nature which will banish their fearsome personifications, inevitably has a scientific aspect.

Magic and religion also meet at this level, since initial efforts to expel problem gods are compulsive, but become precatory as greater sophistication is attained.

Negative and positive numinosity also are found in closest conjunction here, inasmuch as the intrinsic horror turns to sacredness when a problem god who has been insistently present is successfully driven away.

Moreover, solution gods, which are the highest and most culturally sophisticated kind of personifications, are constantly found within the realm of problem gods since it is by appeal to their agency that these autistic shapes of primitive fear are most effectively exorcised.

And finally, it is among these primordial gods which give personal form to the alarming aspects of the natural order and their reverberations within the human psyche, that theology and autonomous symbolism have their first and indeed their most intimate contact; for as the problem gods in their initial formulations become too horrendous to be borne, they are rationalized away, and reality is assigned to more ethically plausible deities, until they themselves are relegated to a place in folklore—and become mere Hallowe'en figures of an earlier and cruder time.

B. Cause-Cure Gods: The Relationship of Bargaining

1. The Ethnic Focus of the Archetype

The next level of personification is that in which a force behind the problem, capable of either causing it or curing it, is the thing personified. Gods of this kind typically represent the major forces of nature—wind, rain, sex or growth. Agencies as important as these are obviously non-manipulable, and their personifications require precatory address. They are thus at a higher level of religious development than the problem gods, who could, for the most part, be exorcised by direct techniques. Nonetheless, typical cause-cure gods are still relatively primitive, and the problems of nature which are their concern are the first to migrate into the domain of science. Of course, we must remember that functions are often assigned quite arbitrarily to a given deity, and that we cannot expect to find a natural force personified *in puribus*, every time a god of this kind is met.

Thus Ishtar, the prototype of all sex goddesses, is also appealed to for success in war, by the Mesopotamians: the sun-god Apollo is made the patron of the arts, and a cause-cure god of illness, in addition to his well-known oracular function, while the Indian Varuna, originally a sky-god, comes to be invoked as a god of righteousness.

The mechanism by which gods of this kind are approached is that of bargaining, with the whole domain of sacrifice subsumed in its extension. The desired relationship is that of a bargain successfully concluded, so that the subject is pleased with its outcome, and is confident that the god is equally satisfied.

These are psychological facts, and essentially simple ones; but the exposition of their details is complex, and its documentation will require considerable reference to the History of Religions, although we seek by our illustrations only to epitomize the mechanism being considered.

We may begin by noting that although we are still discussing autonomous religious experience, which is by definition individual, when we seek to bring it under observation at this level, we are compelled to look at it in a social setting, since a great part of the bargaining which is structural to it is carried on socially, and is for the solution of problems of nature, which are socially shared. Nor is this hard to understand; for when a problem of religious dimensions arises in an area which affects everyone, the ritual cooperation of the entire society is enlisted to deal with it, and its impact upon the individual occurs within this institutional matrix.[37] This is characteristic of the various ethnic religions, and might almost be given as their definition.

Moreover, when we look directly at such experience, what we see smacks of the magical. Much of the ritual that is ethnically addressed to cause-cure deities falls into the pattern we have elsewhere called The Magic Formula, which is to say

---

[37] Also, problems of nature are the only ones acknowledged at this cultural level. Inner-psychic problems are treated as problems of health, and the others are unknown in a vital ethnic situation.

that when such ritual is performed, it is taken for granted that the desired result will accrue. However, we often overlook the fact that the compulsive aspects of ethnic ritual are always accompanied, and indeed dynamized by, precatory ceremonials which constitute the central fact of sacredness for the whole performance.

Thus in Zuni, the entire male population is organized into a dancing society, with precisely delineated gentile groups assigned to each week of the year-long ritual cycle, which is addressed to problems of fertility in the winter, and to the matter of obtaining rain, in the summer. Since the people enjoy it, dancing is held to be what the gods most enjoy, and hence is essentially worship. Indeed, according to a promise primordially made, the *katcinas* will always attend when the people dance, and will not fail to make it rain.[38]

Yet, while the dancers are performing publicly, the priests of the same gens are sequestered in an underground kiva, and there praying with profound earnestness, having been under stringent taboos for several days.[39] Of course the prayers they use are in precise correlation with the public dancing ritual: but the point we are making, is that these prayers contain references, made with the greatest naivete, to the offerings being made, and the benefits expected. *Thus the aspect of bargaining is at the very core of the most sacred part of the entire ritual!* Here are the concluding lines of one of the principal prayers of the rain priests, which illustrate our position fully:

> This day
> With the flesh of the white corn
> Prayer meal, commissioned with our prayer,
> This day with prayer meal
> Four time we shall spread out the mist blanket. (i.e., the meal
>   painting on the altar.)
>
> Our children
> All the different kinds of corn

[38] Bunzel, Ruth, "Introduction to Zuni Ceremonialism," *R.B.E.W.* vol. 47, p. 497.

[39] *Op. Cit.*, p. 515.

All over their earth mother
Stand poor at the borders of our land.
With their hands a little burnt, With their heads a little brown
They stand at the borders of our land.

So that these may be watered with fresh water
We keep your days. (i.e., observe the taboos, perform the ritual.)

That all our children
May nourish themselves with fresh water
Carefully they will rear their young.
And when our daylight children
Have nourished themselves with fresh water
We shall live happily
All our days
This is all.

Thus speaking plain words
I set you down quietly. (i.e., the medicine bundle, in which the
    power of the priests inheres.)[40]

Furthermore, every ritual occasion in Zuni (and many other occasions) is accompanied by the offering of prayer sticks. These are small willow sticks with certain feathers attached, which are the clothing of the gods, and are held to be highly prized by the divine beings. Their preparation and offering involve the use of prayers which both stress the importance of the offering, and specify the favors expected in return. Here is an example:

—And offering our fathers their plume wands
We make their days. (Observe their taboos: pray to them.)
Anxiously awaiting their days
We have passed the days.
After a little while
Your massed clouds,
Your rains
We shall desire.
We have given you plume wands
That with your waters
Your seeds,
Your riches,

[40] Bunzel, Ruth L., "Zuni Ritual Poetry," *R.B.E.W.*, vol. 47, p. 658.

Your long life,
Your old age,
You may bless us—For this I have given you plume
  wands.

To this end, my fathers,
May our roads reach to Dawn lake;[41]
May our roads be fulfilled;
May we grow old;
To where the road of our sun father goes
May our roads reach:
May our roads be fulfilled;
May we grow old;
May we be blessed with life.[42]

In short, as Ruth Bunzel herself summarizes, "In their prayers, Zunis do not humble themselves before the supernatural: They bargain with it."[43]

The same mechanism of mentioning to the god the gifts which are being offered, and the boon which is desired, is manifested in a Mesopotamian ritual of the public cultus, beseeching Enlil of Nippur to bless the soil:

Father Enlil, with song majestically we come;
  the presents of the ground are offered
  to thee as gifts of sacrifice.
O Lord of Sumer, figs to thy dwelling we bring:
  to give life to the ground thou dost exist.
Father Enlil, accept the sacred offerings, the
  many offerings.[44]

Such bargaining is made appropriate by the harsh fact that such a deity must always be approached as the *cause* of whatever problem has prompted the religious activity, and hence must be persuaded either *to cease functioning* as he has

[41] The water that lies on the easternmost rim of the world. This is where the sun comes out, and stands, therefore as a symbol of fulfillment.
[42] Bunzel, "Zuni Ritual Poetry," *R.B.E.W.*, 47, p. 625f.
[43] *Ibid.*, p. 618.
[44] Langdon, Stephen, *Sumerian and Babylonian Psalms*, pp. 278–79. Quoted from *Cuneiform Texts in the British Museum*, XV, 10.

been doing, or *to function in the opposite way*, so as to relieve whatever despite his recent activity has brought about. For the becalmed mariner, the lack of wind is as great a problem as is its wild abundance to one fighting a storm; and in either case, the wind god must be bargained with, *to reverse his field*. Thus in *Iliad* I; 60 ff., Achilles says of another problem,

> But come, let us now inquire of some soothsayer or priest, yea, or an interpreter of dreams—seeing that a dream too is of Zeus—who shall say wherefore Phoebus Apollo is so wroth, whether he blame us by reason of vow or hecatomb; if perchance he would accept the savour of lambs or unblemished goats, and so would take away the pestilence from us.

Observe that he has no doubt that Apollo is the cause of the many deaths occurring among the Greeks, nor does he doubt that the god can stop them: his only concern is what the price will be, for the god to stop causing the problem, and to begin curing it.

Despite the ethnic, and hence social, rootage of bargaining rituals, individual petitions to cause-cure gods are by no means unknown. In Babylonia, each freeholder had a "personal god" from whom he had received outstanding benefits at some previous time, and to whom he would appeal whenever fresh need arose. This was done through institutional channels, with the help of the clergy. As the priest led the suppliant into the presence of the deity, the sacrifice would be mentioned, both as to kind and amount, and the deity urged to accept it, and to meet the suppliant's need, which was presented for his consideration. When such acceptance, and correlative problem-solving on the part of the god took place, the relationship which the petitioner then felt was nothing short of mergence; the god was even thought to dwell within his body, and hence to protect him from demons of disease. Indeed, the official signature of a Babylonian citizen consisted of a seal-cylinder, upon which was engraved a portrayal of the original instance when his "personal" god had given him aid.[45] In short, the deity is now viewed and treated by such a subject as a *solution god.*

2. Bargaining: The Clergy

Much light may be shed on the entire syndrome we are discussing if we investigate this matter of bargaining in somewhat greater detail. We may note at the outset that this bargaining has two levels: (1) that between the subject and the god, and (2) that between the priest and the subject. Since the priest manages the bargain at the first level, and since he speaks for the god, both in *setting the price* for the supernatural favor, and in *issuing the promise of relief,*[46] the bargain at the second level must be concluded first, since his services are so necessary.

a. Setting The Price

Taking these facts into account, we see that the centrality of the clergy in the bargaining situation can hardly be exaggerated. Their own fees are surprisingly modest, probably because they are subject to regulation:[47] it is as bargainers for both the petitioner and the deity that their position becomes truly interesting. While they do not, of course, resort to open haggling as they indicate the amount which will win the divine cooperation, and while the sacrifice appropriate to a given situation may already be prescribed by the ritual, yet the bargain they drive *for the god* will be proportional to the seriousness of the petitioner's situation (not to mention his wealth!) and to the prestige of their own position. They are, in the nature of things, the proprietors of the ritual, of which an essential part is the liturgically approved manner of beseeching the deity to accept the proffered offerings. Its administration is

---

[45] Ward, William H., *Seal Cylinders of Western Asia, passim.*

[46] Indeed, he *dominates* the transaction, since he represents the suppliant to the god, and also reports the reply which the latter gives!

[47] Cf. *Corpus Inscriptionum Semiticarum* 165 for a table of fees allowed the clergy. Note also I Samuel 1:13–25.

a supposedly supernatural technology not elsewhere available to the subject. Moreover, the petitioner is unlikely to complain, since he is afflicted with a religious problem, and so by definition *in extremis*, and likely to accept any arrangement, however ruinous, as preferable to his present distress. The outcome is a bargain of truly supernatural proportions.[48]

Lest we seem too pessimistic about the bargaining proclivities of religious functionaries, we hasten to state that many instances can be found where the price assessed by the priestly intermediary had nothing to do with money, but rather was a demand for ethical improvement, moral integrity, or heroic action. Yet the plaints of Amos, Micah, the first Isaiah, and the author of the non-cultic source of Isaiah 58, all are evidence of the truth in practice of the things we have been saying.

i. Vows   The emphasis we have been putting on the pivotal function of the clergy in bargaining with cause-cure gods will serve to introduce a somewhat parenthetical note on the matter of *vows*, which are a special instance of individual petitioning of cause-cure gods, since vows are frequently made with no recourse at all to the clergy. The story of Jephthah, in Judges 11, is well-known: before a battle, he vowed that if Yahweh would give him a clear-cut victory, he would sacrifice whatever first came out the door of his house, upon the occasion of his return home. It was his daughter who came out, and sacrifice her he did, with her own concurrence, in payment of his obligation. The writer recently saw in the public prints an account of a Roman Catholic bishop, who, some years ago, built a church in Cincinnati in payment of a vow made earlier, when the good bishop was caught in a storm at sea. Having survived the storm, the church was accordingly built.

In instances such as these, the price is always the very

---

[48] A case in point is that of the Brahmins, who, toward the end of the Vedic period succeeded in bankrupting the Kshatriya caste, (originally their social superiors), by urging them to undertake always more expensive sacrifices, in the interest of obtaining a hypothetical deification. Cf. *Satapatha Brahmana*, XIII, 1, i. Cf. Monier Williams, *Hinduism*, London, S.P.C.K., 1882, pp. 39–42.

highest that the subject can possibly offer: "afford" is not a word that applies here, since the problems by which vows are impelled, are, after all, of religious intensity. The only aspect of bargaining that appears, is whether the deity will consider this offering an adequate recompense for reversing the course of his activity, and so deign to accept it.

b. Issuing the Promise

It will certainly be noted that the connection between the ritual (or vow) and the solution is merely ostensible: but we may note with equal clarity that the solution itself is perfectly real, if and when it comes. The supposed connection between the two is provided by the weight of institutional assurance given by the clergy, whose convincingness in ascribing causal efficacy to the rituals is pivotal to the whole enterprise.

Certain men possess an undeniable ability to present and manipulate religious symbols with maximal impact, which gives them a unique effectiveness in conducting religious rituals.[49] Furthermore, it requires only a moment's reflection to realize that until a solution has come to the suppliant, no bargain has been struck: yet a sufficiently experienced and aggressive practitioner can *promise* the solution well in advance of its actuality, thus reducing the anxiety of the petitioner to tolerability much sooner, and so providing a *de facto* solution to his religious problem, albeit not the one primarily intended. Since the solution *which is being promised* may also, and probably will, in fact eventuate, this early assurance of supernatural aid is an important source of whatever numinosity attends the proceedings. Add to these considerations the credulity that arises in a religious subject as the ego is exhausted, and the extraordinary vividness of the whole bargaining syndrome, otherwise somewhat vague and unreal to the scientifically oriented mind of today, comes sharply into focus.

There is still another dimension to solutions of this class. Although a priest who has the routinely professional qualifica-

[49] Cf. Jung, "The Mana-Personality," in *Two Essays in Analytic Psychology*, N.Y., Meridian Books, 1959, pp. 239–253. Note particularly page 245.

tions needs little more than good luck and a flair for theology when he enters into a bargain with a petitioner in a matter of weather, we have a quite different situation when the problem is one involving health: and one who speaks for a deity in this area had better have something more than probability and quick wits going for him. And indeed, this is the case; the very title "medicine man" testifies to this fact. Psychotherapy, direct suggestion, a primitive but sometimes highly effective pharmacopeia, (the Zuni had an antiseptic which kept infections at a lower level than could be attained by the U.S. Army, despite a total lack of sanitation within the curing societies), to say nothing of sweat baths, primitive surgery, and the impact of numinous assurances, were all within the provenance of the religious healer. And if Ishtar, Aphrodite, or some other sex goddess were the one being petitioned, the resources of her earthly representative, in terms of arrangements that might be made, need hardly be spelled out.

3. Bargaining: The Worshipper

Although the advantage might seem heavily weighted in favor of the clergy, yet across the total spectrum of cause-cure bargaining, the favored position must be adjudged to the worshipper at last. A colleague tells of an amusing incident which she observed while on a research trip to Guatemala some years ago: it supports this point beautifully.

> In the midst of a Sunday morning service in a large Catholic church, an Indian from back in the hills marched up to the altar during the sermon. He shook his fist at the altar, harangued it heatedly, although *sotto voce*, and then, going to the rack where votive candles were burning, picked one up, blew it out, and shook his fist at the crucifix again, obviously in a state of indignation at the failure of the deity to fulfill some bargain. Then taking his candle, the Indian stalked out, still muttering. The sermon continued, quite heedless of the byplay.

After all, the connection between any alteration of the course of nature, and some antecedent ritual activity is merely ostensible. Two inherent hazards thus confront anyone who would represent a cause-cure god: (1) The solution, whether promised explicitly or implicitly, simply may not come, and (2) even if it does come, the suppliant may not accept the notion that its appearance is due (a) to this god, or (b) to this ritual! And, of course, once a subject is convinced that a religious activity is unavailing, all that he has to do is stay away: he need not denounce anything, or even take his business elsewhere. He is simply lost to the ritual agency of *this* personification.

If a solution that has been clearly promised is not forthcoming, the subject may have a Problem of Prior Formulation (Cf.V,B,4 of Part One, *supra*): But whether or not the ritual failure becomes in itself a second religious problem, he still has the first one, that prompted his unsuccessful involvement. Either way, however, his condition remains desperate, since his *scientifically* insoluble problem is now seen to be *religiously insoluble* by *this* agency! Various courses of action are predictably open to him.

(1) He may visit a different priest of the same god, at a different shrine, and start over.

(2) He may become a convert to another god. Since most conversions are into institutions built around solution-gods, which are focused on social problems, whereas cause-cure gods personify problems of nature, this reaction may well be due to the efforts of the clergy to convince him that his failure to obtain a religious solution is due to his having broken some taboo, so that he is now a religious—and therefore a social—reject.

(3) He may have a mystic experience, in which an altogether new god is revealed to him. This, however, is very unlikely, unless his religious rejection is shared by many other people. Moreover, such an experience is always non-volitional, so that the subject cannot undertake it by choice.

(4) He may become a total unbeliever. This, in turn, may involve either a tragic sense of disillusioned helplessness, or the grasp of some scientific insight that reduces both ritual and theology to passing insignificance.

It will not matter to the priest who loses him, which of these paths the disenchanted subject follows—he is equally lost to the original institution. Nor is his loss merely a statistical one, for by his withdrawal, the presiding clergyman is by so much discredited.

The enormous leverage possessed by the laity in bargaining with the representative of a cause-cure god, is perfectly illustrated by the situation of the *Wathon,* or hunt leader, of the Omaha Indians, whose annual buffalo hunt was a ritual occasion *par excellence,* involving all aspects of the religious structure, over a period of weeks. The *Wathon* was in absolute charge of its execution, once the date and general direction of the hunt had been agreed upon. His office was hereditary in the Inkecabe gens, which had great religious prestige, as certified by the Sacred Legend of the Tribe:[50] His eligibility was attested by providing the materials for a ceremonial staff of office, the *Washabe,* which he would carry throughout the hunt, and which was a symbol of food. The staff itself was then prepared by the section of the *Honga* gens bearing the same name—*Washabe.* Acceptance of these materials by the group entitled to make the *Washabe* staff automatically qualified him for chieftainship, though it did not guarantee his elevation to that rank.[51] His appointment to the office was made by the officials of this subgens, and confirmed by the Council of Seven Chiefs, the highest tribal authority.[52] The *Washabe* group was in charge of the rituals of the White Buffalo Hide, which had the greatest power of any sacred object known to the Omaha. His manner of life throughout the hunt was characterized as *nonzhinzhon,* "sacred," and its requirements were spelled out for him in ritual detail. The success of the expedition was held

[50] Fletcher, Alice C., and LaFlesche, Francis, *The Omaha Indians.* Twenty-Seventh Annual Report of the Bureau of American Ethnology, 1905–1906. Washington, D. C., Government Printing Office, 1911, (R.B.E.W.), pp. 147 and 149.

[51] *Ibid.,* p. 204.

[52] *Ibid.,* p. 276.

to be dependent upon the strictness with which the Wathon carried out its requirements.[53]

Yet, despite the prestige of the office, backed by these layers of religious endorsement, the earnestness of his own approach to the task, and the sincere counsel of the tribe's wisest leaders, he walked in such peril of tribal rejection that his every command was prefaced by the words "Pity me, who belong to you."[54] Indeed, a surrogate, or "mock" *Wathon* was appointed by the chiefs, to take the blame for any untoward act or disturbance that might jeopardize his tenure; since the failure of the hunt for any reason, however circumstantial, might force him to resign in disgrace.[55]

4. Perpetuating the Syndrome

In spite of the risks involved in undertaking to keep a bargain that the gods have made, the profitability of representing deities of this class has always been such that the clergy keep the cause-cure pattern of bargaining in operation as long as possible. In a few cases, it is discernible even at the present time, if we are careful to remember that any evidence of bargaining entails a cause-cure view of the deity thus addressed.

The delay or non-appearance of a solution to which a cause-cure personification has been pledged by his representative can always be given a theological alibi, since time is on the side of the one making the promise—time, and elementary shrewdness. A rain dance will not be conducted unless rain is due, and the regularity of the seasons makes the likelihood of an acceptable crop a viable dynamic for a fertility ceremonial. When the solution does not follow as promised, supernatural reasons can be advanced, discernible only to the clergy, and which the suppliant has no choice but to accept. Nonetheless, by Plutarch's time, deities of this type were generally regarded as needing rationalization.

---

[53] *Ibid.*, p. 309.
[54] *Ibid.*, p. 280.
[55] *Ibid.*, p. 278.

In addition to the march of science, from Thales to Occam, which eliminated serious consideration of most cause-cure gods, a principal factor in their disappearance was the advent of Solution gods, whose emphasis was on social problems, rather than those of nature. The great redeemer-deities stress the improvement of social conditions as a result of some transformation of the human spirit, rather than making rain, or ensuring tomorrow's sunrise. However, the cause-cure-bargaining syndrome dies hard, and again and again we find it imposed upon one of the newer and more enlightened solution gods, so that even so lofty a personification as that of Christ comes to be portrayed as walking on water, quieting a storm, multiplying food, and above all, healing the sick.

Indeed, survivals of the syndrome we are discussing may be found in this area, even at the present moment.[56] Oral Roberts still urges readers of his literature to participate in what he calls a "Blessing Pact," according to which greater contributions provide the certainty of greater benefits, beginning with health, then extending outward to general prosperity. The enormous efforts of Mary Baker Eddy, both organizational and theological, at the turn of the century, have resulted in most of the apologetic arguments for (a) the possibility and (b) the non-appearance, of faith healings being formalized and made orthodox within the institution that she founded.

Over and above the desperate earnestness of a religious subject who finds himself or a loved one afflicted with an incurable disease, there are a few observations that may shed

---

[56] Although no instances of the application of religion to areas of nature other than healing are presently evident, it is not long since this was practiced. William James quotes Emerson, in a reference to the currency of a naive belief in prayers for rain (*Varieties*, M. L. ed., p. 452, n. 2). Only a generation ago, Augusta Stetson was urging stock-market operators who ascribed their success to her treatments, to give their profits to her as an evidence of faith that through her they could always get more. The writer himself has childhood memories of prayer being offered for a delay of frost, when a crop was in danger.

light on the survival of a primitive religious mechanism in this particular frame of reference.

1. Some 60 to 80% of all disease is psycho-genetic anyway, and hence is amenable to the emotional impact of a "faith cure."
2. Although not to the writer's knowledge utilized in any way by either Oral Roberts or Christian Science, the possession of some esoteric scientific technique, e.g., a new drug, has been widely used to produce "miracles" of healing. The pharmacopeia as we know it, for instance, was developed to a surprising extent by people spoken of as witches, in medieval and pre-medieval times. The use of their own special antiseptic by the Zuni has been mentioned earlier in the present section.[57]
3. Quite apart from psychic *origins* of illness, psychic techniques for attacking disease legitimately have only begun to be explored. Hypnosis, suggestion and auto-suggestion, control of circulation through bio-feedback, voluntary suppression of pain—there is so much to be learned, even at the present moment, that any religious operator in possession of a couple of unexplored techniques would be well able to ascribe his healings to a cause-cure god, and go into business. Moreover, the psychic impact of numinosity *per se* has never been fully calculated: and when we add to all this, the archetypal quality of the healer's personality, the persistence of bargaining with cause-cure deities in connection with faith cures, is in no way surprising.

There is one thing more, so obvious that comments upon it are for the most part lacking. When the religious professional is at the end of his resources, whether of science or probability, he can always translate the whole problem into some metaphysical realm, and issue promises, assurances or threats from this frame of reference, which are impossible to disprove and

[57] Cf. *supra, Issuing the Promise*, p. 117.

heretical to challenge. Thus, if healings are beyond possibility, prayers for a shortened stay in purgatory may be in demand if the pertinent theories have been inculcated earlier. Every Catholic is familiar with the idea of multiple prayers being efficacious in determining the state of the dead. When we reflect that these prayers, if official, carry a price tag, we realize that the precise syndrome we have been discussing is still in evidence.

5. Summary

While everything we have advanced in the above discussion of the cause-cure level of personification has been pertinent, its presentation has necessarily been discursive, and we now seek to state its most salient points, briefly and incisively.

First, the archetype. This is simply something to be supplicated, something to give a personal character to an impersonal force, when a natural disaster overtakes the subject; but it is presented by the clergy as being amenable to financial negotiation, and the suppliants are not averse to this.

Second. The entire syndrome of cause-cure-bargaining is religious *activity*, and is undertaken only against a background of (1) previous personification, i.e., gods already known, and (2) convincedness, faith, that the ritual by which such bargaining is conducted will alleviate the underlying problem. When such is indeed the case, religious *experience* occurs, which is the area of our interest. But once the belief in the likelihood of a solution is dissipated, the syndrome ends, and the pattern of cause-cure-bargaining is over.

Third. Remembering that our basic interest is *religious experience*, as just stated, we must note that at this level, such experience can occur only by *interpretation*, with a few exceptions, acknowledged at the outset. Obviously, if a subject has a vision of Poseidon, saying to him at the moment the wind goes down, "I have just quieted the wind," such an experience is self-authenticating. But typically, the clergy make the interpretation which results in the numinous impact. That is: when a shower follows a rain-making ritual at some plausible time-interval, the subject must be convinced that it results from the ritual activity. The interpretation which gives a supernatural coloration to a natural occurrence is the essence of religious experience within this area, and it is uniformly made by the clergy. It follows that establishing belief in the causal relationship between a ceremonial performed and a solution achieved is the greatest challenge faced by any clergy, just as their greatest hazard is the danger that no result whatever will follow the exercise.

As we have shown throughout the section, when their economic status and prestige are jointly threatened by ritual failure, they display a relentless ingenuity in advancing apologetics which make science seem crass and philosophy callous.

This is the theological enterprise in its simplicity, and here it can be seen laid bare. Elsewhere not inherently meretricious, its essential function is both illustrated and defined in the perpetuation of bargaining with cause-cure personifications, for here indeed is "the rationalized expansion of myth in the interest of ritual efficiency."

C. Solution Gods: The Relationship of Mergence

1. Introduction

The third and final mode in which personification takes place is that of the solution to the problem. Solution gods are to be found most characteristically in connection with social problems, and it is here that they have their rise, although they have found their way into other areas of religious experience, whether by autistic adoption, or by institutional promotion. Consequently, this level of personification has a degree of complexity and importance to which preceding types do not attain, since it involves the entire social dimension of the subject's existence, both past and future.

When the solution to a problem is the aspect personified, the relationship typically sought with the resulting archetypal figure is *mergence*.

Mergence may be defined as the psychological state in which

a subject feels himself volitionally undifferentiated from the force or agency solving his religious problem. It may even become so intense the subject feels complete personal identity with this personification. Since this experience entails a profound modification of the super-ego, it gives us a new and valuable perspective from which religious experience may be examined. Moreover—this mergence-relationship is autistic—the institution's function is to *maintain* it.

2. The Personification: Inner Distinctions In Its Formation

There are two principal ways in which a religious subject arrives at the personification of a solution god—mystic experience and conversion. Alternatively stated, this personification occurs at two levels of religious experience. Qualifications to this position will be discussed following consideration of the two areas indicated.

a. Mystic Experience: Its Varieties

Mystic experience is where personifications of this sort begin: it has both logical and chronological primacy. It is much like conversion in its numinous quality, as well as in the basic fact of personification, but mystic experience is originative, for in it a new and previously unknown archetypal figure appears to a prophet, and reveals to him the imminent establishment of an Ideal Society, which he, the god, will presently set up. A New Morality, appropriate to, and definitive of, the new social order, is uniformly a part of the revelation, and is outlined in it. These features, which define the intent of the deity, are part of the archetype, and are proclaimed by every solution god. The account of Moses at the burning bush (Ex. 3) is our model here.

An important qualification must be noted. Even in originative mysticism, the deity envisioned may be a previously known member of an older ethnic pantheon, who reveals new attributes to the prophet, and is thus transformed into a true solution god, now to be proclaimed as guarantor of an Ideal Society, and author of its morality. Ahura Mazda in Persia, and Allah in Arabia, fit this pattern minutely.

Prophetic experience, whereby the existence and intent of a new archetypal figure are announced, is to be expected in any area of social tension, however located. Such tension need not extend throughout an entire society, but indeed is likely to occur within a minority, who find their discontents reflected and their hopes expressed in such a revelation.

The prophet himself may be any person of religious sensitivity, and generalizations about him can be made only in terms of his religious problem, which determines the universality of application that his revelation will have. (The force of this statement will become apparent presently.) The problem felt by the prophetic personality will be either (1) the common denominator of the problems felt by members of his society, or (2) the inadequacy of the background religion in dynamizing that society. One more thing can be said: the prophet will always have a unique perspective from which he views the problems of his society. He may well be a member of one of its leading classes, who has endured heavy misfortune, perhaps over a long period of time, so that he knows from within how the society is supposed to function, and the reasons for its failure to do so.

Having had the revelatory experience, the prophet makes formulations which constitute the mythos of a new religious movement, which other men will either accept or reject, as they do or do not find it significant for their problems.

Such acceptance, when it occurs, is the Conversion experience. It is altogether secondary, and consists in the symbolic impact of such a deity, already fully formulated, upon a subject who sees it as personifying the solution to his own problem, and thus having archetypal significance for him. Conversion will be dealt with in our next section.

Actually, there are four kinds of mysticism, in the sense of autonomous religious experiences that are unrelated to the adoption of an existing creed or religious formulation:

(1) *Originative* mysticism, in which a totally new personification is made;

(2) *"Second Storey"* mysticism, in which a prophet is seen as himself divine;

(3) *Theological* mysticism, wherein a prophet receives a new revelation from an existing deity, to the effect that a fearful judgment will befall if the prescribed morality is not observed more diligently; and

(4) *Exploratory* mysticism, wherein a religious enthusiast seeks to duplicate the revelatory experience of the original prophet, or to deepen his mergence with the solution god he is already following, by whatever devotional practices he finds appropriate.

The last of these is obviously to be classified as religious *activity,* that sometimes culminates in religious experience, and it is equally obvious that the third, while numinous and revelatory, makes no new personification. The second, while easy to confuse with conversion, is actually a sub-variant of the first, in that a solution god is thereby set up, albeit from a human figure (the prophet), instead of an autistically produced archetypal image. This leaves the first, or originative type of mysticism as the one with which we have to deal.[58]

b. Originative Mysticism: Levels of Universality

The productions of originative mysticism vary enormously in their inclusiveness. At one end of the spectrum, we find the personifying process revealing numinous figures which claim no dynamic for anyone except the subject in whom this mechanism has been operative, but which, none the less, have profound symbolic impact for him. At the other extreme, we find the gods of the world's great religions appearing to their

[58] "Mystic experience" and "originative mysticism" are terms which mean essentially the same thing, and will be used interchangeably in the following material, unless otherwise noted. "Prophetic experience" implies a revelation which is intended to apply to persons other than the revelator, whether or not it is accepted by those concerned.

The reader is cautioned against confusing any of these terms with the expression "numinous experience," which simply denotes any awareness of the sacred.

respective prophets. Between these two extremes, numerous autistic revelations are to be found, all socially dynamized, but exhibiting personifications that merely modify or supplement some existing deity, or else have such localized interest and bizarre characteristics as to have small convincingness in any setting other than their own. Yet whatever their level of universality, solution gods uniformly reveal two things: the early establishment of an Ideal Society which the new god will set up,[59] and a New Morality, which defines and implements it. Of course, in some cases, e.g., Confucianism, these features are revealed only by implication, and a detailed acquaintance with the formulations is required to discern their presence. Also, in the smaller, more individualized instances of originative personifying, these features of the archetype may be incompletely developed, so that one or the other may be present by implication alone, or may be outlined incoherently or indistinctly. Nonetheless, since the problems for which the solution is thus personified are basically social in nature, or else inner-psychic problems having a social rootage, one or both of these characteristics will consistently be found as part of the archetype. Taken together, they constitute its dynamic: a cosmic reassurance that very soon everything will be better, in a cosmically guaranteed fellowship, wherein persons of good intent will merit the approval of the deity by helping one another in an enlightened way. An embellishment that is often found, whether circumstantially or centrally, is the idea that all enemies of the god and his people will soon be snuffed out. Needless to say, the more universal the problem is, by which the mystic is impelled, the greater the likelihood of his revelation gaining acceptance.

The examples which follow demonstrate the varying levels of universality at which originative mysticism may appear, beginning with (i) revelations whose reference is entirely subjective, and going on to (ii) those having inadvertent application to

---

[59] In instances of individualized personification this may simply appear as a set of improved social relationships. See our first illustration, *infra*.

others; thence (iii) to those applying to limited problems; then (iv) those applying to limited problems and groups; and finally (v) to the major prophetic religions, whose claims are overtly universal.

i. Entirely Subjective We cite herewith the record of an originative personification which was brought to the writer's attention some years ago, and which had enormous symbolic impact for its subject, but was never held to apply to anyone else;

> A young mother was tragically widowed, under distressing circumstances. Her husband had been an admirable and outstanding man, and her relationship with him was rather more than that of a sex partner and economic helpmate—it had strongly symbolic overtones.
>
> For some months following his death she was inconsolable, to the point of being unable to manage even routine duties, so that her family feared for her health, and with good reason.
>
> About six months after his decease, the widow had a dream in which she heard a chorus of angelic voices singing "He is risen! He is well!" to the air of a familiar hymn. Immediately upon hearing the voices, she saw her husband approaching her, dressed as he had been for burial, but alive, sentient, and clearly aware of her. He was surrounded by a dazzling white light.
>
> Upon awakening, she found herself calling vividly to mind many things her deceased husband had told her, prior to his death. Chief among these was the explicitly stated thought that death was simply another dimension of life, and a natural part of it: this she felt the dream to have vindicated fully. She also recalled in detail, his telling her that it was his profound wish that she accept life again, following his expected demise: that she care for their children; and, above all, that she must be happy and have no fear. In the light of these vivid recollections, her initially numinous feeling about the dream crystallized into a blinding certainty that it had been a truly supernatural event.
>
> Overnight her depression lifted, and she undertook the responsibilities of her widowed situation with efficiency and cheerfulness. She has subsequently become an eminently successful professional person, and ever since the numinous experience, which is the focal point of her life, her entire approach to living has been one of radiant confidence.

Although she never abjured Christianity, this personally numinous experience has remained the dominant integrative factor of her life, and its personification has been, to her, exactly what we mean by a solution god. In every crisis, she has drawn strength, not so much from any sense of her husband's presence, as from a deeper feeling of his livingness and *support*. She maintains a vital morality, which consists of his remembered admonitions, augmented by further moral insights that she believes he would have known or accepted.

    ii. Inadvertent Application To Others: St. Francis of Assisi At progressively higher levels of universality, various personifications are to be found, symbolizing solutions of more or less subjective appeal, which have none the less resulted in religious movements. The illustrations we advance can only epitomize, since we are seeking to outline the mechanism involved, rather than to write a history of such movements. Thus:

    Francis of Assisi was a wealthy and foppish young man. When he became oppressed by the triviality of a wasteful and possibly dissolute life, he found the solution to his problem personified in the figure of the Lady Poverty, who was revealed to him in a dream of extremely numinous quality, and with whom he merged immediately. The moral imperative to care for the poor which he drew from his mergence with this archetypal figure not only attracted large numbers of converts, for whom the resultant Order became an Ideal Society, albeit not previously announced, but its morality of compassion captured the popular imagination to such an extent that the decadent and faltering Roman Church was at last forced to take cognizance of its validity, and indeed to call upon Francis himself for support. The deplorable misery of the neglected poor would have had an impact upon the consciousness of any person of moral sensitivity, as is shown by the eagerness with which followers gathered about him, once his ministry was under way. Yet, despite the careless generosity of his youth, the needs of the poor were never a primary motivation for him, until he found, at the direction of his religious symbol, *the solution to his own problem* in caring for them. Although his preaching was a literal reiteration of the tenets of early Christianity, all of its dynamic, and all that of the movement which arose from it, was derived from his "marriage to," or in our terminology, his mergence with, the personification of the Lady Poverty.

Thus we see that the institutional results of Francis's central personification were initially unintentional. Now we turn to a formulation appealing to a limited clientele, but which was presented as a viable solution for the problems of persons other than the revelator.

iii. Limited Problems: Mother Ann Lee Ann Lee(s) Standerin or Stanley, 1736–1784, better known as Mother Ann Lee, was the founder of the Shaker sect, of which the correct name was The United Society of Believers in Christ's Second Appearing. Born the second eldest of eight children, her parents were Quakers, residing near Manchester, England. She grew up in a period of social and religious unrest, featured by the impact of the Wesleyan revival on the ravages of the Industrial Revolution, and in 1774 emigrated to America.

Married in 1762, she lost four children in succession, each after a difficult delivery. Following the death of the last one, in 1770, she went through a period of depression, culminating in a revelatory experience which she called a New Birth. In this, she was shown that Godhead is composed not of three persons, but four:[60] God the Father, Christ the Son, a maternal personage known as Holy Mother Wisdom,[61] and a Divine Daughter, which was herself, Ann Lee. She also referred to herself as "The Word," presumably with some reference to the Logos of John I, and as the Bride of Christ.

Concupiscence was the root of every known ill, and, of course, the cardinal sin.[62] Confession *per se* constituted salva-

[60] Note the relationship to the familiar Jungian doctrines regarding quaternity.

[61] Cf. the formulations of Mary Baker Eddy, the Rappites, *et al.*

[62] Cf. Father Divine's identical doctrine.

tion, resurrection, and the beginning of "Life In The Spirit," so that to the convert thus regenerated, the World was at an end. Total chastity was the preeminent moral demand, along with plainness of dress and other typically Quaker virtues: industry, frugality, cleanliness, etc.

The extreme purity of life that she and her adherents sought demanded separation from outside distractions; hence communities were founded, with governing regulations of surprising astuteness.

Worship featured a characteristic shaking dance which gave the movement its name, applied in derision. In this ritual, wherein the head and hands were vigorously shaken, ecstatic states frequently resulted, featuring mediumship, glossalalia and revelations.

The central religious problem by which Ann Lee was impelled was clearly that of tragically harrowing experiences connected with sex and reproduction, and the tenets of the movement attracted many people of surprisingly normal instincts who were appalled at the condition and prospects of womanhood in the marriage state, particularly on the frontier. Limited in scope as this personification was, its function as a solution to the problem felt is clearly apparent. The movement had a peak membership of about 2400 in 1874, declined to less than half that in 1905, and is now extinct.[63]

iv. Limited Problems and *Groups: The Rastafari* Personifications intended to be applicable to entire groups, but of strictly topical appeal, are so numerous that we can only cite them in themselves, since to give complete description to the movements in which they occur would make our study sociological instead of psychological, to say nothing of becoming encyclopedic in size.

A thoroughly typical solution god of this description is found in the Rastafari cult, among the slum dwellers of Kingston, Jamaica. Living in shacks on the city dump, known as the

[63] Cf. Taylor, R. Bruce, art., *Communistic Societies of America*, E.R.E., iii, 781b–783b.

Dungle, they look to Emperor Haile Selassie, defined as the visible manifestation of Jehovah, to liberate them from their poverty, and transport them to Ethiopia, which they declare to be their rightful home.

The name of the cult is a modification of Ras Tafari, which was the Emperor's name before he came to the throne. No post-mortem Heaven is necessary for their belief, which does not acknowledge the reality of death for members of the group as long as they remain sinless according to its definitions. When it does occur, death is ascribed to some moral lapse, or else to "murder" by white medicine, or some other white machination. Jesus is rejected and ridiculed as a white man's deity, who is invisible except to the spirits of the dead: but Jehovah as Haile Selassie, who is altogether tangible, and also black, will presently overthrow the existing social order, and make them all kings.

Their morality rejects any physical contact with a white person, any use of modern medicine, the eating of pork, attendance at funeral services, formal marriage, homosexuality and birth control. It affirms "herbal medicine," in which they would include the heavy use of *cannibis Indica*, ingested in all possible ways, unrestricted breeding, mystical experience and male supremacy.[64]

v. Limited Ethnic Groups The numerous Cargo Cults of the Western Pacific have as their general formulation an Ideal Society soon to be ushered in by the arrival of ships or planes bringing "Cargo" of European goods for the natives: materiél with which they had become acquainted during World War II. This cargo may contain weapons to expel the Whites. After its arrival, work will no longer be necessary. Other aspects of the formulation differ with each of the cults: eternal youth, equality with Europeans, release from primordial guilt, or simply a return to nativistic customs.

[64] Kitzinger, Sheila, "Among Jamaican Outcasts," *The Journal For Scientific Study Of Religion*, vol. viii, No. 2, Fall 1969, pp. 240–262. Unfortunately, Ms. Kitzinger does not include the name of the original revelator.

Personifications of the source of this promised new order are extremely varied. They include primarily (1) the ancestors, (2) various native deities, (3) syncretistic personifications involving Christian ideation and (4) deified prophets, who have had revelations as to one or more of the aspects cited. Europeans, or, more generally, whites, are frequently personified collectively as a problem god or gods, who keep intercepting the Cargo which the solution god is trying to send. Occasionally, Europeans appear as cause-cure gods, who possess the secret of obtaining Cargo, which they might be persuaded to share, if the correct rituals were employed.

Each of these personifications has its own prophet, who has advanced the formulations pertaining to it on the basis of his own mystic experience. That some of the formulations may be cultic, i.e., synthetic and faked, to advance the interests of the formulator, is evident; but some are thoroughly sincere, and even insincerity has its gradations. All of these prophets are named and characterized in the sources listed.

The morality enjoined by these solution gods is deeply immersed in ritual, [as we should expect in a situation so close to the primitive, and is, in general, at a sub-rational level.] Along with elaborate initiation rituals, either the imitation or abandonment of European customs and contacts is its typical expression, together with labored preparations for caring for the Cargo when it comes.[65]

Among the Zulu of South Africa, the solution god takes the form of a "Black Christ," of which there are many. In addition to its generally Christian outlines, such a personification includes much from the native religion: the (resurrected?) spirit of the ethnic king as a tutelary source of well being; possession by this or some similar ancestral ("Holy?") spirit; the ruling majesty of the Divine; and divination, thinly veneered as prophecy in the Biblical sense.

[65] Cf. Burridge, Kenelm, *Mambu*, Harper Torchbooks, 1970, and Worsley, Peter, *The Trumpet Shall Sound*, London, MacGibbon & Kee, 1957. The latter volume has an excellent bibliography.

Such a figure will be embodied by a native of general leadership ability, who is able to inspire numinosity by performing healings and reporting convincing visions: these last naturally contain the message of his own authority as their primary point. Probably the outstanding instance of the type we describe is Isaiah Shembe, 1870–1935, although, as in the Cargo Cults, the pattern is endlessly repeated.

Presently the authority of this leader will be authenticated by visions and dreams occurring among his followers. The attitude of such a personality to his own divinity is exactly that displayed by Father Divine; he never overtly states it, but constantly implies it, and permits his followers to enunciate it without rebuke.

The Ideal Society promised is totally escapist and utopian, since native insurrections have failed repeatedly; but it predictably reflects the era of Zulu greatness at the beginning of the 19th century. The prophet-deity holds the keys to this ideal world, where the color bar is to be reversed, so that no white man may enter, and there will be plenty of land for all Zulus. There the revelator will rule as king, along the lines of Zulu ethnic society, prior to the coming of the whites. The entire heavenly complex is, in each case, identified with the group propounding it, and its geography is named and described in Biblical terms.

The morality that is instrumental to this Ideal Society is a composite of Christian and native practices, and has a strongly ritual character. Here as elsewhere, it varies from group to group. Common features are the avoidance of European medicine in favor of healings by the prophet-king, constant resort to purification ceremonies involving the use of emetics, the encouragement of glossalalia, and, of course, total obedience to the prophet at all times. They may well avoid pork and practice circumcision, and are certain to take a position on polygamy, either advocating or forbidding it.

These movements have ceased to be prophetic, and are to be classified somewhere between Pseudo-Ethnic and Cultic (see Appendix for definitions), but they do show with full clarity the characteristic personification of a divine figure who is the solution to all social problems, purportedly for an entire ethnic group.[66]

vi. Major Prophetic Religions: Formulations Intended To Be All-Inclusive   Of course the major prophetic religions exhibit the characteristics of which we have been speaking, with the greatest clarity. As we have said, our paradigm case for the whole mechanism is that of Moses, whose solution god appeared to him while he was a fugitive from Egyptian justice, and revealed not only the structure of an Ideal Society for Moses's people, but a "land flowing with milk and honey" where it might be established, together with an immediate program for reaching this land of promise, which Moses was commanded to implement.

Islam has its revitalized Mecca, and its Pillars Of The Faith, dictated by Allah, with Paradise waiting to crown all; and Confucianism has its Ideal Empire, whose monarch is geared into cosmic power by the practice of the Five Relations. If primitive Buddhism seems puzzling, look at the Mahayana, in which the Historical Buddha is the deity, and the Order the Ideal Society, complete with its own set of moral precepts. Nor need we shy away from Gotama's original revelation, as regards our pattern; for there the Ideal Society is the world freed from Brahmin domination, then threatening the Kshatriya culture in which the young Siddartha had been reared. This is to be brought about by the practice of the Eight-Fold Path, which as Dharma, is personified at least as clearly as is the *I Ching* today.

And, of course, Christianity has its Kingdom of God, and its Law of Love. A vivid expectation for nearly two generations, the imminent divine establishment of a purified society, to which entry could only be gained by practicing the Law of Love, is the best attested and most central belief of early

[66] Cf. Sundkler, Bengt, *Bantu Prophets in South Africa*, 2nd ed., London, Oxford University Press, 1961.

Christianity. The solution god who first promised this new order was Jehovah, refined into a personification of the love which was central to its morality. Soon, however,[67] this personification became attached to the prophet who had first enunciated it, and the appearance of the Kingdom was keyed to the second coming of Jesus as the Christ, concurrently seen as the second person of a Trinity.

St. John had his New Jerusalem, Augustine his City of God, and down the centuries the formulations of the Christian mythos have been adduced in support of innumerable millenarian movements. Only the details vary; the precise constitution of the Ideal Society, the date of its arrival, and the morality by which it is defined, and by which its coming is ensured. The central theme is unchanging—that amid some set of social conditions that has become intolerable, a divinely instituted utopia is at hand, organized around, and empowered by, a personification of the solutions it will contain: and this personification is the one contained in the Christian formulation as locally understood, plus various embellishments, fanciful or bizarre.

c. Conversion

The second way in which this personification occurs is in the conversion experience. Here, a religious subject finds the solution to his problem portrayed by an existing deity, with such convincingness that the god, whom the subject may have known about for a long time, now assumes a truly numinous quality, and becomes the actual, personal symbol of the solution which the subject then attains, by mergence with what he now sees for the first time, as a Divine Person. While new deities result from mystic experience, it is of the utmost importance to remember that the personifying process occurs with vastly greater frequency in this area. It is in the conversion experience that the basic mechanism of religion—personification and relationship—is typically operative.

[67] I.e., by the end of the first century. By the time the Gospel of Matthew was written, baptism was Trinitarian.

As we saw earlier, in Section I, E, solution gods are very rarely experienced in totally new personifications. Rather: existing deities, not previously important to the subject, and altogether absent from any vital awareness he might have, assume archetypal significance when they are seen as having personal efficacy for the solving of his problem. Such deities have, of course, been previously announced by a prophet, as described in the paragraphs just above.

The conversion experience takes place in predictable ways, on levels that we have already delineated.

i. The subject may find symbolic efficacy in the newly announced deity that some prophet is proclaiming. Differently stated, he may find that this deity portrays the solution to his problem, and that he is able to feel and affirm the personification that the prophet has recently made, or is even then making. The dynamic in conversions of this type is the Cosmic Promise—the proclamation of a supernatural end to social tragedy, and the divinely instituted beginning of a new order.

ii. The subject may find the solution to his problem portrayed by a deity whose prophetic annunciation took place some time ago, and around whom a religious institution has grown up.

As we have seen a few pages back, there are many personifications of solution gods, and many institutions where their promises are cherished. The relation of such institutions to the societies which are their backgrounds, and the sequence of events in their formation, are important matters, but they do not concern us here, inasmuch as it is always in a religious institution that a religious symbol is enshrined, and through such an agency that it is transmitted: and the basic fact is, that as long as that institution is alive, which is to say, as long as the original formulations are actually believed, some facet of the institutional complex will, from time to time, produce symbolic impact in persons who have the same problem as that which brought the religion into being: so that they, in their turn, personify its central archetype as the solution to their own problem. The factor producing this symbolic impact is usually the morality, but when the personifying mechanism is complete, the subject introjects the Cosmic Promise as well, so that the hope of a totally new and fully ideal social order functions to intensify the new convert's commitment to the morality, and indeed to make its performance possible for him.

iii. The subject may come to see an actual human being as the personification of whatever will solve his problem. The mechanisms already outlined are operative here as above, with only a few details demanding remark. Thus: if the person now hailed as divine has already been characterized as such, the subject experiences a *conversion*, obviously enough: and this, whether the supernatural status of the divine person is self-proclaimed, or accorded to him by his followers. Conversely, if the subject is the first to see him as divine, the experience can only be called prophetic or mystic, since it has an originative quality.

It is not uncommon for deification to be accorded to the prophet himself at some later time, by reason of his supposed contact with the supernatural, at the occasion of his big revelation. However, the prophet usually remains simply the prophet throughout his lifetime, and then is given a semi-divine status, in recognition of his selection by the now well-established god, as the original vehicle of the revelation.

In connection with these human foci of the personifying process, the whole problem of cult leaders confronts the investigator. It will be dealt with in Part Four.

d. Solution Gods at the Ethnic Level?

Before leaving the personification of solution gods, and moving on to the relationship they inspire, we must mention two additional matters, as briefly as we can. The first is the apparent intrusion, albeit rarely, of cause-cure gods into this area. Occasionally the cure side of a cause-cure god with whom a subject has struck a particularly favorable bargain, will be acclaimed by that subject as though it were a *bona-fide* solution god. However, the relationship formed, while characterized by gratitude and amenability on the part of the subject, is one of affirmation rather than mergence; and the personification itself thus remains that of a cause-cure deity, since the god has not *become* the solution, but only supplied it.

The second is the question of solution-gods, and the incidence of mystic experience and conversion at the ethnic level. Three borderline cases are outstanding. (1) The Plains Indians commonly practiced a Vision Quest, wherein a personal totem was revealed to a youth of an age to assume responsibility: the youth assumed the character of this personal totem for the rest of his life. (2) Various Eskimo groups depend routinely on shamanistic revelations, obtained from supernatural beings, for guidance. (3) Among the Ihalmiut, many individuals could predict the weather for extended future periods by obtaining revelations about it.

What of these personifications? Are they not also solution gods? And ought not these revelatory experiences to be called mystic? Let us take them one at a time.

i. The Vision Quest of the Omaha   While it is true that in the Vision Quest the youth identified fully with the entity revealed to him, so that he was now an "elk-man," or "bear-man," or even a "mouse-man," if this was the vision showed him, the experience involved salient differences from what we have previously meant by identification with a solution god.

First of all, the symbol envisioned was totally individual, and showed nothing of the archetypal features of the Ideal Society and New Morality, although it might be argued that it contained a moral implication, in that a newly designated "fox-man" would be expected to be clever, a "deer-man" swift, and so on. The totem gained in the Vision Quest simply defined the character of the initiate, and was of no binding significance to anyone else.[68]

Second, primitive and embryonic as these animal revelations are when compared with typical solution gods, there is a perspective from which they can be seen as belonging to this

[68] Cf. Wm. James's second stricture on mysticism, *Varieties*, M. L. ed., p. 414. Note also that societies of initiates who had the same vision existed. Cf. R. B. E. W. xxiii, 1911, p. 133.

class. The youth to whom they came, undertook the Vision Quest "when he was old enough to know sorrow": i.e., when the authority of the ethnos became irksome to him: but once he had the vision which defined his personality, he became part of the authority, and was tendered respect. Hence the symbol which was the content of the revelation might be held to personify a solution. However, since the initiate *gained admission to the existing religious group* by way of his vision, instead of making it the occasion for setting up a new one, the experience is more appropriately viewed as a conversion than a mystic experience.

Most importantly, however, the entity revealed in the Vision Quest was in no way innovative. No new god emerged from this personification,[69] which was rather a means for the initiate to adapt himself most fittingly to the *status quo*. As the numinous event which qualified a new member for admission to the ritual group, its characterization as a conversion experience can be most cogently argued.

Even so, these last two classifications are atypical; the symbols as solutions, and the total experience as conversion. They are advanced on purely formal grounds, as is, we trust, apparent.

The whole procedure of the Vision Quest raises interesting trains of thought, in that as the individual gained deep insight into his own character, he was concurrently given participating status in the ritual group. The relevance of this to what we shall presently have to say about the relationships between inner-psychic and social problems will become apparent when we reach that point in our discussion. Also, these symbols defining selfhood give additional force to Jung's view that Jesus Christ is a symbol of the self.[70]

---

[69] The ritual, however, has been known to undergo modifications as a result of visionary experience: cf. Niehardt, John, *Black Elk Speaks*, and Skinner, Alanson, art. *Siouans*, E. R. E., xi, 576b.

[70] *Symbols of Transformation*, C. W., vol, V, pp. 368, 392 *et passim*.

ii. Group Guidance by Shamanism   In the case of shamanistic experience, whether among the Eskimos or elsewhere, numerous divergences from either mysticism or conversion confront us immediately. To begin with, the deity is typically a problem-god, the personification of the shamanistic frenzy—frequently an epileptic seizure, recognized by all observers, and even by the subject himself, as madness. Further, the shaman does not merge with the spirit or god who gives him information, but rather seeks to escape from its clutches, since this supernatural agent has seized him by force, and forcibly occupied his body. The true mystic hastens blissfully into loving union with the solution-god, and finds his problem solved thereby: but the shaman is invaded and mastered by a force so hostile that he owes his very office to his ability to survive its attacks. Moreover, since the shaman cannot wait for a *bona fide* convulsion each time his professional services are required, he is forced to counterfeit the seizure, so that the very name of shaman is synonymous with the darkest kind of superstitious fraud.

iii. Revelatory Experience Among the Ihalmiut   Our third borderline case at the ethnic level is the ability of the Ihalmiut to get revelations about the weather. If any one of these "People of the Deer" sought insight into the future of the weather (as when a friend was planning a journey), he would spend several days alone, in the open, wearing much less clothing than usual. Upon his return, nearly frozen, his statement as to what the weather would be, had an uncanny accuracy.[71]

This, as the writer sees it, is simply a technique of communicating with the apperceptive mass of the unconscious, which, among these people, would contain generations of subtle hints about the matter that concerned them most. The effort is not unlike that which an author will make in trying to gain inspiration. True, the subject who has gained such insight may, if questioned, ascribe his ideation to some personal entity in the spirit world; but his relationship with such a being is entirely

[71] Mowat, Farley, *The People Of The Deer*, passim.

transitory, and is limited to this one occasion and its single concern. While such a subject might be said to personify a solution, it seems more correct to say that he was trying to account for the whole experience, in the only terms he knew. Revelatory though it is, this interesting phenomenon is quite unlike the production of a true solution god.

A final observation concludes both our review of solution gods at the ethnic level, and the whole matter of their personification. Here it is:

Prophetic experience can occur at any level of religious development, and no level of either intellectual sophistication or primitive credulity is required for its appearance.

Thus, the gods who revealed themselves to Moses and Zoroaster appeared against a background of undeniably primitive religion, as is the case with the deities of the Melanesian Cargo Cults: while Meher Baba is seen as a solution god by highly educated people in the contemporary professional scene.

Solution gods do not appear *within* an ethnic situation; they are always outside it, and seeking to reform it, at a time when its Social Metaphysic—its "taken for granted," unspoken theory of social ranking—has broken down. They may, however, be incorporated into the ethnic complex, if its vitality is sufficiently great. This has apparently happened repeatedly within Hinduism: Vasudeva Krishna is an instance.

Similarly, when one prophetic message has spent its force, another may well appear. Some of the problems precipitating the older revelation may be solved, making it less compelling; it may be misinterpreted and suborned by those it has displaced;[72] or, most typically, its credibility may be lost by the failure of the Ideal Society to appear, with the consequent neglect of the morality, so that social tensions return, even within the circle of the devout. At this point a new solution god may be expected to appear, proclaimed by a new prophet, and

---

[72] Cf. the Magian treatment of Zoroaster's message, and the effort to obliterate Ikhnaton's reform, made by the Theban priesthood.

complete with a new Cosmic Promise of yet another Beulah Land, or Holy City, or Classless Society, and with a morality pertinent to the present need. With this new deity, mergence is once more possible, in which relationship the actual solution is consummated. To this experience we now turn.

3. *Mergence*

Mergence in itself is comparatively easy to describe, but its occurrence is the most dynamic aspect of the religious mechanism, and its analysis involves many complexities. The aversion of a problem god may externalize a fear, or begin the structuring of a value system: the conclusion of a successful bargain with a cause-cure god may be signalized by the solution of a problem of nature, or at least the promise of its future solution, and these are occasions of numinosity for the untutored mind: but when a religious subject experiences the total union of his psychic structure with an archetypal image that represents the answer to his uttermost need, the restructuring of personality which ensues is so profound as to seem supernatural even to the modern sophisticate.

In this experience, the relationship with the personification is accomplished, whereby the solution to the religious problem is completed. This is the final phase of the religious mechanism, as we have set forth earlier,[73] and it has a terminal quality, wherein faith is changed to sight as the subject internalizes the symbol, and knows the hope that dawned with its appearance as present reality. This is not to say that there is any necessary time lag between the personification and the relationship, but merely that the two aspects of the religious mechanism are, in principle, distinguishable.

We have described mergence as the psychic state in which a subject feels himself volitionally undifferentiated from the force or agency solving his religious problem.[74] Interestingly, the subject often finds that he shares not only the wishes of the personification with whom he is united, but other characteris-

[73] Cf. Occurrences of Numinosity, II, E, 2, c, pp. 91–94, *supra*.
[74] Cf. p. 113.

tics as well, such as benignity, courage, or tranquillity, or even a totally new perspective on life. Moreover, these additions to his personality may include new *abilities*, which are not limited to moral and ritual requirements, such as the avoidance of protest behavior, the acceptance of necessary authority, or the observance of arduous taboos, but may very well include profounder psychic modifications, making the subject able in fact to love, or to forgive. They may include enhanced capacities for thinking or organizing, which the subject can utilize in more effective obstacle removing behavior; and even an expansion of his neuro-muscular powers, so that he can endure pain or fatigue, live without narcotics, talk without stuttering, or resist disease as he could never do before. Furthermore, these augmentations of personality may take place instantaneously, so that forever afterward he dates his psychic transformation from a precise moment.[75] Finally, in the more complete instances of mergence, the consciousness of union with the archetypal is frequently so complete that the subject declares himself to be absolutely identical with the god it portrays. Thus Jesus of Nazareth says, "I and my Father are one;" St. Paul echoes him with the statement "Not I, but Christ liveth in me;" (Gal. 2:20) and Angelus Silesius says in one of his hymns,

> Ich bin so gross als Gott
> Er ist als ich so klein;
> Er kann nicht über mich
> Ich unter ihm nicht sein.[76]

[75] Wesley believed that this was generally and possibly universally so. Cf. his statement to this effect, cited in James, *Varieties*, M. L. ed., p. 233. Instances abound, but we may adduce St. John of the Cross, who says of divine "touchings," "A single one of them may be sufficient to abolish *at a stroke*, certain imperfections of which the soul during its whole life had vainly tried to rid itself, and to leave it adorned with virtues and supernatural gifts." *Works*, ii, 320. Italics are the writer's. Many readers will know of someone who has been cured of alcoholism instantaneously.

[76] *Cherubinischer Wandersmann*, Strophe 10. Quoted in James, *Varieties*, M. L. ed., p. 141.

How are we to account for these things?

Baldly stated, the subject first identifies with the personification, and then introjects all of its demands, whether explicit or implicit. Taken together, these two steps constitute mergence, which is different from either of its component aspects. The analysis of this experience involves careful examination of both, in their interaction as well as their internal characteristics.

a. The Structure of Mergence: Identification and Introjection

Identification and introjection are confused throughout the literature. This is as hard to understand as it is unfortunate, since the terms as we shall use them, are readily distinguishable, and clarity has been greatly impaired by the failure to do this. Let us review their connotations.

Identification is mostly imitation, and is altogether affirmative. It may be either conscious or unconscious, and it consists in the subject adopting as many as possible of the traits of another person, real or imaginary, whom he values very highly; together with the corresponding elimination, by repression or suppression, of all negative attitudes toward this person. Reasons for the valuation may be a benefit received, as when a small boy is given recognition by a noted athlete;[77] the basic fact of idealizing, as when a student idealizes a great teacher; or loss, as when someone tries hard to do exactly what he thinks a deceased loved one would want him to do. A factor to be noted is that if the identification is broken for any reason, the adopted traits tend to fall away.

Introjection, on the other hand, is essentially the internalization of social pressures. It is an unconscious process, operating on the principle "If you can't lick 'em, join 'em," and it is always due to fear. This may be the fear of punishment, of retaliation, of rejection, or of mental pain, but is always fear of some coercive action of an authority, official or otherwise.

When introjection occurs, it takes place instantaneously, and produces a complete and even enthusiastic agreement in the

[77] This mechanism is the dynamic for the phenomenally lucrative practice of prominent personalities "endorsing" various products, commercially.

subject's consciousness, who, at the same time, represses the opinion he held previously, and the negative affect he suffered while the authoritarian pressure was being applied. This may involve a radical and highly dramatic reversal of belief and action in the subject, particularly if the required introjection has been long resisted, as in the case of brainwashing by some heinous form of torture, physical or mental. The end, of course, is acceptance as one's own, of the position demanded by the authority, which is now seen as self-evidently right, and metaphysically certain, with an irrational convincedness that is almost impossible to eradicate. This is, of course, exactly what happens to a cultic adherent as a result of the brainwashing process.

The totality of such introjected behavior in any individual's personality makes up his super-ego; and it is interesting to note that this body of introjected material continues to grow while life lasts. We shall return to this element of the personality shortly.

Both of these mechanisms must be present for mergence to occur, although each one resembles mergence up to a point. One who "identifies with" another person for any reason— benefit, idealism, loss, or something else—*affirms* that other person, tries to be like him in as many ways as he can, but does not by so doing attain mergence. That is: he does not feel that he himself *is* the other, or that the object of his identification is simply an extension of his own personality. Others may liken him to this object; e.g., to his father, or little Ernest to The Great Stone Face, but simple identification does not produce the consciousness of oneness that is characteristic of mergence. Similarly, while introjection may produce total agreement with a given position, it does not produce any sense of union with the authority prescribing it. Furthermore, it does not produce the *augmentations* of personality that are so regularly noted in religious experience at this level.

When the solution-god appears to the religious subject, it is clothed with an aura of numinosity, i.e., supreme valuation plus mystery.[78] The supreme valuation hardly needs comment, since, by definition, the god is the symbolic portrayal of whatever will most effectively solve his problem. The mystery is always summarizable in the three questions to which we have already referred on page 100 of Part Three, *supra*; What Is It? Why Is It Happening To Me? and Why Do I Value It So Much?

However, there is an atmosphere of intimacy and pertinence which accompanies a religious symbol, since it originates in the subject's own psyche, and the sense of mystery is thereby intensified. Also, being thus an endopyschic fact, there is a quality of *potency* attached to the pertinence of any religious personification. Just as in a sex dream, the object envisioned is exactly the one that will produce excitement and climax in the dreamer, so in the unconsciously dynamic process of personi-fication, the figure presented to the subject's awareness is precisely the one that will, given all psychic circumstances, most effectively structure the relief of his intolerable distress. Both qualities making for numinosity are thus abundantly present. Thus it is that the initial reaction to symbolic impact is total commitment, i.e., complete identification. An enormous flow of libido moves toward the archetypal personification, which the subject immediately embraces as his own, not without a sense of surprise at the lack of strangeness with which the redemptive moment is imbued.

Nor is this without further explanation: for, as Edinger has succinctly pointed out, every symbol of deity is, in Jungian terms, a symbol of the total Self, the person's objective *identity*, with which the alienated ego seeks reunion.[79] When we add to

[78] The reader is urged to refer again to the section on The Rise of the Personification, if any of the ensuing material is unclear.

[79] Edinger, Edward F., *Ego and Archetype*. Baltimore: Pelican Books, 1973, p. 4. Edinger gives excellent simplification to the multifarious and confusing Jungian definitions of the Self. He summarizes it very simply as the person's *objective identity*, as distinguished from his *subjective identity*, which is the ego. The objective identity obviously includes physical, social and cultural factors which describe the person, and, less obviously, the unconscious aspects of

this the insight of our own formulation, namely, that the deity that is present to awareness in any valid religious experience is the personification of whatever will most effectively touch the subject's insoluble problem: and when we remind ourselves that this archetypal figure is also a portrayal of *how* the subject can best tap the vast reservoir of his own unconscious energies, we are enabled to understand the sense of naturalness and inevitability, as well as the enormous outpouring of love, that always characterizes a subject's acceptance of a religious symbol.

Furthermore, there is another aspect of the experience of a solution-god which may be the most significant of all. We have pointed out that the proclamation of a coming Ideal Society, and of a New Morality by which that Society is defined, are structural aspects of the archetypal figure appearing as a solution-god. Now to a person in the throes of a religious problem, the thought of this morality is the most vivid phantasy that he can entertain. The yearning for someone to help him: for an end to exploitation, for any fragment of compassion, and for kindly people practicing mutual assistance, is necessarily within the content of whatever consciousness remains to him, and it is straight from the Primary Process: for it does not exist for him, he cannot structure its appearance, and he never expects to see it in fact. Thus, when the symbol appears, complete with an annunciation of his dearest hope, he is naturally disposed for its acceptance.

But this is only the beginning. The big hurdle in any symbolic experience is to get it past the Secondary Process—that cold, critical realization that fact is fact and this is only phantasy. However, in the situation we describe, the Secondary Process can only affirm the rightness and inevitability of a benevolent morality, for there is at last no other arrangement by which human beings can live together, and whatever be the details of

---

his psychic structure as well. Unless the two aspects of personality are operating in harmony, the ego becomes ineffective.

its organization, any departure from the principles of mutual aid is a betrayal of rationality.

Hence the solution god who enjoins such a morality, and promises the coming of a society where it will obtain, has not only the dynamic of the subject's own unconscious, where its archetypal pattern resides, but the endorsement of his rational faculties, which might otherwise dismiss the symbolic process as preposterous.

As Primary and Secondary Processes meet in the morality of love, the subject's commitment to its supernatural guarantor becomes absolute, and his identification with it complete.

This, however, is only half the story, for introjection remains to be incorporated in our analysis. At first glance, we might seem to be involved in an obvious contradiction, at least as regards mystic experience, for we have said that introjection is internalized social pressure, and as yet we have no enforcing society: and we have been at pains to make introjection the result of fear, yet there is nothing tangible to be afraid of.

The resolution is not far to seek, for what the mystic fears is *going on as he has been*: hence he introjects the New Morality as revealed to him by the solution god, in a most typical way, so as to be worthy of the change it promises. The early disciples of a new prophetic revelation are hard to classify, since they have not had any revelation themselves, but are merely accepting one, which would clearly make them converts: but at the beginning there is no institution for them to join, and if they proclaim the prophet himself as divine, they become, *formaliter*, prophetic, as annunciators of a new god. However, as regards their introjection of the New Morality, the mechanism is exactly the same as in the case of the original prophet—they fear to continue in their present condition. The society which presently comes into being is made up of these personal followers of the prophet; and their autonomous introjections of the morality constitute the defining pressures of the embryonic social group. Note that these pressures are already in existence as the group becomes officialized, and that they are reinforced, as time goes on, by references to their supernatural origin.

In any event, one emergent fact requires clear emphasis: the mergence which occurs in mystic experience produces a reorganization of the super-ego, as the New Morality is introjected.

The situation is a little different when the religious experience is, (more typically) one of conversion, which obviously entails the prior formulation of the deity involved. Here the subject joins a group that is already in being, and of which some part has affected him symbolically, i.e., appealed to him as being the solution to a religious problem. This may be the ritual, the fellowship, one of the members, or anything—but it leads, on the principle of ancillary attachment, straight to the personification—the deity—around which the group is organized.

As the subject finds the solution to his own problem symbolized and personified by this deity, the identification he feels is essentially the same as that taking place in mystic experience, with one qualification: such a deity never fits his psychic condition quite as perfectly as one rising from his own collective unconscious; and as a result, his responses to it are somewhat rigid and over-intense, and not unlike those of a person trying to learn the genteel manners of a foreign culture.

However, the *introjection* which the convert now experiences differs from that which is met in mystic experience, in that now it has a plainly identifiable origin in the morality of the group to which he is being admitted. This is always understood to be directly enjoined by the god, and whatever its additional content may be, it will prescribe benevolence among the members.

We have said that the super-ego is definable as the totality of introjected behavior in a personality. Hence, when a radically new introjection takes place, the super-ego is sharply modified. This modification is found in two forms in conversion, corresponding to two aspects of the conversion experience.

When the conversion is out of one religious position and into another, the subject finds his super-ego *reorganized* by the new introjection that he makes in the ensuing mergence. The similarity of this to what occurs in mystic experience is at once apparent. Such reorganization may amount to a radical revision of his value structure, as when a Christian joins the Hari-Krishna cult, or it may only be the occasion of shifting the emphasis assigned to certain familiar tenets, and leave major areas of the value-system unchanged, as when an Amishman moves into one of the main-line Protestant churches.

When, however, the conversion is into active participation in an environing religion, about which the subject has always known, but which he has hitherto ignored or neglected, his experience is one of having his super-ego *strengthened*, by the actual introjection of moral demands with which he has long been familiar, but which hitherto have had little or no binding force for him.

This distinction, although it may at first seem trivial, is a decisive technique for differentiating and classifying religious experiences.

b. The Phenomenology of Mergence: An Analysis

i. Instantaneous Personality Change   A certain reorientation of personality is taken for granted as characterizing anything a human being does to surmount a crisis. However, there is a suddenness about the personality change that occurs in this type of religious experience which is frequently its most prominent aspect. The instantaneous character of such change now becomes explainable as an aspect of mergence, entailed by the structure of introjection, which is part of it. This mechanism, which is both involuntary and unconscious, always becomes operative at a given moment, unpredictable beforehand, when the new ideation becomes compelling and the old drops away. When the ideas and/or conduct to be adopted are the commands of a religious symbol, i.e., the personification of which we speak, this moment not only arrives more quickly than in other types of introjection, but less painfully: for in mystic experience the fear dynamizing the introjection is that of continuing in the miserable condition which the subject has been in; and in conversion it is that of failing to merit the enormous consolation that the symbol personifies, by neglecting the institutional morality. Hence, in either case, the internalization is thoroughly congenial to him. However, since identification is also operative, with its intense dynamic of affirmation, the abandonment of what he previously believed or desired, is, if anything, more complete. Hence, in the relationship of mergence, the instantaneous quality of the resulting personality change becomes prominent.

ii. The Augmentation of Personality Probably the most important as well as the most perplexing phenomenon observable in mergence with a solution god is the augmentation of personal abilities that frequently attends or follows it.

We have seen this manifested in the cases of the widowed mother, and of Francis of Assisi, cited above. Malcolm X became able to throw off drug dependency when he joined the Black Muslims. Perhaps the clearest illustration, however, is that of Viola Wilson, better known as "Faithful Mary," who was prominent during the 'thirties as one of Father Divine's principal lieutenants. She was a total derelict when he picked her up, drinking canned heat, and looking back on her career as a prostitute as to an era of lost prosperity. Following her conversion, she was not only able to live without alcohol, but became a competent manager, rising to the successful supervision of a number of Peace Mission restaurants. Her integration lasted as long as she remained in a state of mergence with Sweet Father, but when she broke with him she slipped back into her former habits, with complete inability to manage anything, least of all her own existence.[80]

This phenomenon is to be understood initially in terms of the transfer of unconscious energy into conscious availability for use by the ego. That is what the symbol does, and the manner in which it is done has already been described in connection with the rise of the personification. Briefly restated, the symbol, here the personified solution, provides new structuring for activity which the exhausted ego becomes able to undertake, as

[80] Harris, Sara, *Father Divine, Holy Husband*, Chap. 6.

the subject moves into the appropriate relationship with that symbol, i.e., the god. Its impact comes when the subject recognizes its imperatives as viable patterns of action.

Also, by having its solution symbolically portrayed, the problem itself, typically repressed, is brought back into contact with the ego, and so given access to the adaptive behavior, from which repression has separated it.

Another factor related to the increase of energy *per se*, remains to be noted. Prior to the appearance of the symbol, the subject was traumatized by a devastating problem, which the ego had literally worn itself out trying to solve. Toward the close of this struggle, he necessarily *represses* the desire he feels for whatever it is he cannot obtain, along with the pain of failure, and quite possibly the frustration and hatred inspired by the pressures causing his problem, whether authoritarian or circumstantial. However, following his encounter with the solution god, he either obtains the former object of his desire (e.g., various aspects of normal development: understanding: a benevolent society, etc.), or, more often, ceases to desire it (e.g., prestige, wealth, or revenge.) Thus, in either case, the energy previously wasted in maintaining the repression is made available for use elsewhere.

The ego itself is structured by desire: and what is conveyed in the religious symbolism is awareness of an alternative pattern of action, at least as desirable, and often more significant than the one whose blockage constituted the religious problem. Furthermore, the pattern of activity thus symbolically structured, is *available* to the subject, and this is its most important characteristic. Finally, this structuring of activity, by which his entire psychic life is restored to potency, consists of, or takes place by means of, the things the subject will already be doing, to get himself into the most desirable relationship with the divine figure. As we know, that relationship is mergence, and its attainment involves introjection of the divine commands. Those commands are the morality of the Ideal Society, which is always a morality of mutual aid *in support of what the subject wants anyway.*

Even more light is cast upon the augmentation of abilities in mergence when we inquire further into the modification of the super-ego which is brought about by this new system of introjections, formed as the relationship of mergence is established. Pursuant to the increase of energy we have been discussing, the integration gained in this relationship is bound to make the subject more efficient in the *use* of energy since he is free of conflict, and totally committed to the goals of the Ideal Society. With nothing holding him back, his pursuit of whatever goals are consonant with his new orientation will display a singular effectiveness. Actually, there are two factors at work here: for not only does his introjected commitment to the New Morality free the subject from the temptation to vacillitate, and waste his energy following secondary goals, but he is at the same time *released from the inhibitions* that hampered any course of action he previously undertook. Or again, quite simply: when the super-ego is modified, many repressed ideas can return to consciousness—and they may be all that is needed to solve the problem.

References to the dissolution of earlier orientations in mergence have been made from time to time in the foregoing material without any particular elaboration. As the reader must have gathered, the elimination of the old is just as important as the adoption of the new in this relationship, since when a new introjection becomes fully binding *within mergence,* whatever in the personality is in conflict with it will disappear. This fact is central to our understanding of the remarkable augmentations of ability that are frequently reported in this connection.

Now it is perfectly possible to have elements in the super-ego which are invalid, contradictory, or dysfunctional. They become lodged there by earlier introjections, perhaps even mistakenly: and in the absence of any event dynamic enough to change them, they may keep the subject crippled for a long time. Impotence and frigidity are classic illustrations of this point. The writer once counselled an alcoholic who had fully internalized the idea that it was disgraceful to be anything but rich, and at the same time, the idea that it was shameful to work. This orientation was not inconsistent with the circumstances of his childhood, but when those circumstances suddenly changed, he turned to alcohol in the attempt to dissolve the painful contradictions by which he was then compelled.

However, when both identification and introjection are combined in mergence, and both dynamized by the numinous emotion that characterizes the impact of a personified symbol, former introjections simply drop away in the resulting reorganization of the super-ego, and their pressures are no longer operative. We must never forget that this personification is involuntary, and that it only takes place when the ego has collapsed from exhaustion,[81] so that the subject is in a state of total suggestibility. Also, attention should again be drawn to the endopsychic nature of the symbol to which this transforming acceptance is given. An impaired super-ego is the very essence of an inner-psychic religious problem, whether or not it is consciously identified: but the personification which the subject autistically makes, originating as it does in his own unconscious, is indeed that of the solution to this unconscious problem: and the god whom he encounters in this archetypal experience is exactly the one fitted to disperse whatever non-adaptive introjections are inhibiting him, as soon as his mergence with the new personification has been effected.

The importance of this mechanism for the augmentation of ability that we are discussing, is perhaps most clearly evident in the surprising power of religious experience to dissolve the rigidly introjected *patterns of failure* which make up the syndrome of neurosis. The neurotic, as we shall presently see in some detail, has been conditioned by harsh parental discipline (particularly as to sex) or by other adverse circumstances

---

[81] A recent study by William Sargant, *The Mind Possessed*, Penguin Books, 1975, has drawn fresh attention to the manner in which total psychic collapse, induced by any kind of overstimulation, including ritual, contributes to the reorganization of the ego. However, although he actually describes it, Sargant completely overlooks the fact that the symbolic *restructuring* of personality, as we have been examining it in religious experience, takes place altogether subsequently to the ritually induced collapse.

limiting growth, to fear social, i.e., personal rejection if he makes any move that would be successful, either in gaining love in his own right, or in attaining independent personal adequacy in some other forbidden field. Differently stated, he is forbidden the independent expression of emotion, i.e., love and hostility, apart from the authoritarian center that dominates him. As a result, he can neither love nor believe himself lovable, and he is unable to engage in obstacle removing behavior, i.e., meaningful work, as implemented by the ego. And this, of course, is his religious problem.

Yet, no matter how neurotic he has been before, once the subject has envisioned the archetypal solution to his problem, autistically personified in the god of a religious experience, a liberative sequence is set in motion. His libido flows toward this symbolic figure, in unrestrained identification, since it is the supremely valued personal entity in all his awarness; his super-ego is reconstituted by his introjection of its commands, and his ego finds new structure in arranging the activities entailed by the mergence which is thus constituted. Henceforward, instead of being doomed to repeat a monotonous pattern of unconsciously accurate ineffectiveness, internalized in childhood in conformity to an authority that was either overprotective, itself neurotically blighted, or overtly cruel, the subject is now free to take constructive action in the area that has assumed central importance to him, which is to say, the anticipation and furtherance of the coming Ideal Society, as it is prefigured in the religious institution.

Perhaps the most widely noted augmentation of personality produced by mergence with a solution god is the ability to love, or, stated in a little different form, the insistent and preponderant awareness of loving emotions, which make the subject inwardly affirmative and happy, and objectively likable and pleasant to associate with. Several observations have explanatory value:

(1) Energy itself is erotic, as Freud always asserted. Moreover, the access of energy about which we have been speaking

constitutes the solution to his religious problem, so that the subject now is happy; and James has correctly pointed out the connection between joyousness and tenderness.[82]

(2) As the subject becomes aware of the endopsychic entity that personifies the solution to his problem, (and is, among other things, the symbol of his own completed selfhood—) an enormous quantity of dammed-up libido is released, and flows toward this personification. This in itself is an important aspect of mergence, and a tremendous factor in the solution of his problem.

At the same time, his introjection of the New Morality, which is always benevolent, and may include all humanity in its scope, impels him to express his kindly feelings to those about him. As felt in consciousness and revealed in behavior, these two factors go far to explain the all-embracing love reported and displayed by those who have had the experience of mergence with a solution god.

(3) As his super-ego is modified, the subject, by reason of his new orientation, no longer feels as obstacles the objects, persons and situations that he formerly regarded in this light. Consequently, he needs less obstacle removing behavior, i.e., hostility, to get along. Furthermore, as the resources of his ego have eroded, with the onset of its exhaustion in grappling with the religious problem, his hostility will have turned to hate. Now the hostitity may not have been inappropriate, given the subject's circumstances: but hate is the unstructured and strongly emotionalized wish to destroy the obstacle utterly, simply for the sake of so doing,[83] and as such is very seldom appropriate at all. Moreover, the *expression* of hate is always penalized by society, so that his original problem, itself social, is thereby compounded. Thus, when the new introjection, implicit in his mergence with the solution god, frees him from the inner imperative to continue this circular and self-defeating

[82] *Varieties,* M. L. ed., p. 275.

[83] Cf. Pps. 71–72, *supra,* also *Problems Solved in Mergence With Solution Gods,* pp. 160–, *infra.*

struggle, his relief is profound and his reaction frequently dramatic. The energy hitherto wasted in hate is now directed into the New Morality, as indicated in our preceding point, and it wells up in consciousness as a sense of universal love.

iii. Sense of Total Identity With the Symbol The final aspect of mergence that we shall examine is the sense of total identity with the personification, to which earlier reference was made. Granting that a subject may feel total concurrence with the will of a god, how are we to account for the expressions of complete identity with deity ("I and my Father are one—") or coextensity of the subject's power or ability with that of the god?

The answer is found in the sequence of occurrence. Whereas the augmentation of ability *is* the solution gained in mergence, and the instantaneous aspect of personality change refers to the manner of its coming, the sense of identity with the religious symbol is only met with *after* the relationship of mergence has been established, and is to be understood as a *result* of that experience.

It goes like this: The subject with a religious problem feels "Only a god could solve this problem." Later, when he has surmounted it religiously, he realizes, "But, I am solving it." The logical conclusion that he, the subject, is equivalent to deity, follows; and his emotional beatitude at having found the solution gives credibility to his logic.

Further, it must be remembered that the personification arises from the subject's own unconscious, or from his objective psyche, if that expression be preferred. Hence, as he feels a new force possessing him, objective and personal, he finds it mysteriously his own, and indubitably a part of himself, so that it constitutes *a new dimension of selfhood.* James refers to this experience as "A sense of the friendly continuity of the ideal power with our own life, and a willing surrender to its control."[84] In short, where this sense of total identity is found, it can be understood as the subjective *quality* of the religious solution assuming this form as it appears in consciousness.

[84] *Varieties*, M. L. ed., p. 275.

Instances of ritually induced glossalalia and total divine possession, of the kinds Dr. William Sargant discusses in *The Mind Possessed*, to which we alluded a few pages earlier, ought perhaps to receive some notice here. However, despite their strong resemblance to the states we have been considering, by reason of the exhaustion of the ego on which both are predicated, all cases where this psychic collapse is ritually induced are institutionally sponsored, and are more appropriately considered in that context than in the present one. We shall return to them in Part Four.

4. *Problems Solved In Mergence With Solution Gods*

Having examined the experience of mergence with a solution god in some detail, we now turn to the problems which are solved thereby. As we have repeatedly stated, solution gods arise primarily in response to problems of society, but we shall review all four types of religious problems, since each has some connection with solution gods.

The following observations may aid in orientation.

While problems of society are predominantly the ones solved by mergence with solution gods (i.e., "giving rise to solution gods-"), inner-psychic problems are also, and most logically, solved by mergence with personifications thus made, but *principally by the mechanism of conversion*, or else within the framework of an institution, by the renewal of archetypal contact.[85]

Problems of nature are occasionally solved in this way, e.g., faith healings, but this is a secondary mechanism, resulting from claims made by institutional representatives.

Problems of Prior Formulation necessarily fall into the three categories above, and the paradigm just given applies to the solutions they receive in mergence.

a. *Problems of Nature*

At first glance it would seem as though any attempt to consider the connection of problems of nature with the expe-

[85] Cf. *infra*. p. 137

rience of mergence, obviously pertaining exclusively to solution gods, was a waste of time, since problems of nature do not "give rise to" solution gods, in the sense of precipitating their autistic formulation. However, certain marginal and vestigial instances require consideration, in which earlier types of gods, i.e., problem- and cause-cure gods, are subsumed by solution gods, and problems of nature are brought to solution by deities formulated in religious experiences that originally had nothing to do with that area.

Any connection between these deities and the problems we are here considering can only be understood as the result of claims consciously made at the institutional level, by persons seeking to expand the clientele of the group they represent. To understand how this comes about, we must go back for a moment, and review the rise and development of problem gods.

The first discernible instance of the religious mechanism— personification plus relationship—is that in which the sudden adversities of nature—whirlwinds, avalanches, flash floods, tornadoes and other unchancy circumstances, are directly personified. As problem gods, the relationship sought with these figures is aversion, and it is of their nature to be met with rituals whereby they are placated, rendered inoperative, the subject is made immune to their attacks, or they are simply driven away.

Their tenure as gods is relatively brief, however, since when the big cause-cure gods arise, a more satisfactory rationale is given to the events and situations which were initially personified directly. Furthermore, the earlier problem-gods are portrayed in such horrendous terms as to make the formulations themselves problematic: the newer personifications are invoked to exorcise them, and they presently come to be regarded as demons, with a merely subordinate status. Moreover, the inevitable migration of religious issues removes some of them from the religious realm entirely, by the general advancement of insight: and others are made explanatory of destructive factors in the environment, as in the case of the

Vedic Rudra, who was at last rationalized into the philosophical principle of perishing.

Nonetheless, since what they personify is the immediately
alarming or the intractably terrifying, many of them, in their
status of demons, linger on for a very long time; indeed, until
the present day. Reflecting, as they do, the inner fear, of a
subject who is suddenly confronted by a problem of religious
dimensions, the direct personification of that problem *externalizes* the fear, and permits it to be in some measure removed, as
the demon is driven away.

However, except in the most primitive instances, the basic
principle of exorcism is to expel the unwanted archetype by
summoning another one, of benign intent, and of greater
power, whose command, or even whose presence, rather than
any further ritual endeavor by the subject, is efficacious in
driving out the personified evil. Where a solution god exists, it
is entirely unsurprising to find this exorcistic function claimed
as one of his attributes, even though it may have had no place
in the original formulation.

Thus, Oral Roberts does his healings by casting out demons:
he claims to be able to smell their presence. When such a
healing is performed, the subject is repeatedly urged to have
faith in Jesus, whom Roberts then implores, with deep intensity, to cast out the demon, a moment later announcing, with
great dramatic effect, that this has been done. The deep
mergence of the subject with the archetypal image of Christ, to
say nothing of what he feels for Roberts, must be credited with
whatever improvement is effected in his health. When we
reflect that any valid faith healing entails a psychosomatic
complaint, and when we remember the interconnection of
inner-psychic problems with those having a social basis, as we
shall presently discuss, whereby they are admitted to the true
operating area of solution gods, the amenability of such dis-
eases as Roberts heals, to the techniques he employs, becomes
understandable.

Again, Mary Baker Eddy devoted a preponderant amount of
energy to the exorcism of "Malicious Animal Magnetism," in

the early years of her Christian Science movement. The problem denoted by this term was anything that interfered with the success of her teachings, or rather with her own success, and she personified it at two levels. At the first level, she ascribed failures of belief among her students to the negative thoughts of certain of their number who had broken with her, thus avoiding further exploitation. Two of these, Kennedy and Spofford, were mentioned by name to the point of being made typical problem personifications. The mental, and indeed verbal, abuse which was directed at these guileless young men, in the interest of nullifying their supposed evil influences, was so unseemly, and so heavily stressed as to alienate some of Eddy's other students who were required to practice it. Furthermore, since she taught, and apparently believed, that the teachings of Christian Science were the highest reality, and were to be equated with deity, of which she herself was for a long time the carefully developed personification,[86] it followed that anything militating against this ultimate reality had to have a larger metaphysical dimension. Hence at this level she personified the M. A. M. which caused any kind of failure, ill luck, or organizational opposition, *but particularly illness,* as "The Fiend," or "The Red Dragon," who thus becomes a clear personification of a universalized Devil. For her followers, a deeper mergence into, or with, her teachings, and ultimately with herself, was the only prescribed cure for the Fiend's attacks.

Interestingly enough, she herself never became immune to its onslaughts, but feared it throughout her life as the cause of the hysterical seizures to which she had been subject since childhood. Then, not unnaturally, she was plagued with a variety of illnesses in her advanced age, and from 1882 on, she kept a selected cadre of trusted students about her at all times,

---

[86] She finally stopped trying to develop this emphasis upon herself as divine when it was pointed out to her that it generated too much criticism. Cf. Dakin, E. F., *Mrs. Eddy, The Biography of a Virginal Mind,* N. Y., Charles Scribner's Sons, 1929, pp. 337–38.

to help fight off the personification which she herself had given to her ailments![87]

Although the problems of nature which were paramount in the lives of Father Divine's followers were never personified, they were clearly solved by mergence with Sweet Father, himself a most typical solution god. However, it goes without saying that these problems were social in origin, and the technique of their solution was simply economic cooperation.

A similar mechanism can be observed in the witch-cult of the late Middle Ages. This interesting religious group was made up in large part although not totally, of persons who had been excommunicated, or who feared that they would be, and so had fled to the forests which then covered Europe. There they constituted a small but definite underground society, structured by the pre-Christian worship of an animal deity; and they eked out their clandestine existence by organized thefts of livestock, which provided the basis of their communal "feasts," to which all writers in this area refer. At these ceremonials, a horned god presided, evidently impersonated by a costumed man: and this deity later gave himself to be eaten by the assembled faithful: i.e., a horned animal was slaughtered and eaten.

This underground group was abetted by other persons who kept their residence within the traditional society, but gave their allegiance to the witch-cult in reaction to the Catholic doctrines which held that anything whatever that relieved pain or improved the status of women was bad, since suffering was God's will for the human race, especially women. Inasmuch as the witch-cult was represented as absolute badness, its deity attracted those who were seeking relief from the cruelties called "good" by the official religion.[88] Some of them, although not receiving their basic maintenance from the group, were

[87] Dakin, *Op. Cit.*, pp. 171–186. When closely pressed at the intellectual level, she defined the Fiend as "the error of mortal mind."

[88] This deity, evidently a holdover from a primitive totemism, was not unnaturally regarded as a problem god by all elements of society outside the cult itself.

brought to mergence with this deity as a solution god by their experience of the embryonic healing techniques which were always a feature of his cult.

The point to be noted is that the unfortunates who made up this weird and often unlovely group found their basic problems of survival, i.e., food and health, resolved by their mergence with the horned god who was the focus of adoration in each local coven. Again, the obvious rootage of these problems of nature in profounder problem of social maladjustment is not to be disputed; yet it is undeniable that problems of nature are here solved by mergence with a solution god.

One final word, and a brief one, probably best sums up the fundamental relation between problems of nature and solution gods—namely, that any problem at all is made more tolerable if the subject has some help available.

b. Problems of Society

In previous types of personification, i.e., problem- and cause-cure gods, the individual took his membership in the social order for granted. Indeed, it was defined for him very specifically, in terms of the access he had to the rituals controlling the power of the gods; this ritual control of their power we have elsewhere called The Magic Formula, and have spoken of the definition thereby given to the individual's social status as the Social Metaphysic. Now, however, his own relation to the social order has become the problem, in ways we are about to examine. Hence, in speaking of "Problems of Society," or "Social Problems," we shall be using the terms in this frame of reference, and not to designate some generalized perplexity by which a body politic might be troubled, such as unemployment, inflation, or an outbreak of disease.

The subject whose religious problem is a social one as here understood, will experience it either in terms of his relationship to some group within the total society, or vis-a-vis the total society itself.

i. Intra-Mural Social Problems (1) The subject may be *unable to qualify* for the group to which he aspires to belong, as when a trade-school graduate is denied membership in a learned society, or a *nouveau riche* person is excluded from in-group participation by the local arbiters of what passes for good taste. John Bunyan is an example of this type of religious subject, as are Negroes who aspire to higher status in industrial management.

(2) The subject may have been *expelled from* a group whose membership he valued. While this may take place for a wide variety of reasons, it probably will not occur except for some clear-cut violation of the rules. Examples would be an Amishman subjected to the *Meidung*, or a Mason, expelled from his Lodge for a violation of the adultery clause in the Obligation.

ii. Problems of Relation to the Total Society By the Total Society, we mean the largest group of which the subject is capable of being conscious. For primitives, it would be the tribe: at higher cultural levels, it is usually the national entity.

(1) The subject may be the victim of cultural clash, conquest, or oppression, so that the group to which he formerly belonged, and with which he still feels himself identified, is either disorganized, powerless, demoralized, or all of these things. In short, his own total society has collapsed, and he has no comprehension of, nor sympathy with, the larger and more sophisticated culture that has overwhelmed it, and by which he is now regarded as an inferior. His own position in the defunct total society may have been most secure, but the context for that position no longer exists. As a result, he yearns for any supportive and benevolent society to which he can belong.

Francis LaFlesche describes[89] the tragic melancholy of Smoked Yellow, the last keeper of the Sacred Pole of the Omaha Indians, after the tribe had gone to the reservation. The old man was still keeping this object, once the symbol of tribal unity, in its own sacred tent, set up behind his house; but no

[89] R. B. E. W., vol. 27, (1905–06), pp. 246–250.

tokens of respect were any longer paid to it. Formerly one of the prominent functionaries of the ritual system, he was disoriented and despairing, as a result of the termination of the tribal ceremonials. This man's state of mind, so feelingly described, makes the appeal of the Ghost Dance, which swept the plains three years later, fully understandable. The Jews in Jerusalem at the turn of the era, and the Melanesians and Zulu, cited above, are parallel examples.

(2) The subject may have been expelled from the Total Society. We indicated above that in previous types of person- ification (problem and cause-cure gods . . .) the individual took his membership in the social order for granted, since there simply are no dissenters in an ethnic society. Yet this ethnic unanimity is implemented by the simplistic policy of either killing such dissenters or driving them away, and the plight of one who, like Cain, Esau, Hagar, or Moses, was either cast out to die, or forced to flee, is exactly what we are considering here. Here, again, although Christianity in the Middle Ages was Pseudo-Ethnic rather than Ethnic, it certainly was repre- sentative of the Total Society, over most of Europe. Hence, excommunicated persons who would join a coven of the witch-cult in the effort to survive, provide graphic illustration of this particular problem.[90]

(3) The subject may himself reject the Total Society by which he is surrounded. Although quite satisfactory to most of its members, this society may be tainted by vitiating weaknesses of which the subject is aware by reason of some unique perspective that is available to him. This situation is quite different from the one described in (1), since there, the Total Society that was actually in being[91] was basically hostile to his interests, and there was no reason he should desire member- ship in it, whereas here his acceptance by the society he rejects is complete. A person of great wealth, intelligence, or moral

---

[90] Cf. Michelet, Jules, *Satanism and Witchcraft: A Study in Medieval Supersti- tion*, N.Y.: The Citadel Press, *passim*.

[91] I.e., following the collapse and extinction of the Total Society to which the subject had previously belonged, and in which he felt at home.

sensitivity may come to be so conscious of the discrepancies between his own values and those of the environing social order that he ceases to value any reward it can offer him, or to fear any penalty it might exact, so that for him the society is meaningless, and he derives no sense of support from membership in it. Tolstoi is our prime example of this pattern of experience; the writer knows of no instance more typical, although various members of the American counter-culture, today and in the recent past, insist that they view our society in this light, and with comparable distress. Their discovery of symbolic potency in such solution-figures as Meher Baba and Maharaj Ji, not to mention Jesus, lends plausibility to their assertions.

Yet be all these things as they may, and whatever the permutation in which it appears, the nature of the main problem which solution gods arise to solve should now be fully apparent. For all socially disoriented people, the appeal of a deity who promises a new society, better than the one they have been denied, and who gives authority to a moral system that is just what each of them has hoped for, is so great as to inspire the total commitment we have analyzed as mergence, in which this problem is solved, and out of which new religious movements arise.

We see this pattern exemplified outstandingly when primitives leave a decaying ethnic group to join one of the major prophetic religions, whose solution gods assume symbolic force for the converts by reason of an Ideal Society whose early arrival they proclaim. Indeed, we see it repeated whenever any member of an alienated class aligns himself with a group dynamized by a personification whose announced intent is the establishment of a new social order.

c. Inner-Psychic Problems

Although at the very beginning of our discussion of solution gods we stressed their close connection with social problems, these are by no means the only type of religious issue of which the solution is personified. Inner-Psychic problems are also brought to solution in mergence with such personifications, and to these we now turn.

We must never forget that all problems, of whatever kind, have their impact in the psychic dimension. Even when their true source in another area is recognized, as we have been at pains to do, the psychic distress that they cause cannot be minimized. Indeed, so great is the importance of this area that if the work of the great C. G. Jung has a fault, it is in giving exclusive emphasis to the inner-psychic aspects of religious experience, and failing to notice its connection with problems quite external to the personality.

Malfunctions of the psychic life are among the major sources of religious problems in this area. Fears that are groundless, suspicions that are unwarranted, morbid guilts, and hatreds that the subject cannot relinquish are obvious: but acknowledged phobias, fear of psychosis, guilt over some long gone pecadillo, or hatred of an inadequate ego are also to be reckoned in this accounting: and while all are amenable to therapy, if it is unavailable to the subject, only the religious solution remains.

Of all problems that find relief in mergence, simple grief may well be the most extensive, and it is only classifiable here. This untaught emotional response to the frustration of human desire, and the blighting of human hopes probably impels as many people to find symbolic impact in solution gods, as any other religious issue. Bereavement, in any form; disappointment, whether in the collapse of cherished plans or in the faithlessness of friends; failure, when abilities fall short or judgment is bad; and with these, all the ramifications of injustice, leave the subject in the state of joy-gone-out that is all too familiar to every reader: and times without number, these despairing ones find the only comfort available to them in mergence with a solution god.

Important as these problems are, in the overall extensity of religious experience, they would seem, for the most part, to arrive at the personification of their solutions by a process of conversion, rather than in originative mysticism, coming to mergence with the socially dynamized solution gods on three grounds, all of them laden with symbolic impact.

First, the Ideal Society which a solution god announces is so totally supernatural, so completely unlike and above any merely revolutionary enterprise, that the griefs which mortal flesh is heir to are therein assuaged. Safe within the Heavenly City, all sorrowing ones will be comforted, for the god himself will wipe away all tears from their eyes, and they can lean on the Everlasting Arms, with their fumbling good intentions at last seen as valid, in the Light That Never Was On Land Or Sea.

Second, the morality of this Ideal Society is exactly what those with Inner-Psychic problems need. The mutual cherishing that is its central characteristic is the promise of rest for the heavy-laden, and these embrace the archetypal figure who enjoins it as the author of their salvation. Moreover, the loftier insights of human enlightenment are uniformly represented in such moralities, and those who have found life meaningless for lack of these, gain new relish for existence in their commitment to the ideals of truth, integrity, honor and compassion, seen as divine commands.

Third, these problems have a social rootage which makes them inextricable in practice from those giving rise to the solution gods. Bereavement entails the loss of a personal (social) relationship; grief is hardly ever separate from some form of exploitation; injustice always involves a social reference; failure implies the fear of social censure or the loss of status; and there is no one of these sadnesses that is not ameliorated by the aid or comfort of other persons.

As we thus review the intimate kinship of Inner-Psychic problems with those of society, it becomes abundantly plain why the gods arising out of massive social issues are so appealing to persons who are confused and sad within themselves.

Indeed, these problems are so deeply rooted in those of society that at first glance we might take them for a subdivision of that class; yet, despite this rootage, they stand in their own right; for although many mental states are influenced by social conditions, they are not universally determined thereby. Inner-Psychic problems are not always caused by a bad society, but their cure is always inherent in an Ideal one, where forgiveness, love, and perfect understanding obtain, all within a framework of mutual aid. Furthermore, we must note with some emphasis that the healthful opposites of whatever psychic states are felt as religious problems, are themselves social virtues, generally recognized and affirmed. Hence these problems find their religious solution in mergence with the same god who proclaims an Ideal Society, and enunciates the morality that goes with it.

All Christians are familiar with the idea that God is love; that 'Perfect love casteth out fear' (I John 1:18); and that forgiveness of sins is of the utmost importance. Zoroaster identified his evil principle as Druj, "The Lie;" Vinobha Bhave says "Until you learn not to hate, I cannot help you;" and Gotama's Eight-Fold Path was a technique for eliminating Illusion and Desire. However, even though the symptoms of psychic distress may not be mentioned in a religious formulation, if mergence with the deity about which the formulation is made relieves such symptoms, then problems of the Inner-Psychic variety have been dealt with by a solution god, albeit indirectly.

The really basic problems in this area are fear, hate and guilt. Whatever others there may be are based upon, and formed out of, these. Let us examine them with some care, beginning with guilt, since it is prominent in so many religious formulations and practices.

i. Guilt It is perfectly obvious that one who is known to have violated the mores of a society is penalized by that society, and *ipso facto*, has a social problem. When such is the case, he also has a sense of guilt, at least in the sense of being aware of the social disapproval he has incurred; i.e., he may not be validly sorry for what he has done. On the other hand, once he feels the full pressure of social disapproval, he may become deeply contrite. In any event, his restoration to social acceptance is a valid function of religion, and it involves the removal of whatever overt stigma has attached to him as a result of his trangression, and in token of the guilt thereby imputed to him (the "mark of Cain;" Hester Prynne's "A" for Adulteress; the popular designations of "convict" or "atheist"). Of course such social absolution, when given, entails the general recognition that the offense committed was basically forgivable, according to the canons of the existing culture.

While many if not most crimes have a religious dimension, and so can be called "sins," this mechanism is particularly evident when some ritual offense gives rise to the notion of impurity. In this circumstance, some ceremonial of penance or purification will be employed to restore the subject to social participation. A case in point would be that of a Zoroastrian who had touched a corpse. The ritual known as "The Churching of Women," performed forty days after childbirth, and still in use in the Catholic and Episcopalian churches, gives rise to interesting trains of thought. . . . Such procedures are obviously institutional.

On the other hand, if the offense is regarded as unforgivable, either by the arbiters of society, or by the subject himself, his personally felt guilt brings the problem into the primary area of our discussion, for if it is solved at all, it will typically be relieved in an individually numinous experience of a solution god, from whom the subject receives a supernatural forgiveness that qualifies him for membership in an Ideal Society. Whatever his previous attitude has been, such an experience will be the occasion of his valid moral rehabilitation, as the mechanisms of mergence, already described, operate within his personality.

Since we are dealing with Inner-Psychic problems, we may pertinently observe that many religiously sanctioned social demands have a totally intangible and altogether psychic quality, so that defections from their observance cannot possibly produce any bad results outside the psychic realm, other than the censure of the clergy; i.e., failures of belief, and occasions of ritual neglect. The same is true as regards the breaking of minor taboos, e.g., fish on Friday. Indeed, defections from such demands might even be socially constructive, as would be the killing of rats in India, or the practice of contraception by poverty-striken parents in any culture where it is forbidden; so that as enlightenment dawns in the subject, heavy perplexity is added to his guilt when penalities are assessed for his "sinfulness." Much if not most of the guilt that religion absolves is religiously created, and deals with minutiae having little real relationship to the mainstream of the individual's social existence. Investigators in the field take this as a commonplace fact, yet it has received surprisingly little emphasis in the literature.

Be all this as it may, our contention stands, that one whose social problem is rooted in the actual commission of a socially forbidden act, can only be restored to social acceptance and participation by a process of guilt release, which it is the function of religion to provide.

Now let us look at the other side of the coin. It is equally true, although less obvious, and indeed seldom noted, that one who is socially rejected for invalid reasons, such as poverty, race, or *name* personal peculiarity, will also have a sense of guilt, which cannot be relieved apart from the relief of his social situation. Explicitly stated, guilt and social rejection are so closely related that whatever ameliorates the one will improve the other. The personification of a social solution thus equally personifies the solution of guilt as a religious problem, since mergence with such a figure relieves both symptoms.

There is another aspect of guilt which has remained totally *share* unnoticed, so far as the writer knows: this is its relationship with ego failure. The ego apparently expects itself to be adequate at all points, and when the subject is unable to meet social expectation in areas with which the ego ordinarily can deal, he experiences heavy guilt. Thus, failure to make a living, despite economic chaos or physical handicap: failure to eliminate a persistent enemy successfully, despite the invisible pressures of a power structure: failure to obtain preferment, despite favoritism or prejudice—all are productive of guilt, in spite of the many valid reasons which can exist for the nonattainment of these admittedly routine achievements. Conversely, guilt over past inadequacies is dispelled when a subject finds his ego strengthened and his ability to work correspondingly enhanced by an improvement in his social relationships, which, in their turn, have been made benign by his mergence with a solution god. Indeed, the essential solubility of all these problems in such mergence is clearly apparent, and the resolution of guilt in this relationship is a familiar experience to thousands of people.

ii. Fear Although the most basic of the emotions which devastate the personality, fear is given second place in our discussion because guilt is (a) the problem most obviously and frequently met with in popular religious contexts, and (b) problems of guilt are most closely tied to social relations. Neither consideration changes the fact that fear is the most fundamental of all the Inner-Psychic problems, since guilt is a form of fear, and hate is dynamized by it.

A note of orientation may not be amiss, just here. Although fear has often been said to be the origin of religion, and although all men, from primitives to the most sophisticated, admittedly experience terror in the face of natural catastrophes, and may have religious experiences dynamized by this emotion, such circumstances are not presently the focus of our attention, since the religious response to them has already been considered in our discussions of problem- and cause-cure gods. Similarly, fears of persecution, unemployment, or social rejection are most meaningfully considered in terms of their focus as social problems, and these too, have been dealt with. By the same token, fears of hell, or of the anger of a god, are problems of prior formulation, and will be properly considered in that context. Differently stated, the appropriate area of investigation in such cases is not the fear itself, but the thing feared; since with the removal of the problem, analysis of the fear it inspires becomes merely an academic exercise. It is when fears are morbid, i.e., disproportionate or baseless, that they become part of this class. In short, we are now considering instances where not some horrendous natural event, social situation, or religious formulation is the religious problem, but an inner psychic state, namely fear, which has itself gotten out of hand, and where the resultant personification portrays the solution to it.

The first great instance of fear as a religious problem which is solved by mergence with a solution god is the appearance of an unwanted archetypal image. As Rudolph Otto has ably shown,[92] this experience is always characterized by a *tremendum*, a "need for trembling;" and when a subject is thus overtaken, he finds shelter, as it were, in the more welcome archetype of a religious institution: i.e., in that of a solution god who portrays a comforting society and a pertinent morality. If he can somehow manage to invoke this archetypal image (which, in the vast majority of instances is previously known) he need never come to terms with the autistic one, for the solution god will drive it away.

This mechanism is seen with particular clarity when a problem god is the unwanted apparition; but an archetypal image need not be that of a problem god as we have defined it, to be terrifying when it appears. Actually, the protective function of a solution god is, more typically, to keep these unwanted personifications from appearing at all. It is for this reason that Jung always tried, as a consistent therapeutic policy, to get a patient back into a conventional religious institution if this was at all psychically possible for him; and this is why, at the same time, he held that the process of individuation could not become complete within such an institutional shelter, since the patient who remains there, never needs to come to terms with his own profounder selfhood.

The next great exemplification of fear as a religious problem, and by far the most familiar one, is found in that form of emotional malaise known as neurosis. However, the fear that

---

[92] *The Idea Of The Holy*, 2nd ed., Oxford: The University Press, 1950, pp. 12–14.

dynamizes the neurotic syndrome is repressed, and so unconscious.

While admitting the difficulty of defining neurosis, and
acknowledging that it appears in many different forms, we may
nonetheless note that its most common characteristic is *anxiety*,
whereby the subject is either rendered incapable of constructive action, or achieves it with disproportionate emotional
effort, and with limited success.

Such anxiety is evidenced by premature fatigue, obviously
connected with the emotional friction mentioned; by the acceptance of a selfhood, and a station in life, inferior to the subject's
real potential; by the inability to make changes promptly, and
a proneness to repetitive behavior; by an obvious uncertainty
as to his objectives, as well as to the means for their attainment;
and by a tendency to seek solution to his problems at an
infantile level. One who suffers from neurotic anxiety will
either be unpredictably quarrelsome or excessively submissive,
but he cannot pursue his normal and legitimate interests by the
practice of obstacle-removing behavior, which is to say, constructive work. Most characteristic of all, however, is the
neurotic's inability to love, or to believe in his own lovability.
He cannot appreciate any love extended to him unless it is
accompanied by sacrifice, and in his contacts with the people
around him, he practices a kind of emotional dishonesty,
displayed in a system of emotional shortcuts, whereby he seeks
to *control* them through power or pity, rather than to accept
them on the basis of mutual goodwill, which would require
him to love.

In addition to the routine ineffectiveness and unpleasantness
which commonly express neurotic anxiety, we must take
account of phobias and compulsions, which also are examples
of the neurotic pattern, of which the origins will be described in
a moment. The fear that both of these neurotic mechanisms
illustrate in its dimensions as a religious problem is unconscious, like that dynamizing other types of neurotic anxiety;
and here as there, the entire neurotic syndrome has arisen in
the effort to escape it. The irrational fear, of which the subject

is so intensely conscious in the various phobias, is merely symptomatic, and a displacement of the real fear, now repressed, that has brought it into being.

Our purpose in reviewing these symptoms is not to present an exhaustive clinical description of neurosis, but simply to emphasize that persons having some or all of these characteristics are immediately discernible in any area of religion that one might investigate. The connection between neurotic anxiety and fear per se, becomes plain when we reflect, however briefly, upon the manner of its origin.

The precipitating causes of neurotic anxiety are to be found in three principal areas.

1. The harsh inhibition of sex drives. This is where Freud began, and although he himself, as well as his successors, modified his initial dogma, wherein neurotic symptoms were *identified with* repressed sexual tensions, it remains clear that the frustrating of a major human instinct, particularly when harshly and unfeelingly carried out, is often a crippling experience, and that the agent of such conditioning will be greatly feared at the time of its occurrence, as indeed its very memory will be, later on. And yet this agent will be one or both of the subject's parents, whom he is enjoined by a thousand sources to love. Hence the fear he initially felt for the inhibiting agent, to say nothing of the hatred it dynamizes, is repressed, and only returns to consciousness as a displaced fear of the activity inhibited, or of something which suggests or symbolizes that activity. The various diffused and unadaptive expressions which his reactions to fear then take, make up the content of his anxiety.

The writer knew a woman with a violent fear of *feathers*, which was traceable to a childhood trauma connected with her innocent questioning about the reproductive behavior of poultry, observed for the first time while visiting in the country. Having been shamed by the adults present for her not unnatural interest in what was to her the strange behavior of the cocks in chasing and treading the hens, she was also ridiculed by the other children for not understanding it. The urgency of

178 *Personality Modification*

her questioning (as she later reported it) probably reflected a considerable degree of sexual excitement, albeit not recognized as such.

Although she remembered these experiences clearly, and was sure that her phobia had its origin in their context, she was never able to abreact her original emotions, which must have been distressing to a child of eight or nine. Instead, she saw the whole episode as hilariously laughable; apparently an introjection of the attitude of her peers—and she never overcame her phobia.

2. Conflicting impulses to action. Whether originating parentally, or in a wider environmental context, "situations in which strong and conflicting action tendencies are simultaneously aroused,"[93] are a major source of neurotic anxiety. Reduced to a common denominator, such situations can be characterized as those in which obstacle removing behavior, though intensely desired, and indeed entirely rational, is socially forbidden, and submissive, conforming behavior, though undesired, and even illogical, is highly rewarded.

Whether his parents, an employer, representatives of the law, or someone else is the authority dynamizing the irrational response and forbidding the constructive one, such authority is self-evidently *personal*, and by definition *powerful*, as otherwise no conflict would be set up. In these circumstances, the fear which underlies neurotic anxiety becomes visible as a structural part of the situation.[94]

Under the pressure of these conflicting imperatives, the subject rapidly learns to undertake little or nothing on his own initiative, and to fail whenever he attacks a problem constructively. Instead, he will try to attain such objectives as he is able to acknowledge, by neurotic *aggression*, which is to say, by the exploitation of other personalities. He does this by demanding attention or soliciting pity, with devastating expertness, and by the exercise of power, economic or emotional; sometimes

[93] Wolpe, J., art. "Anxiety," *Encyclopedia of Psychology*, N.Y.: Herder and Herder, 1972, vol. 1, 68b.

[94] This perspective has been outlined by H. S. Sullivan, who defines anxiety as "the state of tension arising from the experience of disapproval in interpersonal relations." The writer agrees fully with this formulation. Cf. Sullivan, H. S., *The Inerpersonal Theory of Psychiatry*, New York, 1953.

openly, and sometimes with a characteristically shrewd con-
cealment.

The compulsions of alcoholism and gambling illustrate the outworking
of this pattern. The subject who is the victim of one of these compulsions is not conscious of the basic fear by which he is driven, which his
obsessional behavior temporarily palliates, until new anxieties, produced by the compulsion itself, come to dominate his existence.

Consider the alcoholic: not only does intoxication anaesthetize him
against the pain of his neurotic conditioning, but by the helplessness
that he cultivates, he obeys the introjected demand for ineffectiveness.
At the same time, he expresses his repressed hostility to the authority
that has crippled him, by the embarrassment that his irresponsible
conduct causes. Sometimes the alcoholic illustrates the neurotic mechanism in a reverse way: by numbing the super-ego with alcohol, he
escapes its prohibitive strictures, and is rendered capable of some
achievement in life, as long as his physical constitution is able to stand
up under the strain of toxicity to which it is subjected. Finally, the social
(i.e., interpersonal) rootage of the whole mechanism is shown by the
way its compulsions are alleviated in the Alcoholics Anonymous.

There, in a mutually supportive intra-mural society, where the
complete acceptance that is accorded him is leavened with complete
understanding, the subject is put into the regimen of a morality tailored
precisely to the solution of his problem.

The essentially religious quality of the whole procedure is evident in
the society's insistence upon its initial requirement, which is that the
subject believe in a god of some kind, whom he is taught to regard as
the ultimate controller of his destiny, and the source of whatever good
he may ever experience; in short, a solution god.

Since the group implements his rehabilitation, and establishes the
morality by which this is brought about, it is thus placed under divine
auspices: and the deity, however vaguely understood, that the subject
acknowledges as his own, becomes the *de facto* personification of the
society that enables him to surmount his neurotic compulsion.

The parallels between alcoholism and compulsive gambling, as to
cause and symptoms, are very striking, and there is a growing
recognition that this latter compulsion can also be controlled by a
supportive social group, into which its victims can merge. The report of
the organization of one such group, called "Gamblers Anonymous,"
recently appeared in the popular press.[95]

[95] Cady, Steve, "The Gambler Who Must," *The Reader's Digest*, Feb., 1975,
pp. 185–188. Condensed from *The New York Times Magazine* for Jan. 27, 1974.

3. Parental Inadequacy. Karen Horney ascribes the entire neurotic syndrome to parental inconsistency and undemonstrativeness, which bring about a "basic anxiety" in the subject, manifested clinically as an unconscious conviction of his own unlovability, which in turn makes him unable to love.[96] The fear of rejection underlying the inability of such a subject to open himself to the warmth of emotional interchange is at the center of the neurotic tragedy.

Now note that in each of the above areas, the neurotic response is *introjected*, i.e., internalized, so that the subject adopts without conscious protest the pattern which society impresses upon him: he ceases the meaningful pursuit of sexual objectives, even along socially acceptable lines; he engages in no obstacle removing behavior ("hostility") although constructive work is its normal expression; and he abandons the endeavor to base any personal relationship on love, least of all with his parents. Introjection is always due to fear of the consequences of non-conformity, and as this fear is repressed, its residue in consciousness is anxiety—the vague, non-objective, generalized, chronic and displaced kind of fear to which we have already adverted.

We hasten to state that all introjection is not bad; indeed, it is the way in which viable habits of socialization are formed. The neurotic pattern of introjection is one in which either excessive socializing demands are made; or they are made with excessive harshness; or some other confusing or vicious set of circumstances impinges upon the subject, in such a way that it gets internalized. It should be further pointed out that the subject who succumbs to these adverse pressures may well lack the normal ability to withstand developmental stresses.

Nonetheless, the entire neurotic syndrome is best understood as a pervasive and intricate system of emotional defenses against a fear of personal (i.e., social) rejection which is

[96] *The Neurotic Personality Of Our Time*, N.Y.: W. W. Norton, 1937, pp. 80 and 112.

associated with normal behavior. Non-adaptive and inappropriate as his anxiety reactions are, the neurotic clings to them tenaciously, since whether the behavior in which they are displayed is active or passive, they are his protection against pursuing the normally effective activities that he so desperately wants, but which, if undertaken, would threaten the repression by which intolerable childhood fears are kept from overwhelming him—fears connected with irrational demands, unreasonable punishments and tragic rejections.

Thus the finally most comprehensive operating definition of neurosis (or neurotic behavior, if that expression is preferred) is: *a rigid but invalid posture of emotional defensiveness.*

When such a subject encounters an archetypal personification portraying the solution to his problem, his reluctant mergence with this figure dispels the fear which has dynamized the entire neurotic syndrome, and simultaneously dissolves the rigidly ineffectual mechanisms of anxiety, by which the fear has been masked.

iii. Hate Hate is the final inner-psychic problem. As we turn to its examination, the reader is reminded of the distinctions between hostility and hate which were introduced at the end of Part Two.

Hostility is simply obstacle removing behavior, and as such, would seem to be a part of the ego—the organizing aspect of the personality. Its principal exemplification is found in *work*; that is, dynamic problem solving. It is definitely structured, and totally instrumental. Once its objectives are attained, it contains no implications of ill-will for its object. The use of this term in popular parlance to denote unpleasantness of address, harsh utterance, and the display of a suspicious attitude, can thus be readily interpreted as obstacle-removing behavior, practiced when no obstacles are present.

Hate, on the other hand, may be defined as the emotion generated by frustrated hostility, and is characterized by the strongly emotionalized wish to destroy the obstacle totally, simply for the sake of so doing. In a prototypical instance, hate is unstructured and inchoate, and characterized by helpless anger, or rage. When a problem resists solution, so that the obstacle cannot be removed by any means available to the subject, emotional pressure builds up, and hatred is the penultimate state known to the subject, just before the final apathy which accompanies the complete exhaustion of the ego. At this point, the *destruction* of the obstacle, rather than its removal, obsesses the subject, so that this destructive urgency obliterates every other purpose he might have been entertaining, and his activity ceases entirely to be instrumental to anything else. Thus hate would seem to be a direct manifestation of the id.

Of course, most instances of hate do not progress to the point of this prototype, any more than most instances of hate become religious problems. Indeed, one might make a plausible case for the thesis that hate *never* appears as a religious problem, at least at the conscious level. Whoever heard anyone bemoaning the fact that he hated too much? Conceivably, a person sophisticated enough to be involved in psychotherapy might voice such a sentiment, but the very insight implied by the utterance removes the problem from the degree of insolubility that might make it a religious problem . . . Or, possibly some *un*sophisticated subject might speak thus after being tortured by a religious promoter, in which case his problem is not hate, but the guilt he has been made to feel about it, or perhaps the social problem of being thus exploited.

Many instances of hate fall into the category of social problems, just as many cases of fear are to be studied in terms of the circumstances in which they originate. A prisoner tortured, a peon exploited, a civilian oppressed by military invaders, a child bullied—each of these will feel hatred, but in none of these cases is hate the primary problem, which is social: and the meaningful therapy in every instance is some profound social alteration. When cases of this sort eventuate in religious experience, its format is that of mergence with a solution god. Everything said a few pages earlier about social problems is pertinent in this connection.

Many cases of apparent hatred, when critically viewed, are

thus seen as valid instances of obstacle removing behavior, and so are formally excluded from the extent of our definition. This would be true of a military man, whether struggling in the frenzy of combat, or planning with total concentration to sink a ship or demolish a fortification. Whatever other problems he may have, hatred as such is not one of them, however much he may be bent on destruction. His focus is on the obstacle *qua* obstacle, rather than seeking to pursue and destroy it *for its own sake*, and without regard to any larger end, to which the destruction is instrumental.

Be all this as it may, among the issues dealt with by solution gods, there remains a hard core of problems which are directly traceable to hatred as their cause, and other problems giving rise to solution gods are so *related* to hate that this is the appropriate place to take cognizance of them. As we proceed to do this, the distinctions we must make between various types and aspects of hate are necessarily precise, and much of what we have to say will be couched in particular propositions.

Returning to the prototypical case of unstructured obsession to destroy, we must add an amendment to our initial description of that state of mind, so as not to confuse it with *rage, per se*. The person who drops every other project in his life to pursue a cold, calculating program of destructiveness must not be excluded from the class of those who hate, despite whatever degree of shrewdness he exhibits in such a pursuit, for note: (a) he has ceased all effort *to remove what was an obstacle to some useful end*, in the interest of destruction *for the sake of destroying the obstacle itself*; and (b) the larger pattern of his life has been abandoned, so that in the deepest sense, his behavior is disorganized, i.e., unstructured, in that the goals he was following before he met the obstacle are now completely neglected.

Thus far, much of what we have had to say about hate has been to disallow this emotion in some way from primary consideration as a religious problem: either to define its manifestations out of validity, or to show that they are more fittingly considered in some other frame of reference. Now, however, we are ready to examine its bona fide appearances as a religious problem, which occur when the hate rather than the obstacle hated is problematic.

(1) Hate impairs the obstacle removing behavior. It would probably strike a more congenial, and certainly a more familiar note to say that hate inhibits love; but *so do the problems requiring removal*. No one can embrace the environment, i.e., love, when the environment is filled with obstacles: their removal constitutes the world's work, and the perennial challenge to the human ego. However, when hate is the dominant emotion, the constructive pursuit of work ceases, in the interest of destroying some particular obstacle; and while we cannot universalize, yet more often than not, such a reaction is *inappropriate*. Remember that we have already excluded such circumstances as exterminating the *anopheles* mosquito, taking time out to kill a poisonous snake, or devoting massive social resources to the elimination of a hijacker. With this in mind, we note that the inappropriateness has several dimensions.

(a) The reaction may be too great for the wrong suffered. Yielding to the urge to destroy the perpetrator of a trivial wrong, by reason of sheer exasperation, is indicative of the erosion of the ego, of which we have spoken.

(b) The hatred may be directed toward an inappropriate object. This may be (i) —something that symbolizes the obstacle to the subject, as when an ethnic group, by a kind of scapegoat principle, comes to symbolize all his frustrations, and is hated proportionately. Obviously, the symbolizing process is private to each individual subject. (ii) —Something that suggests the obstacle to him associatively, i.e., hating a person with a physical resemblance to someone else, by whom the subject has been injured. (iii) —Something that formerly was an obstacle, but has ceased to be one, as the perpetrator of a past wrong, or a former military enemy. (iv) —The forbidden activity, in the neurotic syndrome. Dynamized by fear, when that fear is neurotically displaced, hatred may be directed toward anything to which the fear attaches, instead of the agent of the neurotic inhibition, which might logically have been its object.

(c) Hate impairs the obstacle removing behavior because it is *impractical*. Inappropriateness of intensity and direction, which we have just cited as impairments, also illustrate this dimension; and we must note that the impracticality is present whether the subject puts the hate to which he has yielded into action, or simply broods upon it. Indeed, this leads us to another major consideration, and that quite possibly the most important.

(2) Hate causes other problems. Acting upon it involves the subject immediately in social situations to which severe penalties may attach, thus giving rise to further problems that may well reach the religious dimension: while brooding upon a cankering hatred is so exclusive of all other constructive activity, that the subject can accomplish nothing worthwhile. Also, one who has yielded to the hate syndrome is likely to view too many things as obstacles; and being destruction prone, is in a socially precarious situation. Furthermore, whether the hatred is carried into action or remains merely a matter of phantasy, it gives rise to guilt, and thus to all the problems we have already dealt with, as attaching to that emotion.

We have already noted that hate is rarely if ever acknowledged as a problem in its own right, since it is so generally unconscious, having been repressed because the ego could not deal with it. However, in numerous instances where something else is the recognized dynamic of religious experience, careful analysis will reveal hatred as the sufficient condition of the difficulty to which the solution has been personified. Ulcers, impotence, forgetfulness, accident proneness, uncontrollable irritability and inability to concentrate make up the merest beginning of the list of inner psychic problems that can be caused by repressed hatred. Our earlier reference (Page 25, supra) to the existence and severity of unconscious problems is convincingly substantiated by such an analysis.

The relevance of religious experience to such a psychic situation is clearly apparent. The structuring effect produced in the subject by the rise of the personification, and the relationship he forms with it, restore him to the psychic potency he needs, since hatred is, in essence, a failure of the ego, and the entire religious experience a process of its rehabilitation. The dynamics of mergence, whereby that rehabilitation is completed, have already been presented in detail.

We cannot leave the consideration of inner-psychic problems without one concluding remark. The contraries of these insistent perplexities are the basic social virtues—confidence, love, and an untroubled mind: so that as these problems receive religious solution, the subject gains equipment for reassuring social experience. The intimate connection between mental health and good social adjustment, both before and after religious experience, is brought sharply into focus by the foregoing analysis.

d. Problems of Prior Formulation

Turning now to problems of prior religious formulation, as they are solved in mergence with solution gods, it is immediately evident that such problems are generally if not universally present in experiences of this type, whether or not they take precedence over other problems by which the subject is impelled.

The formulations giving rise to such problems are of two kinds. The first consists of primary affirmations which describe a personification, as, "There is a god whose name is A": and, "A engages in X activities under Y conditions." These stated conditions will outline the basic area with which the god is concerned, including circumstances that can or will anger, placate, excite, or inhibit him: some of these will of course be ritual in nature, and others will delineate the morality the deity demands. These first level statements are, in short, the primordial mythos in which the original revelation has been formulated. They will further include accounts of where the deity came from, and why his concerns are as they are.

The second class of formulations consists of expansions and elaborations of the first. These are made to explain the ritual, to clarify its requirements, and, more fundamentally, to apologize for its failures and perpetuate its influence. We may term the first class revelatory formulations, and the second, theological. Difficulties are bound to arise in distinguishing the borderline types of these two classes, but the obvious instances stand out clearly, and the importance of making this distinction will become apparent presently.

Formulations from both groups become problematic when they fail to come true, when their symbolic impact is negative, or when their institutional enforcement is stultifying.

In addition to being a formally distinguishable group of religious issues which are resolved by mergence with a solution god, there is another significant perspective from which problems of prior formulation must be viewed: they are the dynamics of religious change. When a religious formulation becomes problematic for any of the reasons given, other formulations will follow. This is never necessarily true, for religious problems are only a negative condition of religious experience: but the likelihood of a new formulation being made to replace one that has failed is exactly the same as that of any problem of religious dimensions producing a religious reaction. And of course, when this takes place, and an earlier formulation is replaced by a new one, we have not merely religious experience but religious change.

Thus the examination of these problems in their present context entails the entire history of prophetic religions, since in every appearance of a solution god there has been a prior formulation that has somehow become so unsatisfactory as to make it a religious problem. Indeed, we might say that the entire *sociology* of religion is subsumed by this area of investigation, since it involves consideration of how religious institutions are formed, why they assume the shapes that they do, and the reasons for their being supplanted; all within the context of the societies which are structured by these developments.

This present study of the manner in which problems of prior formulation are solved in mergence with a solution god therefore serves as a natural transition to the investigation of religious experience as it occurs in institutions.

We shall consider these problematic formulations in terms of the issues to which they appertain. Once again, our aim will be simply to epitomize rather than to catalogue.

i. Formulations About Nature Although, as we have seen, problems of nature are, in a few anomalous instances, resolved by mergence with a solution god that has arisen in some other area, formulations about such problems seem to be very little problematic in their own right.

Hunger before the crops ripen, or in time of drouth, cold in the winter, and a certain amount of disease, predictably fatal to the weak, are all taken for granted, and their incidence does not seem to discredit the religion greatly, despite the open commitment of every primitive religion to the prevention, or at least the alleviation, of such circumstances. A ritual intended to deal with these problems can fail signally without its doctrinal framework becoming religiously problematic, so long as that failure occurs within a milieu of cultural stasis. Theology simply takes care of the matter, ascribing the failure either to procedural incorrectness, or supernatural interference.

It is when such failures are accompanied by some type of cultural stress that solution gods arise, but even so, their advent is due to discontent with the social structure and the individual's place in it, rather than with doctrines concerning the gods of nature, themselves.

Nevertheless, after a solution god has appeared, albeit arising from quite other causes, such a deity may well be credited with whatever favorable outcome a problem of nature may have.

Thus: There can be no question that the goddess Isis was a

solution deity in the mystery religion bearing her name. Originally the deified throne, in Egypt,[97] the occupancy of which made its possessor forever a king, she was the mother of Horus, whom every living king incarnated, and wife of Osiris, whom all dead kings became. Once personified, she was credited with the rites that made Osiris able to assume his kingship of the underworld:[98] from this springs her character as a goddess of immortality, which was so much stressed in her mystery cult. As faithful and grieving wife and mother, she became a deity of women. Her tears brought the inundation of the Nile,[99] and from this, she was next held to be a goddess of favorable rainfall. By a continuation of this expansion of function, she became a deity of good weather for sailors, since optimum conditions for navigation came on at the same time as the spring rains. Thus, by the second century A.D., when Apuleius wrote his *Metamorphoses*, the *Navigium Isidis*, there described at length, had become a prominent ritual occasion signalizing the opening of navigation in the spring. Now Isis clearly personifies the conditions for good and safe sea travel, so that one in her charge and under her protection would have no trouble. Hence, when we reflect that Poseidon, a cause-cure personification of the winds at sea, would previously have been the deity addressed to obtain such favorable conditions, we see that the formulations which said,

"Adequate sacrifice to Poseidon will get you a safe voyage,"

—has been abandoned in favor of mergence with Isis, *whose essential nature it was* to give safe voyages. Yet this shift of religious focus is essentially one of conversion, brought about by the obvious availability of a more benign deity, and cannot in any way be classified as an autonomous development,

[97] Frankfurt, Henri, *Kingship and the Gods*, Chicago: Univ. of Chicago Press, 1948, pp. 43–44.

[98] Frankfurt, *Op. Cit.*, p. 183. Cf. also, Plutarch, *De Iside et Osiride*, chapters 12–19.

[99] Frankfurt, *Op. Cit.*, p. 192.

brought about by a sense of the earlier doctrine as religiously problematic.

In this connection, one thing should be clarified. We have traced the development of ideas concerning Isis from point to point as though there were some inner principle of logical continuity that could be followed, as indeed there may have been, in this particular instance. However, this is in no way necessarily so. The expansion of function exhibited by various solution gods takes place simply on the principle that a deity who succeeds in solving one set of problems is subsequently presented as able to deal with others, however different the later ones may be. These expanded claims may originate either with enthusiastic worshippers, or with ambitious members of a clergy, but are always made by representatives of an institution, with the intent of broadening its appeal.

This mechanism is illustrated by Hosea's claim that Yahweh, the solution god of the Hebrews, and basically a god of battles, was also the guarantor of good crops.[100] Then, of course, we have the still more familiar portrayals of Jesus of Nazareth stilling a storm, feeding a multitude, and performing numerous healings, in addition to proclaiming the Kingdom of God.

In summary, we may say that while formulations about problems of nature which (a) themselves become religiously problematic, and (b) find their solutions in the experience of mergence with a solution god, are not unknown, their appearance within this frame of reference is altogether adventitious.

ii. Formulations About Society

(a) The Breakdown of the Social Metaphysic   The outstanding instance of solution gods appearing in response to a religious formulation that has itself become problematic is of course found in connection with the breakdown of the Social Metaphysic, in an Ethnic society. Reference has been made on page 165 to this unanimously accepted definition of tribal status, to which everyone in such a group could turn for the metaphysical authentication of the social position he, and

---

[100] Hosea 2:8.

everyone else, occupied. This was spelled out in terms of the individual's ease of access to, or responsible involvement in, the problem-solving rituals, in the performance of which, the commonly acknowledged problems of the tribe were dealt with in lieu of science.

When a substantial minority within such an Ethnic group becomes dissatisfied with the status thus assigned to them, we may expect one of their number to come up with an archetypal experience wherein a solution god inspires mergence by his announcement of the imminent arrival of an Ideal Society, which he, the god, will presently set up.[101] This mechanism has already been described in depth. Whether the older formulation is regarded as powerless or as pernicious, the newer one, involving the solution god, clearly arises in response to a previously existing religious position, now felt as a religious problem in its own right.

That is: the Social Metaphysic says, in effect, "It is the will of XYZ god that you occupy such and such a position in the ritual structure;" and this is documented by reference to the mythos. When this prescribed social status is felt to be not good enough, or if and when the ritual structure itself collapses, a new formulation occurs through the agency of the prophet, as described. Thus religion structures society, for when an existing formulation, giving format to a social pattern, becomes intolerable, the desired change receives both structure and dynamic in the revelation of a solution god.

(b) The Failure Of A Cosmic Promise An exact parallel to the above situation is seen when a Cosmic Promise[102] fails to materialize. While this failure is not always observable in the dramatic completeness that characterizes religious collapse at

---

[101] Members of the minority indicated need not all come from the same stratum or segment of the society, although this is likely to be the case. Dissatisfaction with the existing society can be felt on many grounds, and from various perspectives.

[102] I.e., the proclamation of the Ideal Society, as repeatedly outlined.

192   *Personality Modification*

the Ethnic level, following cultural impact or conquest,[103] the non-appearance of an Ideal Society that has been categorically promised by one who claims divine authority for his proclamation, gradually infects those who await its coming with an incredulous despair. Increasing numbers of them become open to whatever newer revelation is at hand, or may presently appear. This may be either another prophetic announcement, or a cultic promotion. (See page 137, supra.) However, the very incredulity with which the failure of a prophecy is met, delays its ultimate extinction by giving time for various theological formulations to be made, which may perpetuate the movement for a long time, until they, too, are felt as problematic.

iii. Formulations Regarding Inner Psychic Problems   Our earlier treatment of Inner-Psychic problems as they are solved in mergence has made their intimate connection with social problems abundantly clear. Thus *formulations about* religious problems in this area which have become problematic in their own right, are subject to most of the statements we have made in the section immediately preceding, as well as to those regarding the constantly expanding functions of solution gods, made in connection with Formulations Regarding Nature.

An instance in point is the Brahmanic formulation which made social status dependent on Karma accumulated in past lives, and at the same time made the entertainment of any human desire or attachment productive of negative Karma in this present one. The history of Buddhism is a record of Gotama's response to the problematic impact of these doctrines. If the nihilistic ideas he personally advanced (clearly in an attempt to make the issues migrate out of the religious realm!) do not seem to bear out our thesis, the reader is urged to look at Mahayana Buddhism, appearing only a few centuries later, wherein Gotama himself is elevated to the status of a solution god, in response to the austerities of his own teaching,

[103] Cf. however, the failure of millenarian movements, to which precise dates have been attached.

now felt as problematic. Similarly, Christian formulations condemning "lusts of the flesh," originally made to exalt pure spirituality by contrast, or to enforce a viable morality, have burdened generations of sincere people with guilt that found its resolution in mergence following conversion.

The ascription of persistent fear, hate, or guilt to the activity of a problem god, i.e., the devil, a ghost, or a demon, will be the occasion of summoning a solution god to drive him or them away; and mergence with the latter typically keeps the unwanted personifications at a distance. The comments made in the paragraphs dealing with the devil, in our earlier treatment of Problem Gods, are germane here.

If these problems are incompletely personified, their presence may be charged to a lack of religious intensity in the subject, who will be urged to cultivate a deeper and closer relationship with the solution god. The solution itself follows, in the subject's attainment of (or return to) the euphoria of mergence, following the exhaustion of his ego. The religious conflicts of Luther, and their resolution in his major insight regarding salvation by faith illustrate this situation perfectly.

iv. Theology When we come to the discussion of prior formulations about prior formulations, the course of our argument would seem to have lost itself in formalism, until we remember that this is *theology*, in which are found a number of problems not elsewhere encountered, and which are also solved in mergence with solution gods.

Much of theology is innocuous, and indeed is of good repute, seeking to correlate archetypal experience with philosophical insights regarding ultimate origins of the universe, in the interest of identifying some definable entity pertaining to both, that will, at the same time, be fully reverenceable. Since the archetypal image is highly valued by anyone who feels its impact, numinosity being, let us remind ourselves, supreme valuation plus mystery, it is not unnatural that a true believer should seek to commend the personification with which he has found relationship, to others whose vision of his great Reality is unclear. Such an enterprise is for the most part harmless, and we might add, correspondingly ineffective, since archetypal immediacy loses all compellingness when it is intellectualized.

However, when a revelatory promise that has gained some acceptance fails to come true, so that those who have accepted it without reserve are disillusioned, there are always those who seek to modify or expand the revelation, i.e., the mythos, so that whatever clientele has been generated by the hope which the promise contained, will not be lost to the influence of its promulgators. These are the hardcore theologians, since theology at last can only be understood as the rationalized expansion of myth, in the interest of ritual efficiency. The formulations made in this frame of reference, i.e., second level statements concerning earlier revelatory material, generate the problems presently under consideration.

To discuss these problems meaningfully, we must begin by pointing out that in so doing we have actually begun the consideration of institutional religion. The formulations here encountered as problematic have not been made autonomously, but are rationalistic elaborations of spontaneous revelatory material, made in the interest of shoring up organizational structures that are beginning to lose credibility.

Precisely on this account, the problems created by theology are of great emotional intensity. Revelatory material, albeit sometimes grotesque and always irrational, is essentially benign, since at its core it is the unconsciously produced symbolism of problem solving. Theology, on the other hand, in seeking to perpetuate formulations which have lost their symbolic impact (i.e., which no longer solve problems), gives them a literalistic interpretation, in terms of which preposterous explanations are advanced, and horrendous sanctions imposed. Adherents of a failing institution, already distraught by the collapse of cherished certainties, find these new and threatening formulations distressing in the extreme.

As might be expected, a careful scrutiny of theological *dicta* reveals fundamental differences among them, of which we must take account.

First, it is necessary to distinguish between apologetic formulations made to justify or excuse ritual failure, and threatening doctrines, advanced to ward off apostasy by depicting its punishments. The former are frequently inoffensive, and may be merely expository, while the latter are intended to terrify. Within the group of apologetic formulations, a further distinction is to be noted.

In ethnic religions, where the problems attacked are fundamentally those pertaining to nature, the failure of a ritual to solve a problem is explained by a fairly predictable syndrome of formulations; incorrectness of procedure, unfitness of the subject to engage in ritual activity, interference of a problem god or demon and anger or disaffection on the part of the deity addressed. These are among the techniques of bargaining, employed by the clergy who represent cause-cure gods, and have been referred to in that context. However, it is only when problems of this class are accompanied by radical social discontent that they expand to religious dimensions. When this occurs, they will be resolved in mergence with the solution god of a prophetic religion, in the manner that has already been described.

In Prophetic religions, on the other hand, the non-appearance of the Ideal Society is at first uniformly ascribed to negligence in practicing the New Morality. As time passes, however, the morality is progressively equated with ritual prescriptions, until the religion has an Ethnic appearance; this we have elsewhere called the Pseudo-Ethnic stage of religious evolution. At this point, the Ideal Society, originally an expectation of radically improved conditions on the local scene, will either be identified with the religious institution itself, or with immortality.

An alternative stratagem is to propound various supernatural and/or metaphysical explanations, which are logical enough, in view of the alleged supernatural origin of the promised Ideal Society. Thus, when a 1914 prediction made by the Jehovah's Witnesses failed to materialize, whereby Christ was to return to establish His Kingdom and end the rule of

Satan, the failure was rationalized by widespread assertions that the whole thing had occurred in heaven: Christ had, in fact, ascended to His throne there, and the devil had been cast down to earth.[104]

In this frame of reference are to be found the various pseudo-scientific strictures by which sagging religious authority tries to bolster the credibility of an outworn cosmology, upon which the authority of its myth depends. Thus we find a straight-faced insistence upon Aristotle's 55 prime movers, and of creation *ex nihilo* in Catholic orthodoxy, and upon creation in seven days, in Protestant fundamentalism. Preposterous as claims of this type are, they do not usually become religiously problematic until their acceptance is made the condition of institutional endorsement in a setting where this is necessary to acceptance by the larger society.

However, when all apologetic efforts fail, so that a religious movement loses the greater part of its symbolic impact, its adherents naturally begin to drift away. This is when the theological formulations are made that are inherently problematic, and require nothing less than archetypal reassurance to assuage the anxiety they create.

Gods that are angry, penances that disable, moralities that impoverish or render ineffective, demons that terrify before they harass, an impending judgment of cosmic proportions, and hell after all for those who ignore any of these terrors—all are tailored with maximal ingenuity to secure compliance with existing ritual structures.

Doctrines of impending universal judgment are probably the most obvious instances of this mechanism. They agree in predicting an early and fearful cosmic division between members of the religious group and all others, whether they have left the group or failed to join it. Members will immediately enter some realm of bliss, variously described and located, and the rest will be consigned to some correspondingly fearsome

[104] Braden, C. S., *These Also Believe*, N.Y., Macmillan, 1949, 374f.

existence, of which the inescapable permanence is not the least of its terrors.

It is thus apparent that the reinforcing theologies by which operatives of a discredited institution seek to prolong its existence, become at last, by their very intensity, one of the strongest dynamics whereby the institution they were intended to preserve is displaced by whatever solution god can dispel the terror which they inspire.

It is also apparent that the theological formulations which become problematic, and as such, receive solution in the experience of mergence with a later solution god are clearly *social*, in either their reference or their intent. In different phrasing, the purpose of theological statements is to prescribe the social status of institutional adherents, either in their present environment, or in some future abode.

Another pattern of theological dogmatizing leading to this end seeks not so much to *retain* members in the ritual group as to *arrange the content* of such a group, by altering the emphasis of an earlier formulation, or otherwise manipulating it. Since status within, or in relation to, the ritual structure largely determines status in the total society, the problematic quality of theological statements made in this area is due to the threat of social rejection that they contain.

The Brahmin drive for social supremacy in India, from 1000 to 500 B.C. illustrates this pattern explicitly. They were a group whose uniqueness seems to rest upon their arrogation of priestly power, inherent in a set of magically potent sacrificial ceremonials, supposedly arising out of the earlier Vedic religion, and over which they presided. They were, of course, custodians of its mythos, and spokesmen for its ritual requirements and expectations. By persistently promising outright deification to members of the Kshatriya caste in return for exorbitant sacrifices (from which they naturally profited), they managed to bankrupt whatever members of this group survived the bitter intramural struggles in which the Kshatriyas were currently involved. As a result, the status of the Kshatriya caste was reduced from that of the nobility to the merely military, and the Brahmin priesthood, originally secondary to the Kshatriya, came to outrank them.[105]

The Brahmins consolidated their primacy in the ritual structure of Hinduism by the manipulation of the doctrines of Karma and transmigration which are structural to all forms of Indian religion. Originally, these doctrines arose as explanatory of the social situations of millions of people whose lives had been uprooted by one or another of the conquests which had convulsed India, at least from the time of the Aryan migrations. However, as the Brahmins relentlessly pushed themselves into power, during the centuries between 1000 and 500 B.C., they twisted these doctrines to support their own position, so that instead of brute fact in the background of any life being cited as the cause of bad circumstances, a deplorable human condition was now ascribed to *moral* ill, in one or another of the subject's past incarnations: and transmigration, instead of being a new chance the next time around, became an interminable series of punishments that could only be terminated by rebirth as a Brahmin, since they alone could die without rebirth when their time came.

It was under the pressure of this debilitating and morally paralyzing theology that Siddartha Gotama, himself a Kshatriya, and son of a Kshatriya chieftain, came to his great revelation of the Middle Way, which has at its center the idea that once its major insights are understood and adopted, there will be nothing left to transmigrate, since the only entity that can be reincarnated is *produced* by Karma, rather than merely having its nature thus determined: and all accumulation of Karma will have been stopped by the practice of the Noble Eight-Fold Path.

If these nihilistic ideas (clearly advanced in an attempt to make the issues migrate out of the religious realm) do not seem to bear out our thesis, the reader is urged to look at Mahayana

---

[105] Cf. "The Satapatha Brahmana," XIII, 3, 1, i, in *Sacred Books of the East*, XLIV, p. 328. Quoted in Noss, John B., *Man's Religions*, 5th ed., N.Y., Macmillan, 1974, p. 95.

Buddhism, appearing only a few centuries later, wherein Gotama himself is elevated to the status of a solution god, mergence with whom solves all problems.

Again, the twisting of emphasis in some part of the mythos is used to *restrict the membership* of the ritual group. Thus, the account in Genesis 3 of the Fall of Man is an aetiological story, advanced to explain why men must work, and women experience distress in parturition. However, the medieval stress on the inferiority of women, *as a social imperative*, invoked the myth of Eve's creation from Adam's rib, along with that of her beguilement by Satan, and her subsequent seduction of Adam with the apple, but with the frame of reference so altered that it could be cited as proof that women not only deserved the miseries of their condition, but were inherently unworthy of any better lot. The enormous popular appeal of the Reformation doctrines to *women*, has never, as far as the writer knows, been adequately delineated; but their attractiveness to the exploited half of the population cannot be overlooked as a vital factor in the rapidity of their general acceptance.

Similarly, in the original account of Ham, the son of Noah, being assigned a servile status, because he, Ham, had broken the taboo against seeing his father's nakedness (Gen. 9:18–27), the intent is obviously to provide an apologetic for the ruthless conquest of the Canaanites, who are declared to be his descendents, and so must inherit the curse. Also included in the list of Ham's progeny (Gen. 10:6) is Cush, the eponymic ancestor of the Ethiopians, who are thus labelled as occupying an inferior social position at that time and place. However, amid the social insurgency of the last hundred and fifty years in the United States and elsewhere, the same story has often been cited to show that Negroes *should*, by religious necessity, occupy such a social position. The eagerness of these people to attain not only a better social status, but the metaphysical justification for it, is seen in the eagerness of their mergence with Father Divine, and with the Black Muslim version of Allah.

Perhaps a word of summary should be given to put all of this in focus. If so, it is simply this:

When theological formulations become religiously problematic, they eventually find their solution in mergence with solution gods, whether these are already in existence, or made known in new revelations.

D. The Emergence of the Religious Institution

We said early in the preceding section that the discussion of theology involved institutional religion. We now advance the proposition that theology is the specific difference of a religious institution, and that the institution, primordially viewed, comes into existence with the advent of theological activity.

The religious institution, *per se* is much less differentiated in an Ethnic society than in other types of social organization. Indeed, one can argue that it does not exist in its own right, paradoxical as this may seem. What does exist is a massive establishment for the administration of myth and ritual, but which is simply the metaphysical dimension of the society, and not a discrete organization, separable from the total fabric of political, intellectual and moral functions by which the society is constituted.

Another way of expressing this would be to say that although personifications of value (problem- and cause-cure gods) and experts to deal with them (priests) are obviously present, the functions of both are so interwoven with the vital functions of the tribe that they are inextricable from the operations of government, economics, morality, and the regulation of social precedence. In short, *the religious establishment and the total society are indistinguishable, and this is the essence of the Ethnic situation.* It is when explanations for ritual failure become necessary that the religious elements permeating the Ethnic complex first become (a) self-conscious, and (b) socially differentiated. Should an apologetic be required for the social order that has been archetypically prescribed, in what we have called the Social Metaphysic, the actualization of the religious institution is complete, but at the same time the Ethnic situation is gone, so that the Ethnic religious institution, by the time it has been fully articulated, is already vestigial. A tribal society may linger on for some time under the trappings of its original Ethnic integrity, but when the clergy must advance rationalistic amendments to its mythos in order to obviate ritual neglect or social insurgency, the Ethnic situation is dead, even as its archetypal foundations become institutionalized.

By the same token, a prophetic movement is not a religious institution until its hope has largely failed. Until then, it is merely an informal group of believers who are awaiting the coming of the Ideal Society as promised by the prophet, sharing its common hope, and practicing the morality which is instrumental to its fulfillment. When failure threatens at this level, theological activity begins, just as it does when earlier Ethnic formulations collapse. Its essentially apologetic stance signalizes the self-perpetuative efforts of a group that previously had no need of this function, and indicates the beginning of institutional life as such. Within this syndrome we find religious activity increasing, even as religious experience diminishes; and the activity takes on an officialized quality, as its functionaries seek to preserve their perquisites and prerogatives by retaining or recapturing the situation as it was before any apologetic was needed. Theology as the specific difference of a religious institution is thus seen to be promotional as well as apologetic in its intent.

This brings us to our final observation concerning the institution's emergence. We have tried to show that the birth of institutionalism, as distinguished from the melting trustfulness of autistic piety, is coeval with the appearance of theology. Thus theology is a necessary factor in the group's continuance, and the institution's origin. *But this factor is always the work of professionals.* As long as the primordial mergence of the early collectivity obtains, the religious professional is neither necessary nor evident, although persons of unusual expertise in myth and ritual, or of ulterior motivation will admittedly be found within its membership: but it is only when a ritual group requires the services of a specialist in order to remain in being, that institutionalism is born.

Moreover, once the institution has become distinctive and

identifiable, its activities are invariably a compound of two things: first, the autistic, cooperative impulses and efforts of those who still find symbolic impact in some aspect of the revelation, and second, the consciously systematic endeavors of others, who, as we have seen, expand the mythos into whatever dimension they must, in their determination to keep the faltering collectively going for their own ends[106]: ends largely unconnected with the original religious problem. Whether we describe these two aspects of institutional life as characterizing believers and promoters, laity and clergy, or the symbolically and the selfishly oriented, the dichotomy is clearly evident to anyone who pursues religious experience into its corporate manifestations; so that the first question that must be asked about any phenomenon to be investigated in this area is which of these two sectors has been its point of origin.

[106] E.g., so they can continue to collect a salary: so that their earlier formulations will not be discredited: so that they will not lose the prestige of an earlier prominence within the group: so that they can sell something to the group, as ritual articles: so that they can manipulate the group for political reasons: so that they can be known as belonging to the group, for various reasons,: or so that they will not be embarrassed by having to confess that a prior commitment is now in error.

Part 4

The Institutional Reference

I. Introduction

An institution *per se* is a group of people having some common interest, wherein a standardization of the status attaching to roles has been established. A *religious* institution has three aspects: ritual, myth and theology: and the focus of its interest is the members' relationship to some archetypal figure or figures whose acts, promises or commands have inspired numinosity in them.

These archetypal events are recorded in the mythos; the ritual is the embodiment of the divine commands; and the standardization of the status pertaining to roles is established by the theology. Such an institution comes into being when the myth and ritual cease to be autistic, i.e., the spontaneous acts, utterances and beliefs of a group of people to whom a revelation has come. This typically occurs when the promises of a Prophetic religion fail to materialize, or the rituals of an Ethnic complex fail to produce the expected results. The efficacy of the ritual then becomes questionable, and the credibility of the mythos dissolves. At this point, theological formulations are made, which rationalize and modify the claims made by the myth, in the attempt to strengthen or restore ritual efficacy.

Without such formulations, the association arising out of earlier numinous experiences would disintegrate; and as they are made, the institution *per se* assumes definitive form. Two features may be taken as identifying factors of an institutionalized religion: (1) a creed, which presents the beliefs necessary for membership, and (2) some form of ordination, whereby the professionals or specialists who make the formulations are accredited.

As we have said earlier, the religious institution is a blend of activities: those performed by the true believers, and those carried on by promoters who are seeking to manipulate them. It will be our somewhat perplexing task to sort out which institutional characteristics are to be assigned to each group. This process of distinguishing will be to a large extent focused in the area of theology, and the perplexity in it is caused by the fact that wherever the promoters come from, and whatever be their intent in the emendations that are made to the myth, these doctrinal formulations are always given the appearance of emanating from the very most orthodox center of the institution.

In order to facilitate all aspects of our discussion of religious experience in institutions, we have put into an appendix a concise description of the forms or types in which religious institutions appear, as the writer has come to understand them. This resumé will not only serve to clarify earlier references in which this developmental model was mentioned, but will relieve us of the need for making an expository detour, every time that reference is made to a particular type of institution.

However, apart from whatever acknowledgement of differences in form and function is necessary, our emphasis in what is to follow will not be upon the institution *per se*. While we cannot, in the nature of things, escape occasional references to the sociological and anthropological dimensions of institutional phenomena, our intent in the present discussion is to minimize such involvement as far as is consistent with the exposition of the psychological factors which are our concern. Specifically stated, our effort here will be to point out the internal relationships between the acts and facts of institutional operation, and religious experience as we have described it, and then to show how each has structured the other. To this end we shall approach the religious institution from the perspectives of ritual, myth and theology, which are its component aspects.

II. The Institution As Living: Implementing The Religious Solution

A. Ritual in the Institution

1. *Ritual as Maintenance of Relationship*

As often stated, the basic mechanism of religious experience is the personification of some aspect of a religious problem, followed by the formation of an optimum relationship with the personified figure. *The overriding aspect of religious experience in an institution is the maintenance of that relationship.*

There is, however, this radical difference. In individual religious experience, the subject seeks this relationship with the god for its own sake, and does so on the strength of motivations that are for the most part unconscious, or at any rate ingenuous. In institutional religious experience, on the other hand, the protagonists of the institution seek to maintain this relationship of the subject to the personified figure, not for his, the subject's, interest, but for their own; because in the relationship of mergence the true believer will obey any command whatever, if given in the name of the god, and so can be exploited to any degree.

None the less, as long as the central personification around which an institution is structured remains sufficiently numinous to make this quest for perfected relationship with it a matter of dynamic importance, the institution is a living one, even though theological effort may be required for its perpetuation. From another perspective, an institution may be regarded as living as long as some part of it can produce symbolic impact, at least occasionally. Reflection will show that these two sentences describe virtually the same set of circumstances; for as long as the central personification retains its numinous quality, the institution where this experience is enshrined will have some symbolic force in its own right, both within and without the circle of its membership.

From one perspective, everything pertaining to institutional religion is anti-climactic—the formalized aftermath of a massive archetypal event in which the subject gained new energy through a new orientation. There is, however, another perspective from which institutional religion can and must be regarded. Here we can see the Solution spelled out, the *telos* made evident: here is the living happily ever after—the Faith State in its enactment, wherein all members may lean upon the Everlasting Arms. Stated less imogistically, the institution is a group of subjects enjoying the flow of psychic energy which is available to them by reason of their continuing relationship with whatever archetypal symbol had the power to release it in the first place. Obviously, that relationship is primarily determined by implicit obedience to the divine commands: and these are embodied in the ritual and morality around which the institution is structured.

a. Ritual As Morality: Obeying The Divine Commands

There is a profound sense in which ritual and morality overlap in the living institution: both are understood to be divinely ordained. Indeed, if we press the analysis of their characteristics at all, the lines dividing them have a tendency to blur: for while it is easy to say that ritual consists of activities addressed to the superworld, and morality of the regulations for getting along well with other people and with the natural order, how are we to classify Jewish circumcision, Amish repudiation of motor transport, and the Hindu refusal to kill rats, in terms of these categories? Yet, granting the difficulty of making sharp distinctions between them, these two salient aspects of institutional religion still provide us with our points of departure in what is to follow. We begin with ritual, which is a primary means of maintaining the desired relationship with the personification, since in and through it the archetypal commands can be tangibly and overtly carried out.

i. Ritual As Supernatural Address

(a) Ethnic Ceremonials   Although the individual experience of numinosity, as we have been at pains to describe it, hardly occurs at all in Ethnic religious institutions, except in certain

initiation rites, yet in the collective ceremonies, the felt relationship of each participant to the deity addressed is very real. The problem- and cause-cure gods that personify the collective needs of the tribe are patently those aspects of the natural order upon which the welfare of the society depends, and the maintenance of a proper relationship with them is the explicit purpose of the ritual structure.[1] All members of an Ethnic group are preoccupied with this endeavor, since each one has a precise ritual function assigned him, which defines his social position in terms of his agency for the common survival. Indeed, the relationship of the various elements within the Ethnic society to the natural order, as personified, is so intricate, and at the same time so insistently maintained that the entire structure may collapse when confronted with cultural change.

This becomes transparently understandable when we remind ourselves that the ritual, primarily a matter of supernatural address, is also the total morality of an Ethnic group. Procedures for hunting, farming and making war, as well as for all aspects of domestic and political life, are included in the ritual structure, so that the individual who is ritually painstaking has no further moral responsibilities, inasmuch as anything not included in the ritual is simply not a moral issue.

(b) Prophetic Ceremonials   At the Prophetic level, the individual has had his own archetypal experience, solving (prototypically) the problem he feels when the Ethnic situation collapses. Alone and forlorn, he finds new hope, and the ground for life's continuance, as he meets a solution-god. As repeatedly described, this archetypal figure promises the early advent of an Ideal Society, supernaturally established, and defined by a morality of mutual benevolence, the observance of which is instrumental to its coming. Since this is a new religion, its adherents are *converts*; this entails several things. (1) There are several of them, (2) They have shared a common problem, and (3) The nature of the solution they have found implies fellowship. Their comparison of experiences is ecstatic, and their

---

[1] All ritual procedures are of course understood to be divinely prescribed.

common dedication to the archetypal commands they have received is absolute. The ritual and moral duties which are the content of these commands are all instrumental to the appearance of the Ideal Society, and the expectation of its coming is the dynamic of their mergence with the deity who has announced it. Since it is his act that will establish it, the maintenance of relationship which is central to all ritual comes to be seen as the effort of adherents to assure themselves that the Cosmic Promise will really come true. Thus we may say that while the *morality* of a Prophetic religion pertains to the Ideal Society which is hoped for, *ritual* is an absolutely integral feature of the *institution* which arises among those who await its coming.

These rituals may celebrate and affirm the morality as the Lord's Supper celebrates the *Agape* in Christianity, or as Propriety (*Li*) was stressed in the Confucian performance of the ancient Chinese ceremonies. They may provide direct visionary evidence that the new world order is getting closer, as was the case in the Ghost Dance: they may embody a technology for advancing toward the Ideal State, as in the Hebrew formulae for picking up and setting down the ark,[2] and in the various stages of meditative progress toward Nirvana, in Buddhism. Again, they may be merely occasions of "spiritual refreshment," wherein the worshippers, by some practice of mutual recall, e.g., reciting the divine attributes, can enhance their sense of the god's reality, and feel again the wonder of his primordial appearance to each of them. But whatever the activity in which they engage, and whatever the circumstances in which it is undertaken, maintenance of the valued relationship with the solution god is the basic function of any prophetic ritual.

ii. Morality as Ritual   Another salient aspect of relationship maintained by the performance of divine commands is of course the morality. Instructions given by the god for the management of social relations, and for a proper adjustment to

[2] Numbers 10:35f.

the natural order, afford an obvious opportunity for implicit obedience, whereby mergence can be kept unthreatened. Also, the morality in a prophetic religion is precisely the attack upon their problem which the adherents most desire; so that the real dynamic for the enduring institution is found here, in the dream of a social order that is truly supportive and constructive.

Here, of course, are the definite moral requirements which characterize the world's major religions: Christian love, Jewish loyalty to Yahweh, the early Zoroastrian cherishing of cattle, combined with the ethic of combat against all alien things, the Muslim avoidance of wine and gambling, plus pilgrimage and holy war, Confucian propriety, and the Buddhist negation of selfhood. In every case, the precept followed is understood to be a divine command.

However, upon careful scrutiny of religious institutions *as we actually find them,* morality is seen as subsidiary to ritual, and this is our reason for classifying it as we have done.

Morality has two aspects. The first is that of which we have just spoken: the body of rules, contained in the original revelation, which outlines the social behavior that will solve the basic problem. It may also contain prescriptions for dealing with the natural order. This is the central dynamic of prophetic religion—the solution which the deity personifies, and the essence of the new movement. As such, its practice is undertaken immediately, in joyful anticipation of the new world to come, and with such dedication that it becomes in itself another dimension of ritual behavior.

However, as the hope of the Ideal Society, fades, *secondary elements* are added to the morality, trivial and particularistic, but intended to be reassuring: i.e., supplementary or overlooked divine commands, which are now declared to be essential to the new order or its appearance. These are, of course, the productions of theology, and it is such emendations as these which signalize the appearance of the religious institution as strictly understood. Such features as an exaggerated purity of sacrifice, circumcision, or other ritual mutilations, peculiarities of dress (the Sikhs, the Amish . . .), sabbatarian-ism, and other non-adaptive regulations presently become ingrained in the day-to-day morality of the institution. When even these attenuated prescriptions at last fail to restore expec-tation by their observance, the Ideal Society will typically be equated with immortality, or with the institution itself. At that point, such moral trivia become the insignia of institutional adjustment, with no reference at all to any appearance of an Ideal Society, however far in the future. Dietary requirements in various religions, the Catholic prohibition of contraception, and the Hindu refusal to kill rats are all cases in point: other illustrations of this mechanism will occur to the reader.

Thus, we see that as institutionalism replaces numinous expectation, morality becomes increasingly subordinate to rit-ual, and comes at last to be a matter of institutional conformity rather than of the radical problem solving which initially characterized it.

b. Ritual As Community

Ritual in a prophetic religion also keeps mergence alive by its aspect of *community*. Those who have found their problems solved in the attainment of this relationship with a personified solution are eager to speak of what they feel is their favored condition; but only those who have had the same experience can understand what they say, or will affirm it. In ritual participation, those who are entitled to take part gain the recognition as adepts which they feel is their due in the light of the tremendous experience which they have had. Along with a sense of social cohesiveness, rising out of the mutuality of action that ritual entails, they receive a reinforcing resonance for the numinosity they feel, since all other participants have not only had similar archetypal experience, but unite in pro-claiming it as wonderful.

Moreover, this resonance extends to the beliefs they share about the nature of the cosmos. Such beliefs, derived by implication from their numinous experience, are centrally im-portant to all the membership, but may not be accepted at all outside the institution. In the ritual, these beliefs can be recited and affirmed without ridicule or contradiction, and thus clarified and consolidated.

Their mastery of ceremonial detail is in itself a form of cultural superiority, for which every ritual occasion provides an opportunity of expression.

The mutual belongingness which such a group engenders is intense, and within its circle the morality of benevolence becomes practicable.

All these elements are part of the solution which is personified in the archetypal image, and subsumed by the activity which is instrumental to mergence with him.

Maintenance of relationship is thus integral to ritual in its aspect of community.

2. Ritual as Problem Solving Behavior

a. Inherently Problem Solving Activities

There is a slightly different perspective from which ritual can be viewed, namely that of problem solving behavior. While similar to maintenance-of-relationship, this function of ritual signalizes the rise of institutional autonomy, as distinguished from the autistic numinosity which prevails initially among those who have accepted a new revelation. As the institution assumes the function of carrying out the promises of the deity, and of implementing his directives, it is in effect seeking to become the thing that the archetypal figure personifies, and thus is acting as the surrogate for the Ideal Society. As such, it obviously must attack the problem, and if possible, keep it solved. Thus the ritual will consist of whatever activity serves this purpose, since the prime requisite of any ritual is *efficacy*.

Certain types of characteristically ritual behavior are *inherently* problem solving. Feasting relieves hunger, dancing provides exercise as well as tension release, social action obviates loneliness, and sex, alcohol and drugs all diminish anxiety. Furthermore, since all of these keep the subject's attention occupied, they have an inherently *instrumental* function, in that they *reduce the intolerability* of his primary religious problem. This is, of course, one of the basic ways in which it is possible for such problems to be solved.

Also, the *importance* which the subject attaches to the problem *may be substantially diminished* by the promises which motivate the ritual, as well as by its immediate effect upon the participant. This is another of the irreducible possibilities for solving religious problems; and the otherwise perplexing longevity of institutional religions becomes understandable as we realize that in their rituals, these two basic mechanisms *can be set in motion volitionally.*[3]

In just this connection we must mention the healing rituals of such groups as feature them. While not *inherently* problem-solving, the mass excitement which is their most prominent feature is definitely contributory to whatever psychosomatic improvement the participants may enjoy.

b. Instrumentally Problem Solving

Whatever their inherent characteristics, the typical orientation of religious rituals is *instrumental*—the solving of more or less specific problems. Thus, much of ritual consists of repeating behavior that was successful in the past. Whatever the subject happened to be doing when the solution overtook him, will be mimetically repeated, in the not unreasonable hope that it may work again. When this is a dramatization of some validly correct procedure for problem solving, however accidentally discovered or unconsciously formulated, we have the birth of science.

However, great numbers of totally invalid procedures have been employed apotropaically on this same principle, as when noise is made to drive away an eclipse. Past successes, alto-

---

[3] However, there is no certainty that the inherently problem-solving character of some ritual acts will produce numinosity in any given subject on a given occasion; nor can we predict *when* symbolic impact will occur, in the event that it does. Hence these observations are not in conflict with our earlier statement that religious experience is involuntary. All religious activity is of course open to volitional control, and is *intended* to produce numinosity.

gether due to the transitory nature of the crisis, have served to perpetuate such rituals.

Ritual frequently dramatizes the desired result, as when clouds and thunder are simulated and actual water is poured, in a rain making ceremony. The same mechanism is illustrated when ritual participants assume the character of the gods by wearing costumes or masks, and thus attired, act out the things they would like the gods to do. Theological fiction may even equate such performance with the benefit sought.

The definitely instrumental character of sacrificial rituals in attacking specific problems by summoning supernatural help has, of course, been remarked many times. Such ceremonials combine the inherent benefits of feasting, which commonly accompanies the slaughter of food animals, with the ritual reminder to the god that his price has been met, and a bargain thus concluded. The benefits expected are always recited, so that the instrumental quality of such rituals is unmistakable.

3. Ritual as Recall

Another aspect of ritual, related yet distinguishable, is its employment to produce vivid recall of archetypal events which are primordial to the institution. These events are, of course, the *acts* of the solution god, and are as much descriptive of his character and intent as they are of the institution which is their resultant. The ritual recall of these acts and facts contributes to the maintenance of relationship with the deity who is thereby affirmed ("praised"), and imparts a renewed sense of the relevance of the Ideal Society, as the promise of its coming is repeated. The primary process is thereby stimulated, and as the desired solution is envisioned more clearly, the sense of its reality is heightened.

Such recall may be accomplished by a simple recitation of the mythos, always a feature of ritual, or by some dramatic reenactment, symbolic or literal, of the events celebrated in it.

Thus, celebrations of the Passover in Judaism, and of Easter in Christianity, recall the *original problem-solving events* to which these institutions look back for their ultimate authority.

The promise of a future solution may be the archetypal fact recalled. We see this in the ritual of the Ghost Dance, which culminated in visions of the promised early restoration of primitive Indian ways.

The Christian Eucharist explicitly recalls *the establishment of the ritual itself* by the direct command of the archetypal Founder. Furthermore, although the average worshipper probably has no conscious awareness of them, the symbolic impact of this ritual is almost certainly intensified by two antecedent factors in its development: the Agape, an *inherently* problem-solving ritual belonging to Christianity's pre-institutional period, and the Messianic Feast, which was one of the most cherished *promises* of later Judaism, and is reflected in the several accounts of Christ feeding the multitude miraculously.

4. Ritual as Exhaustion of the Ego

Along with the dramatic recitation of the myth, bringing vivid recall of archetypal figures and events, whereby the primary process is stimulated and a heightened sense of reality given to the scenes portrayed, we find the exhaustion of the ego to be a consistent ritual practice, in every stage of the institutional life cycle.[4] This complements the production of recall, and engineers its numinous acceptance.

The effects of this dulling of the subject's critical abilities have been fully discussed above, in connection with *The Rise of the Personification*[5] and are well understood: the archetypal material, presenting some desperately desired solution, is experienced by the ritual participants as assured reality, carrying numinosity with it by entailment. This is, of course, the end sought.

The repetitive and emotionally fatiguing practices of singing,

---

[4] The Ghost Dance and Voodoo exhibit this phenomenon as *living* institutions, the Wesleyan movement as an *expanding* one, taken against the backdrop of a decadent Anglicanism, and American Revivalism of the eighteenth and nineteenth centuries displays it in the framework of institutional *decadence*.

[5] Cf. Part Three, II, B, *supra*, p. 84.

drumming, dancing, or chanting, which are familiar to any investigator, thus fall into place. Sooner or later, the secondary process collapses under the stress of such artificial frenzy, just as completely as it does when the subject has been struggling with a real life problem. The moment when this collapse will take place cannot be predicted, but when it arrives, as it all but inevitably must, the archetypal material comes flooding in, to be felt as real and authoritative.

Fastings and vigils that are frequently required before ritual participation are contributory to the same end.

Another well known device for exhausting the subject's critical judgment is the reiterated public insistence on the literal truth of some preposterous claim, together with the importance of accepting it fully. Along with this, repeated pleas for "Surrender!" will be made, and above all, by implication, conventionalized ritual reference, and overt statement, the idea will be advanced that the subject is unworthy and even depraved until he has placed all his faculties under the domination of the archetype, or of its local representative, whether or not any vital need will thereby be met, other than alleviating his artificially stimulated guilt. All this will be accompanied by references to the supernatural bliss of "enlightenment," i.e., acceptance of the institutional claims, and to the unforgivability of their rejection.

This combination of pressures seldom fails to bring about the collapse of the subject's ego, even though he may have previously had no religious problem. Moreover, in every religious institution there is a peripheral clientele of emotionally insecure people, uncertain of their ultimate worth by reason of their lack of any profound social rootage. The impact of such ritual procedures upon this group is, of course, devastating, and contributes to its institutional effectiveness.

It is just here that we find the roots of Exploratory Mysticism: for as the idea is more and more strongly advanced that the sole and supreme value in life is numinous experience, simply for its own sake, certain subjects of idealistic bent and more than average suggestibility will seek to attain this value in its

ultimate manifestation, and to reproduce the experience reput-
edly undergone by the archetypal founder. Their devotional
excesses, undertaken in the interest of exhausting their egos
are well known—hair shirts, flagellations, starvation, sleepless-
ness, and prolonged prayer, all kept up for incredible periods,
in the effort to bring about visionary experience. It is unfortunate that this type of mysticism has too often become the
referent envisioned whenever the term is used.

B. The Mythos in the Institution
    As we turn from ritual to the mythos, our frame of reference
is basically the same, since the mythos is not merely a static
body of dogma, but a living part of every ritual performance,
and so must be seen as a part of the overriding institutional
effort to maintain relationship with a personification already
arrived at.
    The chronological primacy of myth vs. ritual has been much
debated, albeit inconclusively. It is probable that in Ethnic
religions, ritual precedes myth, which comes into being later,
to provide rationale for autistic group behavior, spontaneously
initiated in response to some crisis, at a *very* primitive level.
    However, in Prophetic religions, the myth is clearly a record
of the original revelation, and of the commands given to the
prophet in that primordial moment. As such, it contains
directives regarding the ritual itself, and thus is prior to it both
logically and chronologically. Of course, it is the defining
function of theology to keep expanding the myth rationalisti-
cally in the interest of ritual efficiency.
    What then is to be said of the operation of the mythos as this
is related to religious experience in the institution?

1. It Is The Rationale Of the Ritual
    The myth is the rationale of the ritual, even as the ritual is the
recitation and enactment of the myth. Although, as Clyde
Kluckhohn has pointed out,[6] this correspondence is far from

    [6] Harvard Theological Review, 35:142, page 49.

absolute, the generalization is nonetheless valid enough to be taken as a point of departure. Although substantial portions of the myth may be external to the ritual, the latter will always contain some part of a central narrative that answers the question, "Why are we doing this?"

The mythos is a record of the divine commands, beginning with the injunction to perform the ritual in the first place. The word "celebrate," always used in connection with ritual procedures, carries the connotation of "memorializing"; and this is exactly what a correctly designed and executed ritual does: it calls to mind what the solution god has directed his adherents to do. Thus the ritual is not only *explained* and *justified* by the mythos, but derives its content from the same source.

2. It Reinforces The Morality

We are thus led directly into the second function of myth. It reinforces the morality, and gives it a conclusive *raison d'etre*, by recalling its origin as a divine command, whereby it is metaphysically authenticated.

A morality thus religiously based has always had a greater compellingness than one developed from strictly rational principles, however lucid these may be. The god to whom it is attributed is highly symbolic, and the system itself contributes to this by its intense pertinence to the problem for which the deity personifies the solution. The mythic claim to the divine origin of the morality, reiterated in the ritual, thus completes the dynamic for its total acceptance, so that the supernatural penalties attaching to its non-observance are hardly noticed until much later.

Moreover, we must not forget that the various stories of saints and heroes which make up a large part of any sacred literature are also a part of the mythos, although admittedly ancillary to it; and these illustrate and commend the kind of moral action that is divinely approved, thus contributing to its reinforcement.

3. It Provides a Standard of Excellence

The mythos provides a standard of excellence, in terms of which ideals can be structured and values formulated. We tend to forget that *the realm of the sacred is simply the secular as it ought to be*—who has ever seen this elementary concept in print? Yet, as the account of the archetypal personification is given currency, along with those of the Ideal Society he will establish, and the morality he has commanded, all prior concepts of value fall under judgment, clarity is imparted to aspiration, and new insights regarding personal achievement and social interaction are inevitably generated.

4. It Provides Id Release

The mythos in a living institution *provides a great deal of id release.* Since this idea has not been much stressed in the interpretation of religion, we hasten to point out that id-release is by no means limited to the expression of sexual imagery, although this is certainly not absent from the major mythologies, as witness the loves of Krishna in the Bhagavad-gita, and the various amours of the deities of the Greek pantheon, to say nothing of the grosser materials in the creation myths of many religions.

Being chosen and loved by a cosmic figure, and being part of a group whom he has commanded to love and sustain each other—concepts which appear in the majority of the world's religions—have been dynamically liberative experiences for centuries, to people who were lonely and forlorn. Likewise, rehearsing the sorrows of a god, as in the "sad feasts"[7] of Isis mourning Osiris, or as Christians do in brooding on the passion of Christ, provides opportunity for worshippers to sublimate their personal griefs into those of a cosmic figure.

Further, the hostility release that is gained by contemplating the victory of a solution god over his adversaries is no small thing; consider the emphasis placed on it by the Jehovah's Witnesses. Indeed, Jehovah has always been a god of battles, and in Judaism the Psalms of hate for his enemies, have been

[7] Plutarch, *De Iside et Osiride*, 68, 378–71, 379D.

a significant part of that faith for twenty-five centuries. Similarly, the lure of *jihad*, "holy war," for orthodox Muslims, is something to be reckoned with down to the present moment. The same mechanism is activated by reflecting upon whatever ultimate damnation the mythos may prescribe for enemies of the faith and the faithful, at the time of a final judgment.

Again, the portrayal of some great and beatific success, attained by the archetypal figure after fearful struggle, and promised to those who are merged with him in the faith, is a source of fantastic id release to any religious subject in the throes of suffering or persecution.

5. It Describes and Guarantees the Archetype

Above all else, the mythos describes and guarantees the archetypal figure. It recalls the personification, and shows why it is symbolic, by reciting the problem it has solved, and the circumstances of the solution. It is, in short, the absolutely central factor in any religious system, the repository of sacred information, and the focus of authority.

First hand awareness of its claims thus signalizes membership in the company of the faithful, during the pre-institutional period of numinous enthusiasm, and acceptance of those claims on faith is the condition of entry to the institution when it appears.

6. It Provides Something To Appeal To In Crisis: "Archetypal Contact"

We are thus brought to the final function of myth of which we shall speak, and the most important one: *By its presentation of the archetypal figure, the myth provides something to appeal to in crisis.*

This may well be the most important kind of religious experience there is, simply on the ground of its extensity: for mystical experience, particularly of the originative sort, is very rare indeed, and experiences of conversion, although not unknown, have a once-in-a-lifetime character: whereas *Archetypal Contact*, as we shall term the experience here to be described, occurs with surprising frequency. Indeed, this is one of the more benign characteristics of institutional religion—the opportunity it affords to those within its fellowship, not only to enjoy mutual assistance and human affirmation, but to have recurrent symbolic communication with the archetypal figure who personifies everything for which the institution stands.

Actually, Archetypal Contact contains two sorts of experience; Recall, and Supplication, both involving the focus of the subject's attention upon the myth, wherein the archetype is enshrined and guaranteed.

a. Incidental Recall

In the first, the subject gains energy release, with its accompanying sense of numinosity, without any unusual or specific religious activity on his own part, as his awareness of the archetypal figure is renewed or intentsified, however incidentally. Simply to contemplate the mythic portrayal of the solution god, whether this is ritually presented, in all the tender beauty of a sacred ceremonial, or autonomously recalled, under the pressure of a problem situation, produces great symbolic impact in one who is discouraged, and whose sense of a religious solution once known, has become faded with time and adversity.

i. Review of Symbolic Impact

Let us look at this experience, and at the nature of the symbolic impact which it entails. First, the problem: and here again, there is a distinction to be made.

The problem may be minor. An institutional member, beset by emotional distress, may derive notable beatitude from the Archetypal Contact obtained in customary ritual participation, although his trouble, admittedly poignant, has never had the dimensions which are the condition of autonomous religious experience.

The problem may be highly subjective, or new. Although the institution itself is the answer to social collapse, and serves as the interim surrogate for the Ideal Society that is expected, and although it may constitute a viable solution to a social problem the individual once had, he may now have an inner-psychic problem: he may be disappointed in love, bereaved, guilty, or ineffective. Even within an institution dedicated to mutual aid, the personal griefs of a person with one of these difficulties may be neglected, so that, *simply on account of its subjectivity*, his problem may assume religious proportions.[8]

It is altogether natural that such a person will be attracted to the religious activities of the group, where he will, in the course of things, encounter the archetypal figure whose mythic attributes are being ritually recalled. Note, moreover, that a person who has had one kind of religious problem solved, will have complete trust that the deity who solved it can solve any other kind, since he has already experienced this god as unlimited in power, and is fully committed to him, through membership in the institution. Hence, when the Archetypal Contact occurs, even by incidental recall, the subjective problem, akin to, but not identical with, the one solved in the mainstream of the institution will be alleviated by the symbolic impact of the personification thus encountered.

In just this connection, let us look again at the experience of symbolic impact, and review the mechanisms which make it dynamic. The term is, of course, inseparable from the idea of energy release, and indeed can be taken as synonymous with that expression for all practical purposes. We must also remember that "symbolic" has repeatedly been defined as "problem solving" for the present frame of reference. Thus we are in reality seeking to explain how and why problems are solved and energy released when the subject renews his contact with an archetypal image. The observations which follow have been discussed at length in earlier parts of our study, and are simply offered in review here.

First, the religious symbol, always a personification, is a love object, and as such, inspires a pronounced flow of libido toward itself. Libido being energy, the subject is thereby liberated.

---

[8] Presumably it is unnecessary to remind the reader that subjectivity is one of the characteristics of a religious problem.

Second, the personified symbol inspires the quest for relationship. This inspiration is renewed whenever Archetypal Contact occurs, illustrating again the predominant institutional function of maintaining optimal relationship between the subject and his god. It goes without saying that full observance of the ritual and moral requirements of the institution is always a part of this.

Third, the pattern of action given in the ritual and the morality is *available*, thus giving the subject something he can do without inhibition, and in the doing find his problem solved, since the activity involved in this quest for relationship is itself a form of energy release.

Fourth, the symbol is desirable, and the ego is structured by desire. As we have previously stressed, the primary and secondary processes meet in the morality which the deity personifies and commands: the subject dreams of a realm of mutual benevolence, and his reason affirms the phantasy as the only social order that can finally prevail. Further, this moral order is perceptually tangible in the institution, and its availability not only gives verification to all else that the revelation has claimed, but provides an area where the recently exhausted ego can assert the claims of reason and practicality, in pursuit of a profounder and more rational desire than was previously known. Hence, whatever the nature of his problem, the subject finds his ability to deal with it enhanced, as its intolerability is lessened by contact with the deity who personifies and guarantees this panorama of well being.

b. Supplication

All of these factors come into an even sharper focus when the problem felt by the subject is of such dimensions as to move him to active *supplication*, which is the second sort of Archetypal Contact. The fact of explicit prayer and its answer probably provides the most vivid instance of numinosity to be found in institutional religion, and is without doubt its strongest support. The syndrome involved requires our careful consideration.

As a child begins to mature, he is compelled to introject the imperative to self reliance, not only by those in authority, but by his peers as well. Particularly is this true of the prohibition against weeping. Indeed, his own sense of advancement into maturity will be measured by the progressive mastery of whatever skills will protect him from the embarrassment of needing to entreat parental assistance, or, what is worse, from the surrender to desolation and helplessness of which weeping is the evidence. This introjection is likely to become so complete that in adult life he will pretend a tough-minded adequacy long after his resources for dealing with a problem have been exhausted. As we have already seen, this introjected demand for ego-adequacy is so general and runs so deep that failure of any kind, however unavoidable, is accompanied by guilt.[9]

However, at the same time he is being required to internalize this imperative to self-sufficiency, another set of pressures is calling for his introjection of religious attitudes, many of which run counter to those described. Thus, surrender of selfhood to the institution, acknowledging the will of the deity as supreme, obedience to all commands of the god, and seeking to know the will of this deity in every kind of perplexity, will all be presented to him as eminently desirable, and indeed, morally mandatory procedures. Although their omission will be entirely overlooked if he becomes successful in some secular aspect of the society, despite the exaggerated lip-service, which is tendered them, yet, paradoxically, these religiously oriented injunctions really do represent the value structure of the society of which the institution is a part, and certainly of the institution of which the subject is a member.

Hence, when a subject in such an institutional setting is confronted by a problem of sufficient magnitude as to produce religious activity, the very fact of his beginning to pray is productive of a whole series of interesting reactions.

We must remind ourselves initially that in so doing he

---

[9] Cf. Part Three, III, C, 4, c, i, *supra*, page 171.

confronts the archetypal figure, so that everything we have said about the rehabilitating effects of symbolic impact comes into play, as described above.

Note also, that although he has introjected the prohibition against seeking parental aid, yet on any occasion in which such aid was vitally necessary, e.g., serious physical injury or crushing disappointment, such assistance would be extended to him, whether or not requested. Thus, as he now surrenders to an attitude of supplication, he unconsciously *expects* assistance to be forthcoming.

The very fact of total surrender, and the ending of struggle brings about a sense of relaxation which is itself welcome. To put by all pretense, and admit that a problem is beyond one's ability, has an aura of reality and rightness which will not be denied, however reluctantly this attitude is assumed. Furthermore, the presence of the archetypal figure provides something to *surrender to*[10]: a larger, vice-parental source of security, which is socially approved.

Moreover, the act of praying is in itself the source of inner affirmation from his super-ego; for in so doing, he is accepting the dictates of the highest level of morality that he knows.

These factors—relaxation, expectation of help, and inner affirmation, taken in conjunction with the exhaustion of his ego, may of their own dynamics bring about such an improvement of feeling tone that his problem ceases to be intolerable, hence less important, and is in effect, solved. Moreover, these same factors are the same ones upon which autistic experience depends, and visionary or hallucinatory experience may indeed come to the praying subject. However, the god he sees will be the god of the institution, and the words he hears, except in the rarest of instances, will be drawn from its format, and congenial to its tradition.

Furthermore, the supplication of one who prays will frequently assume some form to which a conventionalized reply can be made; either directly, by the clergy, or through his own

---

[10] Cf. "Leaning On The Everlasting Arms."

recall of some ritual utterance, or some passage from the myth. This will typically take the form of a *promise*; and the expectation of a *future solution* to his problem has the same psychological impact as having it solved out of hand, for it *is no longer insoluble.*

The enormous importance of the doctrine of immortality becomes apparent at this point. As the ideal society which never arrives on earth is translated into a realm beyond the sunset, its function may even be enhanced: for now it is more than a supportive commonwealth, and certainly more than the mere prolongation of human existence. It has become the place where all tears are dried, frustrated hopes and ideals fulfilled, physical ills healed or transcended, and where broken loves are reunited in the Communion of Saints—the Beautiful Isle of Somewhere . . . It is probable that the expansion of any deity's function is brought about more frequently by the judicious issuance of promises of future solution to new problems, in immortality, than by any other means.

Yet another factor must be taken into account here. Many of the solutions we have been describing have been either neuro-muscular (relaxation, improved feeling tone) or intellectual (some phrase or statement from the mythos as pertinent to a new problem). As such, they require *interpretation* to make them numinous. This the institution does, through all its channels, endorsing them as evidence of divine intervention and aid, in the subject's behalf.

Thus the simple turning of the mind back to the formulations of the myth, whether passively, in simple recall, or actively, in supplication, is at the root of the most important aspects of institutional numinosity, by reason of the Archetypal Contact which it entails.

These considerations shed whatever light is needed on Jung's dictum that, although commitment to an institutional religion protects the subject from the dangers of premature confrontation by unconscious imagery, it also precludes his full attainment of individuation.[11] For Jung, this completed unfold-

---

[11] *Two Essays On Analytical Psychology*, Meridian, 1956, p. 236.

ing of the personality is the result of the subject's coming to terms with his own autistic, archetypal experiences: but these the institution virtually precludes by insisting on the metaphysical ultimacy of an archetypal figure already in existence; by persistently directing the subject's attention to this figure, in the interest of maintaining his relationship of mergence with it, and by making contact with this archetypal figure, of the type we have been discussing, so readily available that its numinous glow comes to seem volitionally attainable. Being thus shielded from first hand experience of his own unconscious (i.e., archetypal . . .) imagery, the subject cannot of course, come to terms with it, and is thus denied individuation in the interest of psychic tranquility.

C. Theology and the Institutional Life Cycle

1. Pre-Institutional Theology?

Although we have spoken of theology as though it were an exclusively institutional phenomenon, there are certain traces of it at the pre-institutional level.

The true believers are trying, in whatever they do, either to make the most of a religious solution recently promised, or to solve some related problem that has arisen subsequently. Since revelatory material is always irrational, it is inevitable that those to whom it has come shall seek to reformulate it in ways that will make it less abstruse, and easier to describe to the uninitiated, and which will provide a clearer authentication for the morality, which will itself be given such minor modifications as make it most applicable. However, these modifications are essentially *expository*, and neither promotional nor apologetic. Furthermore, they do not reflect any doubt whatever concerning the absolute validity of the revelation itself. None the less, some of these reformulations may be contributory to the institutional format which the collectivity eventually assumes.

2. The Institutional Profile: A Theological Construct

Institutional existence begins at the moment when persons of influence within the collectivity first view the group itself as more important than the doctrine which brought it into being. In a prophetic religion, this moment arrives when some inner circle of members, possibly less sincere and more opportunistic than the rest, realize for the first time that they will have to wait a little, for the Ideal Society to be established. It is not even necessary that they shall have lost faith in its eventual coming, but since they must wait, the manner of waiting becomes important to them, as does the question of who shall direct it. That is: How is the date of the Ideal Society to be recalculated? And why, in fact, has it been delayed? Do we work until it comes, or merely pray? How is the property to be held? Who or what is to authenticate the morality in this embarrassing interim, and who is to supervise that authentication? Are we doing the ritual correctly? What shall we tell the new converts? What is the status of the dead? Countless administrative decisions and pronouncements must be made, and the people who make them are at pains to see that their own efforts in so doing are given adequate recognition. This is the moment when the less committed members of the collectivity become its effective power majority, and aware of the desirability of perpetuating the group for their own ends. As they realize the enormous advantages of every kind, ranging from spiritual dominance to substantial economic gain that can accrue to them *if the group survives*, they are impelled to a high level of organizational ingenuity, which finds its most typical expression in theology. They do not hesitate to speak for the god, and to interpret his will in detail, in the interest of making sure that the group remains in being, and that their own positions of leadership are fully consolidated.

As soon as their own administrative roles have been established as preeminent, the relative importance of other functionaries within the fellowship will be carefully defined: the ritual specialists, the primordial revelators, if any are left, and then, finally, the order of prestige among the laity will be spelled out, always, of course, with such further claims of divine guidance as are needed to ensure acceptance of the status assigned.

This standardization of institutional roles involves definite modification of the original revelation, since in a Prophetic religion there is no social metaphysic for the present. All statements in a Prophetic revelation regarding the order of precedence among believers refer solely to *future* rank in the Ideal Society, when it shall have been established, and are calculated in terms of the integrity with which its morality, both ritual and social, has been practiced.[12] Institutional prominence, on the contrary, is a matter of manipulative skill.

Along with standardization of roles within the group, standards of *belief* are established in a creed, and standards of authority are incorporated into some sort of ordination procedure. At each step of the way, the mythos is either appealed to, in order to authenticate what is prescribed, or additions are made to it, upon whatever pretext, so that its authority will undergird the stipulations which transform the erstwhile numinous collectivity into a permanent institution.

Central to all these matters is, obviously, the continued existence of the group, and so, in turn, the relationship of the members to the archetypal figure which has been its dynamic. Thus we see *the institutional imperative to maintain this relationship* begin to operate. The first place it is needed is to provide some plausible explanation for the delay in the coming of the Ideal Society. The apologetic offered runs through a predictable sequence: wrong calculation of the date, negligence in practicing the New Morality, equating the Ideal Society with immortality, and finally, identifying it with the institution itself.[13]

In all of this we must remember that in spite of any setback their faith may have received, numbers of the original true believers, whether more credulous or more committed, will still be clinging to their primodial hope, and speaking of it in

[12] Cf. Mt. 20:20–28. Parallel examples are to be found in every prophetic religion.

[13] This has already been given some consideration in Part Three, III, C,4,d,iv, pps. 193–200, *supra*.

glowing terms. To these the organizers can point with pride, as living evidence of the viability of their theologically attested system. Their practice of the morality, in particular, lends much credibility to the institutionalized group.

None the less, every effort will now be made to *produce* numinous experience. We have already noted the institutional emphasis on Archetypal Contact, but in addition to this, vigorous institutional promoters will ascribe every favorable and/or unusual occurrence to some act of the deity, in their effort to keep the clientele religiously sensitized. Also, various objects,[14] locations,[15] and events[16] will be declared sacred, so that as the members encounter them, exaggerated claims of numinosity can be made. Extraneous, neuro-muscular and intellectual solutions to religious problems will be stressed, since their numinous quality in every instance depends on subsequent interpretation.[17] Problem solving aspects of the ritual will be emphasized, so long as the solution can be promised at some future time, and whenever possible, effective techniques for the actual solution of problems will be given a ritual character.[18] Also, the ritual itself will consistently aim at

[14] The altar, the priest's chalice, his costume, costumes of the gods, sacred statues, eagle feathers and red paint for the Ghost Dancers, fire for the Parsis, the Ark of the Covenant, sacred relics, etc.

[15] Locations: Mt. Sinai, the Wailing Wall, the Kaaba, the birthplace of any founder, Canterbury, the Vatican, etc.

[16] Events: All visions seen and voices heard: the birth of a Dalai Lama; the sprouting of a sacred tree; the elevation of the Host, etc.

[17] Cf. Supra, Part One, VI, A-B, 1-2, pages 26–31.

[18] Sacred substances are as often medicinal as they are psychedelic. Just at a venture, compare willow bark, containing cinchona (quinine), much used by the Plains Indians, and deadly nightshade (belladonna), commonly employed in the medieval witch-cults, with the ubiquitously mentioned mushroom.

Also, the problem solving may take the form of some divine apparition addressing, manipulating, or even inhabiting some of the ritual participants, as in Voodoo, whereby those who are thus "mounted" seem to gain a sense of significance that makes their otherwise sordid existence tolerable. Cf. Sargant, William, *The Mind Possessed*, Penguin Books, N.Y. & Baltimore, 1975, Chapters 18 and 19.

ego exhaustion, so that suggestibility will be heightened and critical judgment blunted throughout the clientele.

In short, any device that will contribute to maintaining the close relationship of group members with the Archetypal figure who originally personified the solution to their problem, or any technique that will authenticate and guarantee the predominance of the administrative class, will be added to the mythos by the latter group, for whom the institutionalized religion is the vehicle of their own ends, and whose prime concern is its perpetuation.

Feature after feature of institutional procedure thus becomes orthodox as soon as its effectiveness is proven, until presently all of them are matters of dogma, supporting a rigid organizational structure, and themselves impermeable to change except by further theological development.

3. *The Expanding Institution: Theology as the Growth Factor*
Religious movements do proliferate on their own merits, and we must not lose sight of the fact that a primordial revelation may be so pertinent to the problems of its time and place as to gain it widespread acceptance at once, without theological expansion. Thus, Moses' Jahvistic revelation, which was intended for a precisely defined group of people, and was instantly fulfilled by the crossing of the Red Sea, was unanimously accepted by those for whom it was meant, and went on to be authoritative, with only minor modifications, for a very long time.[19] Christianity, whose doctrines were already a blend of all the near-Eastern religions, had widespread acceptance among the lower classes wherever it was taken, and early

[19] Note, however, that Moses took advantage of the vast primitive credulity of his day, in reporting repeated "revelations" from Yahweh, as these became administratively expedient. That Mohammed later used the same technique, issuing his own directives in the name and by the authority of Allah, cannot escape our attention: this is precisely what we mean by theology. Indeed, the suras of the Koran are dated in this way: the short, autistic ones are assumed to be early, and the long, particularistic chapters by common consent are taken to be later. The same phenomenon is observable in the Book of Morman.

Buddhism spread with similar rapidity, although its freedom from theological refinement by the monks who formulated the oral tradition is doubtful.

However, careful examination of the world's religions will show that all but a very few have had their greatest growth only after assuming institutional status, which is to say, after they have undergone notable modification by the theolgians. As we have seen, this only takes place after their original promise of cosmic reform has been to some extent discredited.

Thus we see the early agricultural reforms of Zoroaster giving way to the elaborate eschatological doctrines of the Saoshyants, and note that the movement did not enter upon its phase of definite growth until after the prophet's clear-cut ethical dualism had been replaced by a cosmic dichotomy of good and evil beings and substances, far less morally demanding, but ritually acceptable to the common people.

Similarly, the reformulation of Buddhism that changed it from a resolute psychological discipline to a lush redemptionism is well known: and the fact that Mahayana is a theological development of Hinayana, successfully designed to give it greater competitive advantage against a liberalized, popular Hinduism, is a commonplace of the History of Religions. The entire history of Confucianism is an account of the theological modifications which finally established it as the epitome of Chinese culture. Note also that the movement of any prophetic faith into a new geographical-cultural milieu involves its accommodation to local ideas as much as it involves the reform of those ideas, which the transplanted faith is supposed to be undertaking.

As the nascent religious institution is given shape by those who are promoting it, it frequently assumes very attractive proportions, so that simply by the fact of its own existence, it produces a considerable amount of symbolic impact, both upon those who are outside it, and those who are either within it, or closely peripheral to it. Numerous converts are often gained as a result.

(1) In the first place, any numinously affected group of

people is, *ipso facto*, impressive. They are filled with hope and optimism in the prospect of a cherished dream presently coming true, and their personal relationships, guided by the morality of mutual aid, provide a center of radiant contrast with the folkways of the surrounding society. This numinous glow may arise from the original revelation, or something that it implies, or it may be the result of recent theologizing: but whatever its source, to the extent that this condition obtains, it is an important dynamic for institutional growth, simply in its power to produce symbolic impact, which is preliminary to conversion.

(2) A growing religious institution is bound to appear well organized and highly effective. The clientele is filled with enthusiasm, and the organizers are most earnest in their efforts to keep them so. Converts themselves only recently, and hence able to remember the stringencies of social maladjustment, the theologians who are promoting the group are now looking down vistas of power and prestige which serve to inspire them to a sincerity that is unequalled by any other executive class. Volunteer assistants are available in great numbers, needing only the assurance that their efforts are pleasing to the deity, to stimulate them to patient and dedicated attention to details. Indeed, the will of the god is adduced for everything that is done throughout the group, which produces a unanimity that presently makes it a most effective power structure. Of course, the theologians are at pains to credit all organizational prosperity to the approving favor of the deity, with the clear implication—spelled out explicitly, if need be, that the reason for this felicity is the institution's perfect conformity to the divine will, which is to say, its metaphysical correctness, and indeed cosmic ultimacy. Although its organizational machinery may be less closely articulated than would appear to an outsider, the overall effect of an expanding religious institution is one of numinous and irresistible power.

As a result, the institution may become a political force in its own right: and when we reflect upon the willingness of promoters to ally themselves and their followers with existing power centers[20] as well as to oppose them, and upon the logical tendency of rulers to rally new constituencies to their own support, we see that the names of Vishtashpa, Asoka, Constantine and Sitting Bull, royal patrons respectively of Zoroastrianism, Buddhism, Christianity and the Ghost Dance, appear in the history of these movements by a relentless logic. Of course this comes later; the proponents of a new social order will at first be adjudged seditious, and efforts made to exterminate them. It is when the theologically organized institution has (a) survived, and (b) accommodated itself to political reality that it receives official sanction.

Be all this as it may, once the institution receives royal, or even official support, its theologians will so embellish the imperial sponsor and the burgeoning institution with divine attributes and authority that additional converts will come in, touched with symbolic impact by the sheer refulgence of the expanding group.

(3) At this point we must give some consideration to the peripheral seekers who follow the expanding institution—the constituency from which these converts will be drawn. We make this expository detour with a view to understanding the manipulative techniques the institution will employ in order to gain their committed support.

Some of them will be family and friends of those already converted. These will necessarily have had a great deal of contact with institutional activities, and may even have been attracted to the original revelation, *simpliciter*, and so indeed be drawn into the institution by the promise of the coming Ideal Society, even as this hope begins to fade. On the other hand, they may only be worried about the strange aberration that has brought their relatives into the institution to the detriment of other relationships. Some may be drawn to the morality, but repelled by the metaphysical assertions that undergird it.

The key, however, to understanding the peripheral clientele

---

[20] As in the case of the author of Second Isaiah, trying to equate Jahvistic monotheism with that of Zoroaster, to gain the favor of Cyrus. Cf. Isa. 45.

of an expanding institution, is to remember that *it is an institution* they are following, and not a revelatory leader, nor a popular movement.

This entails certain definite observations that must be noted.

The message of a truly autistic revelator is by definition irrational, and those who accept his prophecies of world cataclysm are truly desperate people, since actually to take seriously the notion that an Ideal Society will be supernaturally established in the near future implies a mental condition in which archetypal material can dominate the psyche. This can only refer to the state of ego exhaustion which follows prolonged struggle with problems that we have designated as having the religious dimension—totally insoluble, important to the point of touching the very life, and emotionally intolerable. Here and only here is autistic material either produced or accepted.

Now the camp-followers of an institution are not this desperate, and the institutional message is not this radical: it promises a generally improved social status, and the most efficient route there is to contact with the solution god, who is unswervingly declared to be the personal manifestation of ultimate reality. And although these people do indeed find their problems insoluble, they do not feel them with that final edge of intolerability that is the efficient condition of autistic numinous experience. This is due at least in part to their being among the beneficiaries of whatever part of the New Morality the True Believers have been able to put into effect. We might describe them by saying that their bare survival is not threatened, but that they are unhappy, and aware of being without significance. They are shallow, ignorant and credulous, and lacking in social rootage. They would appreciate a leg up economically, but even more than this, they desire some kind of automatic respectability—some notable improvement of status, that will not cost them too much.

Members of this peripheral constituency observe the numinous glow of the True Believers, and without understanding it at all, desire a state of verve and confidence similar to that produced by true mergence. They are, however, totally un-aware of its terrible price of Archetypal confrontation and personality reorganization, and would be quite unwilling to undertake it, even if it were understood. They may even fail to distinguish the inner radiance of those who are numinously affected from the complacent social adjustment of merely institutional members, and desire nothing more than the latter situation.

However, their most profound yearning, deeper than that for economic betterment or even social recognition is for some simple—or preferably supernatural—solution to the burden-some futility of their own selfhood. As a matter of fact, the very intensity of this desire keeps it repressed most of the time. None the less, the most pervasive characteristic of the clientele from which converts to a religious institution will be drawn is that its members are either unwilling or unable to organize any effective ego structure, by reason of the unrealistic alternatives and neurotic conditioning to which they have been subjected. This is the central problem for which they need and want a religious solution, and it is a problem that the institution itself has created.

For note:—

Quite apart from their initial disinclination to face the lack of authenticity within themselves, and over and above other problems that may have afflicted them, they have been thor-oughly propagandized by the institution, to the effect that only within it are the words of life to be found—i.e., that only there can valid answers to any problem be obtained. This is the theology of promotion, implacably presented, and being close enough to pick it up is one of the defining characteristics of the people we are describing. Moreover—and this is crucial—they have been relentlessly indoctrinated with the idea that to pit their own judgment against *any* problem, instead of seeking the "divine," i.e., the institutional answer, is not only folly but presumption: and more than this, that *to differ with* such an institutional dictum is frowardness unspeakable. As a result, ordinary ego activity comes to be all but impossible for them: it makes them guilty and confused, and they become progres- sively more vacillating and dependent.

Hence they are quite willing to abandon this burdensome psuedo-selfhood for anything purporting to be a religious solution; which is to say that they will repudiate the clear evidence of the Secondary Process—ordinary rationality—if any pronouncement, any program, or any promise is given them with enough prestige behind it to silence their question- ing, and which will hold out to them the sense of inner clarity that they can neither define nor achieve by themselves. It goes without saying that "enlightenment after surrender," "sight following faith," and "understanding opened by belief" are promised in fulsome and unreserved expression, along with the cosmic significance which will accrue to anyone who makes contact with the Solution God.

Once a prospective member has experienced the personify- ing process, so that the institutional archetype is real and personal to him, the sense of clarity, certainty, and above all rightness that he feels is absolute. This is the experience of conversion, and the quest for relationship which is its culmi- nating phase is completely satisfied in the opportunities for Archetypal Contact which the institution affords.

As the new convert moves into the institution, rejoicing in the sense of authenticity and psychic autonomy that mergence with the archetype always gives, and marvelling that his resignation from reason has had this numinous outcome, he receives certain other immediate benefits. Being a member of any well established group is always reassuring, and all the institutional resources await his exploration, many of them accompanied by supernatural claims which he finds attractive.

Moreover, certain outright economic advantages may accrue to him. Social acceptance is itself a protection against the more overt forms of exploitation, as we see in the conversion of Hindu untouchables to Christianity, or of American Negroes to the Black Muslims. Then too, the full benefits of the morality of mutual aid are now available to him; in a contemporary institution this may well be the means of his finding employment, or obtaining promotion. Programs of thrift and literacy, commonly featured in such moralities, make for a gradual rise to prosperity among the entire clientele.[21] As this came about among "the people called Methodists," John Wesley made a point of urging them to do business with each other, and to give the brethren preference in employment; the same policies were understood and followed by the Quakers. An elaborate program of relief gave early converts to Islam a share in the loot that persistent conquests were bringing in. Thus we see that although prophetic religions do not have the primary economic emphasis by which certain cults are characterized,[22] the material benefits of joining such an institution, while admittedly incidental, are not to be overlooked.

However, important as the survival aspects of religion are at its inception, and pleasing as its material advantages may be at any time, the emphasis is elsewhere in a growing institution, although every instance of improved circumstances among its converts is naturally acclaimed as evidence of divine favor, and, by implication, of institutional effectiveness.

Nonetheless, the benefits typically sought and supplied at this stage of development are cosmic rather than mundane, and the techniques for obtaining them are more dramatic than

[21] Note also the elementary training in accountancy which arises out of the demand for tithing!

[22] Consider the Father Divine movement, the ill-starred People's Temple cult, the Hare-Krishna cult, and that of Maharaj Ji, all of whom assume complete responsibility for their adherents, thus relieving them of the need for ego activity, in return for absolute commitment, and, in effect, supplanting their ego-structures by institutional provision. Thus they gain clientele either by creating dependency, or by attracting already dependent people.

Of course these economic provisions have a deeply numinous impact on many of the adherents: others simply take them for granted in the light of other magniloquent promises the leader has made.

We must, however, point out that cultic groups constitute a distinct class, inasmuch as the founder has frequently had no numinous experience at all, as far as research can show, except the success of the cult itself, and is simply exploiting the need and credulity of those who follow him. Cf. the section on Cultic Religions, *infra*.

economic cooperation, and less arduous than self-improve-
ment. Easy access to the supernatural is the prime demand,
whereby the new convert can maintain and deepen the flow of
energy that accompanied his conversion. Since Archetypal
Contact is its principal stock in trade, the institution makes this
available, not only through its rituals, but by extra-curricular
techniques, guaranteed to be mechanistically effective in producing supernatural results. Buy a candle and light it, and your
prayer will be favorably received; buy a St. Christopher medal,
and be safe while travelling; go on the *Hajj* to Mecca, and be not
only sinless but prestigious forever after; bathe in the Ganges
and escape transmigration; make a pilgrimage to Canterbury
and obtain expiation; to Lourdes, and be healed. In every
instance, the Archetypal Contact to which the prescribed
activity is supposed to lead comes to be identified with the
action itself. The institution does nothing to discourage this
development, since each routine is purchasable and lucrative.

Thus we see the institution making its greatest growth, and
attaining its greatest popularity through its most exploitative
operations. Nor is this difficult, or even hazardous to its own
credibility, since all that is necessary is to transfer the promised
benefit into some metaphysical dimension where verification is
impossible, or into the future, where failure, if detected at all,
can be blamed upon some intervening fault of the suppliant.
The converts themselves revel in the assurance, grounded in
the mythos by theology, that they can tap the supernatural at
any time by some readily accessible act or practice.

Of course, the intensity and validity of the putative contact
with the archetype eventually become lessened and diluted in
exact proportion to the tawdriness of the mechanism by which
it is supposedly brought about: a concurrent factor in this
ultimate diminution and failure is the policy of labelling whatever happens at the end of one of these shortcuts as archetypal,
whether or not it has any numinous characteristics. This
institutional decline takes a very long time, however, since the
institutional guarantees are convincing, and the people involved are reluctant to admit that they have been duped.

Concurrently with these developments, the authority of the mythos will be adduced in support of a resolute program of missionary activity, whereby the benefits arising from commitment to *this* deity rather than to any other, are disseminated as widely and convincingly as possible. An invariant feature of this approach is to stress the terrible culpability of anyone who, after learning of this institutional faith, fails to embrace it immediately.

Then, as the converts come in, the theologians continue their drive to *produce* numinous experience[23] by claiming any doctrine or practice that is gaining success in a competing group as a prerogative of the deity worshipped in *this* institution, and the new claim will be authenticated by appropriate divine utterance, opportunely discovered or revealed as belonging to the original mythos. The ability of their own institution to solve any new problem of sudden, widespread stringency will, of course, be claimed by the theologians, whether or not such a problem is the focus of a competing institution.

4. The Mature Institution: Theology Triumphant

The maturity of a religious institution is reached when it is accorded complete acceptance throughout the total society, which is to say, the largest social complex of which its members are conscious. This is not merely an uncaring tolerance, but the acknowledgment of its valid sacredness and symbolic efficacy.

It is predominantly recognized as the custodian and administrator of the Archetypal Figure with whom all members of the society seek contact for spiritual refreshment: comfort in sorrow, reinforcement of their ideals, guidance in perplexity, or in any other circumstance where their flow of psychic energy needs to be renewed. As institutionally presented, this deity is the locus and source of all popularly accepted values, and is quoted constantly in support of the institution and its every activity. He is still a solution god, but now is the sovereign of a heavenly kingdom, which theology has located in the realm

---

[23] Cf. *Supra*, in Part Four, II, A, 4, p. 214, s.v. Ritual As Exhaustion Of The Ego, and also II, C, 2, p. 227ff. The Institutional Profile.

of immortality, where its idealized outlines extend far beyond the sociological, and from whence his divine promises of reunion, consolation, healing and eventual mergence are brought to the populace with a pertinence to the longings of the clientele that certifies the ingenuity of the theologians.

This supernatural realm thus provides a locus for the eventual solution of problems of nature, as well as all inner-psychic problems: and insofar as it still reflects the Ideal Society of the original revelator, it is conveniently out of the way, so that no embarrassing comparisons with the present social order need ever be made.

Indeed, the Ideal Society, originally proclaimed as imminent, is now mentioned only rhetorically, yet its memory remains. Whatever elements of mutual aid provide the dynamic for the present society have been drawn from its outline, and it is to the archetypal originator of this ideal system that present leaders turn, through whatever institutional channels, when their need for guidance is sufficiently acute.

There is, however, one clear understanding. Although the religious institution, which previously was seeking to gain acceptance, and to make converts, has now attained full ascendancy, its adoption involves an explicit dichotomy between the realm of the sacred, which is represented by the institution itself, and the secular realm, made up of the rest of society, and generally considered to be the "real" world. By common consent, the religious institution does not intrude upon the secular realm without invitation, except in clearly exceptional situations, which is to say, in moments of crisis. Yet the theological enterprise has so arranged matters that this separation is not absolute, so long as the institution is indeed living; for all secular authority is endorsed and sanctioned by the sacred, which in turn gives nominal recognition to the head of the state as head of the church.

Within this frame of reference, the rituals of the mature institution are refulgent, and will have proliferated to fit every possible situation, as is illustrated by the cycle of the Christian year, the daily prayers and fasts in Mohammedanism, and the seasonal ceremonies in Zuni. Their presentation is dramatically compelling, aesthetically satisfying and their efficacy is mechanistic. The explicitly avowed presence of the deity (or deities) during their performance makes them strongly numinous: it may be guaranteed by the costumes of the celebrants (Zuni), the words of the liturgy (Christianity), the place where it is conducted (Islam), or, in fact, by anything whatever that is agreed upon. Moreover, their appeal is widespread; for although their actual celebration is now restricted to specialists, large numbers of the laity have definite ritual functions, and still more are able to enjoy the limited participation of observers, joining in the responses, singing, and assuming the appropriate physical attitudes of genuflection, kneeling, or prostration. The ultimate source of their numinous impact, however, may well be found in the doctrinal assurance, painstakingly inculcated in every participant, that the ritual is being performed in his behalf, and that in some undefined way, he, the individual subject, is deriving benefit from it.

However, impressive as the rituals of institutional maturity are, and effective as they may appear to be in maintaining relationship with the deity, there is nonetheless an actual diminution of Archetypal Contact during this institutional heyday. As custodian of The Sacred, the institution now presumes to regulate the personal forms of this most intimate experience, so that such contact by recall must be submitted to institutional certification, and that by supplication must be conducted through channels that the institution designates. In short, the ritual system, resplendent though it is, is now *de facto*, the only source of Archetypal Contact, which constitutes institutional power.

Nor is this all. Having limited Archetypal Contact to the channels under its control, access to these ritual channels is closely monitored and carefully restricted. Non-members are not admitted at all, and of those on the membership list, only those whose dues have been paid, who are in conformity with the doctrine and the morality, and who have observed the taboos of the time and place may participate—unless they have purchased the privilege of having these things overlooked.

Since there is a necessary spontaneity about the experience of symbolic impact which is lost in these formalized arrangements, the very nature of what is meant by religious experience becomes greatly modified: so that instead of some need being met in a way that arouses valuation so intense as to be mysterious, it is now understood as a prestigious kind of social recognition: of little meaning in itself, but valuable for the institutional endorsement it represents.

Indeed, on the original principle of the institution coming into being when the group becomes of more value than the doctrine it is supposed to represent (See page 227, *supra*), we may now say that in the mature institution, the relationship stressed is with the institution itself, rather than with the solution god who is esconced therein.

More precisely analyzed, it becomes apparent that the Archetypal figure himself is still sought, but is surrounded by so many intermediaries, interpreters and spokesmen, all clothed in so much ritual protocol, that however sincerely the subject may be groping toward psychic reality, his quest can only lead him to some institutional surrogate of the god he is seeking, who will give him an officially approved answer to his problem, and support it by such assurances of its supernatural origin as are most convincing at the moment.

Nonetheless, the assurances are there, and however transparent they may be to analytic thought, their impact, received in the warmth of his belongingness, makes the average member fully amenable to whatever directives may be given for the large scale programs characterizing the religious institution at this stage; let us make conquest of the infidel, let us reclaim the Holy Sepulchre; let us build so great a cathedral that men will think us mad for having attempted it.

We shall return to these ideas presently.

The morality of the original revelator has by this time been made as rational as may be without giving up its claim to supernatural authority. It is thoroughly adapted to the secular society, by whom it is unquestioningly accepted and sincerely affirmed, despite expected deviations in practice.

Actually, this morality, understood by all to have its origin within the realm of The Sacred, i.e., the religious institution, constitutes the defining factor by which the entire secular order is structured, so that failure to observe its tenets is *ipso facto* social deviancy. Minor infringements will be overlooked, especially in one who is otherwise successful, but major derelictions will not be tolerated. It thus constitutes an important bridge between the Sacred and the Secular.

As we should expect, the moral code is careful to ensure the privileged status of the clergy, along with that of the ruling class.

Although performance of the rituals does not by any overt definition exhaust moral responsibility, this attitude becomes implicit as moral trivia are absorbed into the ritual structure,[24] and as the latter is assigned greater importance. If one observes the ceremonial cycle, marries within the faith, has his children baptized or circumcized, observes the food taboos, wears the prescribed dress, and is generous with the clergy, so as to pile up whatever passes for merit, he will be asked very few questions about weightier matters of the law. Morality, in short, tends everywhere to become ritualized, and thus subsidiary to ritual itself, and the appearance of this tendency is a clear indication of institutional maturity.

One more tendency requires mention: the appearance of clearly negative, or counter-productive morality. As the institution approaches maturity, practices are advocated on moral grounds that are overtly detrimental to selfhood, in that they inhibit one or more aspects of its development. Originally presented as completely certain routes to numinous experience, they are retained and developed by reason of their undoubted advantage to the institution, until they come to be regarded as highly desirable if not altogether imperative.

---

[24] Viz., covering or uncovering the head in worship, Buddhists sleeping on low beds, Mennonites and Amish fastening their clothing with hooks and eyes, and a multitude of dietary regulations that will occur to the reader.

Monasticism, in particular, is a case in point. Its tenets of poverty, chastity, and obedience bring free labor and social quiescence to the institution in return for a certain aura of superior holiness that can be readily bestowed. Other instances will occur to the reader: e.g., the institutional opposition to various medical advances which has been observable in our own time and the recent past.

Persistent commitment to such negative morality is an important reason for institutional decline, and an unfailing characteristic of an institution that has already died.

The mythos, of course, will be adduced as the basis for all these developments, so that divine authority for everything that is done with institutional sponsorship can be shown to derive from this source, either in some direct statement, or by what such a statement implies.

Theology is the rationalized expansion of myth, in the interest of ritual efficiency, and the religious institution is its product. Generations of theological effort are presupposed by the institution in its maturity: all of its aspects have been articulated into a panorama of symbolic efflorescence, and set upon a ritual stage by those who have made it their vehicle to power. Upon that stage, and as participants in the drama there enacted, the theologians are now able to manipulate the vast religious establishment for their own ends. The quotations they cite as divine commands have been added to the mythos by unimpeachable discoveries, and the interpretations they make are backed by every resource of tradition and scholarship, so that to question their authority is made to seem not only personally foolhardy, but academically ridiculous.

As we look beyond the intramural characteristics of the mature religious institution, we see that its social polity has two outstanding characteristics.

It is basically a power structure, of course, and the first and most obvious use of its power is *financial*. All institutional services now carry a price tag; special offerings for various "charities" are mandatory, and fiscal accountabiltity is indignantly repudiated as beneath the purity and holiness of anything within the Realm of The Sacred, so that the laity are without recourse as to learning whether their contributions are in fact put to their declared uses. Emergency situations are not wanting, for which substantial capital sums must be raised, whether famine relief or the rehabilitation of shrines. Vast building enterprises may go on for centuries, as did the Age of the Gothic in Europe, and that of Buddhist temple building in Burma,[25] as well as the financing of world-wide colonial enterprises for the spread of the faith.

The second characteristic of institutional polity is *political*, and again two aspects must be distinguished.

(a) Within its own milieu, the mature institution tries to enlarge the realm of the sacred so that it takes in more of the secular. Thus we have Henry IV standing in the snow in Canossa in 1077, and the Ayatollah Khoumeni displacing the Shah of Iran in 1979; both are historic triumphs of institutional religion over environing secularism. Moreover, society itself is now structured by the religious institution, so that its various gradations are held to be divinely ordained.

(b) At this point the power of the religious institution is such that it exploits the entire secular society for its own ends, impelling it to wars of conquest whereby the society is expanded, and its own area of influence correspondingly increased. Thus we see the Muslim conquest sweeping the world from 635 to 732 A.D., and the Crusades assuming primary historical importance from 1096 to 1350. The various wars of the Reformation period illustrate the same pattern.

What began as the archetypal vision of an Ideal Society, proclaimed by a friendless mystic as supernaturally impending, is thus brought to imperial dominance. The systematic modification of its cosmic promise has solidified it into the institutional format which makes this possible, so that its dynamic of hope is at last warped into the same tyranny against which it was originally a protest.

[25] Interestingly enough, at about the same time: i.e., 1050–1300 A.D. Cf. Garrett, W. E. art, "Pagán, On The Road to Mandalay," in *National Geographic*, vol. 139, no. 3, March 1971, pp. 343–365.

III. The Institution As Dying: Self Perpetuation As Self Defeat

A. Introduction

When a religious institution dies, the evidence is partly objective, for all to see, partly internal or subjective, i.e., felt by its disappointed adherents, and partly discernible only to the experienced investigator, and that with varying degress of clarity. Moreover, an institution never dies in absolute totality; there is always the possibility of a religious subject receiving symbolic impact from a personification that has long since been abandoned if not discredited in the popular mind, as well as that of some circumstance in which a ritual, long regarded as obsolete, becomes filled with meaning. Then too, the authorized functionaries of such a system may go through all its motions long after they have entirely ceased to matter to anyone else. Hence we speak of the institution as dying, rather than dead.

These evidential distinctions are hard to make, since they are so completely interlocking. Nonetheless, we shall attempt to draw them, admitting that our classifications may be less than absolute, partly because the facts can be viewed from different perspectives.

We shall then indicate the reasons for institutional deterioration, and finally, consider the measures such an institution undertakes in the attempt to perpetuate itself a little longer.

Following this examination of the dying institution, we shall attempt to indicate the patterns that religious experience takes at this stage, both within and without the institutional framework.

B. Objective Evidences of Obsolescence

1. Neglect of the Rituals

The most obvious symptom of institutional decline is, of course, the neglect of its rituals. Resplendent though they are in the institution's maturity, the populace at length comes to regard them as less interesting than the ancillary customs which attend their celebration: i.e., the Mardi Gras quite overshadows the beginning of Lent, and the clergy are sorely tried to "Keep Christ in Christmas."

Furthermore, except at the highest levels, the personnel who are supposed to celebrate the rituals tend to become careless in the performance of their duties; the monopolistic security of their tenure naturally contributes to this situation. Consequently, the people presently cease to understand the import of the rituals, even to the point of being ignorant of the symbolisms involved. Hence they lose interest in the very procedures which were originally intended to keep them in touch with the source of their psychic energy, and omit most of them, restricting their religious activity to certain minimal occasions upon which the clergy still insist.

2. Clergy Inferior

The clergy of a dying institution tend to be of inferior type. The truly outstanding members of a society structured around such an institution seek other professions, and the majority of postulants are those who have either failed elsewhere, are merely seeking a sinecure or who, lacking the mental acumen to cope with the rigors of science, are of necessity, preoccupied with the symbolic. As a matter of fact, the duties many of them are called upon to assume are so trivial that their performance involves no difficulty.

Of course, a few heroic souls of real ability are to be found, who, with sincere commitment, are trying to utilize the vast resources of the institution to alleviate the ills of the moment, but within this class of able practitioners, they are far outnumbered by those who, with regrettable correctness, see the institutional structure as perfectly adapted for manipulating the masses, with no interest but a selfish one.

Moreover, this last group of clergy will characteristically be in power; indeed, as we have seen, they are the ones who have determined the institutional structure from the first. As the institutional decline gains momentum, these clerical administrators demand greater and greater efforts from the lower orders, in the attempt to stem the retreat: until as last, the duties required of them are so arduous, the judgments they are compelled to render upon the common people so harsh, and the moral compromises they are required to make so repugnant, that they leave the institution in large numbers, until an actual shortage of clergy occurs. This migration of the lower orders of clergy out of the institution is followed by a surprising number of those in high places, whether motivated by a sense of futility in betraying confidence on so great a scale, or merely by sensing that opportunity will be greater in some other area of endeavor.

3. Assumption of Temporal Authority

A third evidence that a religious institution is dying is its assumption of temporal authority. However flourishing it may be, such an institution is no longer religious, but simply a political entity that has managed to evade its responsibilities.

Another way of expressing this would be to say that while an institution reaches maturity at the time it is completely affirmed by its environing society, it dies when the situation is reversed, and the religious authority completely affirms the society which is, in effect, its own creation.

This is perhaps the essence of the Pseudo-Ethnic situation: for a Prophetic religion in its vigor has no social metaphysic, except for the Ideal Society which is to come, and that in terms of faithfulness to the New Morality which defines it; but it is of the nature of an Old Ethnos to define the status of every individual, in terms of his ritual function, and its supposed benefit to the society.

While this might seem to be simply a definition of institutionalization, we must note that Ethnic religions are prescientific, and that the status assigned by one of them cannot be changed, except through ritual channels: whereas in the definition of an institution by which we are guided, there is nothing to prevent the individual from changing roles. Of course, if and when he does this, he must perforce accept whatever status attaches to the new role he has chosen to assume.

Be all this as it may, we must remember that temporal authority involves areas beyond the political, and that when a religious institution assumes it, not only is political autonomy at an end, but the very principle of free investigation is under attack, so that along with social mobility, science itself is doomed.

The decadence of the religious institution is thus visible in its assumption of temporal power, in that, instead of being the representative of a Solution God, and implementing the solutions that he personifies, it now *creates* religious problems in several dimensions.

4. No More True Believers

A fourth evidence of institutional decline is the all but total disappearance of true believers. These are to be distinguished not only by their unquestioning acceptance of the early coming of the Ideal Society, and the radiant confidence in the future which rises from this belief, but also by their practice of the morality of mutual aid, which in its literal performance identifies them instantly.

Their absence removes a force for institutional cohesiveness that is important beyond calculation: neither the problem-solving force of their integrity, nor the power of their example can be replaced. Recent and contemporary converts may display a certain enthusiasm, but the inner authority is not there.

Moreover, as an institution comes to maturity, conversion itself loses meaning, for new additions to the clientele are not required to make any radical modification of their personalities as they enter it, and receive little or no numinous impact from the experience, but merely a kind of initiation. Even this is all too frequently shallow and undemanding, and represents nothing more than a recognition of social respectability as institutionally conferred.

The dynamic of the original revelation has long since been dissipated: indeed, it predates the institution's earliest existence, and all that the institution ever pretended to supply was its memory. But now, even the opportunity for the members to obtain contact with the archetypal Source of that revelation has been obscured by organizational priorities, and nothing remains that can transform personality as the True Believers were transformed.

5. Venality

The fifth objectively observable symptom that a religious institution is moribund is the appearance of venality in its policies. When the time comes that, in addition to setting a price on all its services, the institution will rationalize serious moral transgressions for a sufficient consideration, that institution is dead from any religious perspective. It may still have a great effectiveness as a political or an economic establishment, but its power to arouse any sense of sacredness has been irretrievably lost.

6. The Rise of Competing Religious Groups

A sixth observable symptom of institutional decline is the presence of competing religious groups throughout the society. As dissatisfaction with the major religion grows, the first to appear are the *sects*, which purport to be within the general tradition of the dominant institution, but which stress some restricted part of the older faith in a way that gives them an institutional character of their own, despite their insistence that they seek only to purify the doctrine and sharpen the appeal of the parent body. Thus glossalalia, faith healing, foot washing, snake handling, apocalypticism, and various ritual modifications and doctrinal revisions, to say nothing of numberless peculiarities of dress and diet, have all been given centrality as the *sine qua non* of true religion in sectarian groups, the part in every case being taken as the whole. Such groups arise while the parent group still has considerable influence, and in many cases are indeed intended to augment its efficacy.

Cultic religion is a later phenomenon, coming to prominence when the principal religion has been thoroughly discredited.

Since cult leaders are fraudulent from the outset, an atmosphere of religious cynicism is entailed by the presence of cults, which, in fact, signalizes the imminence of major religious change.

C. Subjective Symptoms of Obsolescence

1. No Symbolic Impact

From the standpoint of the institutional member, the predominant symptom of institutional decay is the failure of symbolic impact. Now symbolic impact is what releases energy, and the term "symbolic" has repeatedly been identified with "problem solving" in our frames of reference. Thus a defunct religious institution solves no problems and releases no energy.

Note further that a religious symbol is always a personification: but the central figure of moribund religion no longer stands for anything of problem solving importance to its members, and so does not activate the basic religious mechanism of personification-and-relationship within them. That is: since the personifying process, always an essential part of numinous experience, does not take place, there is no imperative to relationship: the deity is simply a statistic—historical, sociological, or whatever. And since the central function of a religious institution is the maintenance of relationship, it is suddenly empty, as there is nothing of symbolic importance to relate to.

There are, of course, various factors which contribute to this situation, and we shall attempt to review them in Section D, *Reasons for the Demise*, which follows.

2. Rituals Attended for Wrong Reasons

The second subjective evidence that an institution is dying, is the attendance of the clientele upon the rituals *for the wrong reasons*. We have already observed, objectively, that the rituals are neglected, and now we note that when the members do indeed patronize them, they are clearly conscious of doing so for various secondary purposes, rather than for that of obtaining the Archetypal Contact that the ceremonials were designed to provide.

To gain a reputation for respectability, to obtain prestige by being at the head of something, to achieve publicity that is valuable in some secular area of endeavor, to collect recognition for charitable generosities, superior piety, or ritual skill—these are the things members mention to their intimate friends or to their analyst, as their real reasons for participation in the rituals of a dying institution.

Add to these the inability to resist the promotional blandishments of the clergy, the presence of morbid guilt, too often created by the institution itself, and the not unworthy feeling of a responsibility to shore up the faltering institution, which is regarded as a force for social stability, and the actual motivations for ritual support are pretty well summarized. And even granting that some of these reasons have a connection with definite religious problems, it is apparent that the rituals are without serious meaning to those whom they are supposed to benefit. The intimate congruence of this observation with the fact of their neglect cannot fail to impress the observer.

3. Institution Itself Felt as a Problem

A third subjective evidence that a religious institution is dying is a logical extension of the two already given: namely that it is felt as itself a problem, possibly even of religious dimensions, by the very people it is supposed to be helping—its own members. There are three outstanding reasons why this is so.

a. Negative Morality

We note first the institutional employment of negative morality. As the individual member tries to go about his lawful concerns, he is constantly stumbling over some requirement that is either entirely trivial, or clearly inimical to his interests, and contrary to the dictates of his judgment, but which carries a religious penalty if not observed. Thus, whether it is fish on

Friday, the prohibition of birth control, or the institutional proscription of symbolic logic, he is bound to feel the institution as productive of problems, whether merely irritating, or seriously inhibitory.

b. Archaic Cosmology

A second aspect of institutional decline that is felt as a problem is the adoption or retention of an archaic cosmology. A mythic account of the universe may have powerful appeal in some poetic context, but when its literal facticity is insisted upon, and acceptance of this is set forth as a moral demand, the institution requiring such intellectual subservience is bound to be felt as a problematic force.

c. Systematic Creation of Guilt

Lastly, and probably most importantly in this connection, is the systematic employment of guilt to create situations which the institution can then assuage, and so continue to have some ostensible function, at a time when its functions are being lost. Moreover, this stress on guilt serves to reinforce the negative morality which perpetuates the problems making the institution necessary, and the outdated cosmology, which either negates present science, or reinforces the system of rewards and punishments upon which the institution is based. Both of these, in their turn, stimulate the production of guilt *per se*, for which the conscientious member must obtain absolution. Over and beyond these dynamics, however, is the more insidious doctrine of metaphysical guilt, whereby humanity itself is held to be inherently tainted, and thus in need of some ceremonial purification which the institution stands ready to administer.

D. Reasons for the Demise

Thus far we have described the stigmata of decay, as seen from both outside the institution and within it. Now we seek to identify the causes of that decay, whether among its symptoms, or underlying them.

This requires careful consideration, as there is an obvious

sense in which all symptoms of decay are causal, inasmuch as every defect of structure or function in an institution may contribute to its eventual dissolution. Again, the things an institution does, in the effort to perpetuate itself, once it is aware of its own decay, are similar in kind to those that have killed it, when undertaken earlier, so that cause and effect are confused.

Our present task is to identify whatever circumstances, policies or procedures, voluntary or involuntary, have had such a negative influence upon the institution, that as a traceable consequence of their appearance, its efficacy as a vehicle for religious experience has been measurably diminished.

1. The Migration of Religious Issues

The most basic element in the decay of a religious institution is the migration of religious issues. The progress of civilization, both scientific and social, is, after all, responsible for the alleviation of many religious problems, thus making the institution redundant. Although we are not dealing primarily with the Ethnic emphasis upon problems of nature, we cannot forget that the initiatory event in the coming of Judaism's Messianic Kingdom was the Messianic Feast,[26] four times attributed to Jesus in the Christian Gospels.[27] Israel's Promised Land was to flow with milk and honey,[28] and Zoroaster's initial message was that the Ox Soul was to be cherished by the preservation of cattle.[29]

As agriculture develops, as problems of distribution and transport are solved, as medicine becomes more than embryonic, as the morality of mutual aid gains some acceptance, and

[26] Cf. Isa. 25:6–8, 55:1–3, Psa. 132:15 and Ezek. 39:17–20. For fuller discussion, see E. R. E., v, 541a–542b.

[27] Mt. 14:13–21, Mk. 6:32–46, Lk. 9:11–17 and Jn. 6:1–14.

[28] Ex. 3:8, 17, 13:5 etc.

[29] Moulton, James H., *Early Zoroastrianism*, London: Williams and Norgate, 1913, pp. 345–357. Moulton Cites Yasna 29:1–11, 31:10 and 32:19 most convincingly.

the secular society is unified for defense by its religious structuring, the fundamental insecurities of the original adherents are to some extent alleviated, so that their religious imperatives are lessened. Hence the Ideal Society is less in demand, even as some of its aims are achieved.

Of course, as long as the original problem continues, the institution capable of dealing with it effectively will survive: and this is, of course, the reason why dying institutions try so hard to keep religious issues from migrating.

2. *Archetypal Image Loses Numinosity*

The second cause of institutional decay is closely related to the first.

An institution declines when its archetypal figure loses force, and this inevitably goes on over any period of time. He may be rationalized into an abstract principle, interesting enough academically, but not dynamic; or he may be so literalized that his numinous quality is reduced to ludicrous or horrendous detail, inspiring only ridicule or dismay.

When the time comes, as inevitably it does, that secular agencies can provide better solutions than the religious rituals and morality, then the god who is supposed to dynamize those procedures no longer arouses any numinosity: such valuation as is still accorded him is far from supreme, and whatever mystery still adheres to his person is beside the point.

The problem itself for which this figure originally personified the solution may have migrated to such an extent that the solution is no longer needed, and the deity has no further appeal.

The morality which the institution has attached to a particular deity may have become so inappropriate that the deity himself is seen as merely primitive and repulsive. Differently expressed, we might say that the progress of science and morality is such that the symbolic figure is less good than other factors in the environment.

An archetypal figure may lose *credibilty*. A religious solution almost never *comes*: it is *promised*: and a living institution works to implement the promise, to some approximate degree. The institution is dead when the promise fails completely, and the deity is thus discredited.

Finally, instead of personifying any kind of solution, the archetypal figure may be so obscured by the institutional structure that he is merely its figurehead; and since it is felt as problematical, he shares in that quality. The consequence of this is that any relationship whatever with him is undesired, and the institution is thus seen to have precluded its own function.

3. *Exploitative Intent of Leadership Recognized*

Of equal importance in institutional decay is the exploitative intent of the leaders, and its eventual recognition by the clientele, however long this may be delayed.

As the institution comes to maturity, its position is most secure. It is the sole custodian of the Archetypal Image; its rituals afford, if not the only, at least the primary, contact with that figure, and it is accepted throughout the environing society. Hence the leaders make the fundamental mistake of supposing that it will be permanently desirable for its own sake, and neglect the meeting of religious needs, devoting themselves rather to the production of "revelatory" material that will serve their own interests along strictly temporal lines. As a result, the group becomes effective in this direction, rather than in doing what it must to remain alive: namely implementing its own revelation in the achievement of a cohesive and benevolent fellowship of mutual aid, with truly comprehensive concerns.

Presently more and more members find their contact with the Archetype devoid of numinosity as they see the functionaries who are supposed to mediate that contact suborning the values for which the institution is supposed to stand, and citing unimpeachable quotations from the mythos in support of their own avid pursuit of material prosperity, or the power upon which it is based.

The progressive worsening of this situation, despite its

camouflage of supernatural endorsement, eventually produces a disillusionment which makes it impossible for the institution to communicate any sense of sacredness at all.

4. *The Institution Attempts to Monitor Archetypal Contact*

Another indubitable cause of institutional decline is the attempt to monitor Archetypal Contact. As we have seen, (P. 241) the institution in its maturity demands that Archetypal Contact by recall be given institutional certification, and that by supplication be carried on through a ritual pattern, assisted or supervised by the clergy.

That is: such experience by recall must be reported to the religious authorities for their verdict as to whether (a) it was really archetypal and (b) it was correctly understood or interpreted. And anyone presuming to pray, is asked to do it through channels, with his petition duly censored, and its presentation to the deity duly formalized.

In advancing these demands, the institution is, most obviously, seeking to limit *all* contact with the deity to ritual occasions. This would, naturally, be advantageous to any structure seeking to control society: for such contact by recall might well yield autonomous insights unfavorable to the dominant institution, and that attained by supplication might express religious concern with some institutional pressure that the individual felt as a problem, but which the institution would never admit to this category.

In short, by demanding that *no archetypal experience whatever* take place apart from its supervision, the institution is trying to make certain that *no archetypal critique* of its policies or procedures shall ever appear among the clientele.

This, however, is psychologically impossible, and organizationally preposterous.

There is an inherent spontaneity in the experience of symbolic impact so necessary that to attempt the supervision of individual religious experiences is simply to preclude their occurrence.

The only place the Archetypal figure can appear is where it

exists: namely in the mind of an individual. The institution can perhaps stimulate the individual's recall, and reinforce his awareness of such a presence, but can never *supply* the Archetype, *per se*. It can enshrine and ensconce the Archetypal experiences of many individuals, providing each one with the resonance of the others' acknowledgment and affirmation, but if any one of them is limited to the institutional portrait *alone*, to the exclusion of his own unconscious imagery, the experience is nullified.

Moreover, all ritual occasions are fundamentally directed to the aspect of *relationship* with the deity, whereas *personification*, which is the first half of the basic religious mechanism, is an intensely subjective, individual experience: and this is just what is going on, in the types of Archetypal Contact that the institution destroys with its attempted censorship. Furthermore, let us remind ourselves once more, that unless personification *does* occur, there is nothing to relate to. We have seen, a few pages back, how this can occur when the Archetypal Figure loses his numinous quality.

Another psychological observation is pertinent. Conversion into an institutional group provides personal authenticity for many of its members, who thereby solve the religious problem of its lack, as their neurotic inhibitions are resolved in the experiences of Archetypal Contact which institutional membership makes available to them, so that within its circle they enjoy a freedom of action, clarity of purpose, and completeness of personality not otherwise attainable. In particular, they gain the courage to practice the morality, to a surprising degree.

To tell such people that their most liberative moments of religious recollection must be screened for orthodoxy, and that their intimate supplications for integrity must be run through a ritual pattern, is to advise all of them that they are being manipulated. The trauma of this discovery nullifies their religious solution, and drives them back into the morass of neurotic futility from which the institution had temporarily lifted them.

Turning to the organizational perspective, it would seem

fully evident that the more Archetypal Contact the institution can purvey outside the ritual structure, the greater will be its degree of livingness, since here we have an autistic process bringing secular concerns into the domain of the sacred for their amelioration, and this with no coercion, promotion, or official pressure of any kind.

Moreover, the members who have the moments of Archetypal Contact of which we are speaking, are the sincerely committed ones, and are already ritually involved. Thus, whatever Archetypal Contact they experience over and beyond the stated ritual celebrations not only brings additional benefit to the individuals involved, but enhances the efficacy of the institution. To drive these spontaneous and deeply personal contacts with the deity out of existence by trying to bring them under institutional control is clearly a diminution of sacredness, and an institutional mistake.

Again, we may note that Archetypal Contact is an experience characteristic of the state of mergence, not of its lack. Now organizationally, it is a commonplace fact that a member who is merged with the Archetypal Figure will unhesitatingly obey any command that purportedly comes from Him. Thus, even from the most cynical point of view, it can be seen that it is organizationally detrimental to impair mergence by forbidding its most intimate expression, while at the same time creating skepticism by the tacit admission that the institution does not trust the most sacred moments of its most committed members. Indeed, by this attempt to monitor and control the individual's contact with the Archetype to whom it has guided him, the institution forfeits its ability to communicate any experience of sacredness at all.

5. Growth to Excessive Size

Another reason for institutional decay is the sheer size to which the institution may grow. As long as it is limited to a small group, the intensity of religious recollection produces a degree of resonance that contributes to further archetypal contact, and even when it reaches moderate size, i.e., a few thousand members, a great deal of communication takes place in non-religious areas, leading back to shared confidences of religious experience, which, of course, is Archetypal Contact *by recall*. This, combined with their fervent expectation of the Ideal Society, produces visionary experiences in at least some of the members, which will presently be communicated to the entire fellowship, thereby intensifying the general sense of numinous involvement.

However, when the institution attains massive size, the inevitable contact with virtual strangers brings a steady lessening of communication. Some of the individuals met by any given subject will be uncongenial to him, some religiously insincere, others culturally dissimilar, and no matter how skillfully the organizers strive to maintain the integrity of a very large group, it loses its religious character rapidly. For a time it can be held together by the Archetypal Image *per se*, but presently even this central symbol will be seen from so many different perspectives, and in such different lights, that the ideal it originally personified falls into confusion and disrepute, simply by reason of the lack of any real intimacy among the majority of its adherents. Being unwilling or unable to converse with ease and confidence, their insights concerning the Archetype cannot be correlated, and disinterest follows the sense of disunity rising from this failure of communication.

The religious quality of the movement is further undermined by the inevitable struggles for ascendancy that are bound to take place, whether they are related to leadership, sectionalism, race, or economic class. These controversies will be veiled in theological terminology intended to make them seem to be matters of proper doctrinal interpretation: but those who understand what is going on will be filled with bitter enmity, and those who do not will be bored to death.

Finally, splinter groups will form along sectarian lines, and the process will repeat itself, simply by reason of the unwieldy size to which the group has grown.

6. Dilution of the Fellowship

Even in the early moments of its existence, a religious collectivity requires *some* professional leadership, if only to run errands. Typically, it involves much more than this: i.e., expertise in ritual, early contact with a revelator, some unique ability, or an unusual depth of commitment. Given the theological, or promotional, aspect of leadership, vastly more may be involved.

Leaving these things to one side for a moment, we remind ourselves that at this early and totally sincere stage of institutional or pre-institutional development, membership is by its very nature defined in terms of strongly numinous experience. Those who are members at this stage may have known the revelator and heard him speak, may have themselves had some kind of revelation, and at the very least have committed themselves to the movement in complete belief. This may be on the testimony of a close friend or relative who belonged to one of the groups just mentioned, or it may be the end result of long brooding on the problems to which the revelator speaks. Furthermore, *all* of these early adherents, no matter what other distinction may be drawn among them, share one massive fact in common: they are *sure*, with the sublimest of certainties, that Salvation is theirs; that their place in the Ideal Society is secure; that its coming involves no great delay; that whatever moral impediments might have kept them out of this Abode of the Blest have been removed; and that whatever price they have already paid, or must still pay for admission to it is little enough, in view of the bliss which will soon be theirs. Meanwhile, in the immediate present, their mergence with the Archetypal Figure who guarantees all of this is absolute, and each subject values the others because they too, have been redeemed, have known the Redeemer, and are citizens of His Kingdom.

For these True Believers, the New Morality is not merely a meeting of the Primary and Secondary Processes, but is a sacrament: it is not a duty, but a celebration. Accordingly, their unstinting practice of its tenets of mutual aid is productive of enormous symbolic impact for the embryonic institution, and along with their utter fearlessness, provides the dynamic for many conversions.

The leaders, meanwhile, however sincere they may have been at the outset, are all too prone to become ambitious. More than this, if they do not become so, they are likely to be displaced by individuals who are: see the material on the institution as a theological construct *supra*, in section II, C, 2, p. 227, surpa. As these leaders consolidate the influence which their position carries, they gradually lower the standards of membership, in the interest of obtaining a larger clientele. This is all too easy to do, since in the very nature of things there are bound to be differences of intensity, if not of sincerity, among the religious experiences of the truest of true believers. Moreover, when the faith of a member wavers, the others hasten to "edify" him i.e., build him up: moral lapses are forgiven when duly repented, and those untutored in the doctrine are promptly instructed in everything that has been declared, together with all that it implies. Consequently, when converts of slender experience are admitted, the true believers tend to embrace them with compassion, and to assume their sincerity as seekers, redoubling their efforts to imbue the newcomers with their own numinous certainty of the imminence of the Ideal Society.

But the process of dilution continues, until presently overt moral derelictions come to light among the newer members. The promoters quiet the outrage felt by the true believers by arguing the qualitative difference between even a totally committed follower who is nonetheless finite, and the infinite perfection of the Archetypal Figure, by this time solidly established as a historical personage.

As the institution burgeons, it is to be expected that numbers of reasonably sincere adherents will accumulate, who are nonetheless deficient in either numinous authenticity, or in belief, i.e., the expectation of such numinous experience. To accomodate their presence, the theologian-promoters will begin to define the fellowship of believers not as Those Who Have Been Saved, but as Those Who Are Seeking Salvation.

Sooner or later the ardor of the original True Believers cools. Perhaps not much, but the delay of the Ideal Society's coming, and the multiplication of various practical concerns, have their effect. Also, many of them die, so that their numbers carry less influence than at first. And so it is, that under the unremitting pressure of constant expansion, backed by a convenient missionary imperative, and coupled with official propaganda intended to stimulate guilts for the institution to absolve, its dominant atmosphere suffers a complete reversal. Instead of being a fellowship of the redeemed, among whom doubt is impossible and duplicity unthinkable, it now stands in contented laxity, its hope gone with its integrity, and proclaiming that We're All Poor Sinners Anyway.

This rationalization fulfills itself rapidly, both within the group and outside it: and as religious experience disappears from the institution, its pretended emphasis upon the religious quest becomes correspondingly vacuous.

E. The Institutional Reaction

1. Efforts to Produce Numinosity for its own Sake

When the leaders of a religious institution become fully aware of its obsolescence, their initial reaction is to attempt the artificial stimulation of the experience of numinosity. Such awareness is brought home to them by the failure of their promotional efforts to rouse any serious desire among the clientele for relationship with the Archetypal Figure.

Now numinosity, as we have seen, is the emotional accompaniment of energy release, which is to say, its movement from the unconscious, organic level, into conscious availability. This emotion, together with the energy it accompanies, is always brought into consciousness by some type of archetypal experience, i.e., an experience involving symbolic impact; and these experiences, always autistic when authentic, are precipitated by the presence of religious problems, as we have defined and described them. Such problems are brought to solution in the numinous experience, as repeatedly described and analyzed above. As we know, the emotion itself is a compound of supreme valuation and mystery: it is otherwise known as sacredness.

Of course, the archetypal image may be brought to the attention of a religious subject by the functionaries of an institution in such a way as to recall a former occasion of energy release, and so renew and revitalize his numinous emotion: but the attempt to generate sacredness simply for its own sake is self-evidently meretricious.

Since Archetypal Contact is the vehicle of numinosity in the institution, the leaders now try to increase the incidence of this experience, much as a business man would try to increase sales, so that the deity is kept before the public in a sort of advertising campaign. The essential artificiality of these efforts is evident in the emphasis upon the mysterious and uncanny aspects of the experiences generated, to the neglect of true problem solving. Nonetheless, since the Archetypal Contact which the institution typically makes available is itself the agency of some energy release, even these contrived efforts have some religious efficacy, until their essential falsity is exposed.

a. Ritual Proliferation

The first area where this may be observed is in the proliferation of ritual. Ceremonies for every occasion are developed, and elaborate precautions are taken to purify and refine their performance. Thus, the Parsis will use nothing but genuine sandalwood for the sacred fire upon which their shrunken faith is focussed. The Essenes stressed ritual bathing with complete immersion before doing anything important: the preoccupation of the Greek Orthodox clergy with costume is well-known, as is the Roman absorption in ritual appurtenances and procedures. In fact, it is the tendency of every liturgical system to become sacramentarian. Doctrinal reasons for every detail of action and object are advanced, with the clear implication that correctness of celebration will have a mechanical efficacy in producing a divine response. Certain precise moments or acts in the ritual drama are held to signalize the deity's appearance; e.g., the sound of a bell or the consecration of the host, and much is made of this supposed "presence" of the divine.[30] However, in the meantime the religious issues have migrated; secular agencies now provide solutions for the problems to which the rituals are addressed, so that the ceremonials have only an antiquarian interest, and the supposed ritual appearances of the god become commonplace and uneventful.

b. Epiphanies
Independent epiphanies of the deity will be arranged, outside the ritual structure, with attendant messages to the faithful wherever feasible, but always with maximal attention to credibility. The recipients of these synthetic epiphanies will be assisted to publicize them widely, and in the course of time will be beatified. Similarly, any event sufficiently unusual to be *interpreted* as supernatural will be thus classified, so that utterances and acts of the god will abound.

2. Manipulation of Religious Problems
Although the institution has for some time ignored the meeting of individual religious needs, and so lost the chance to

[30] The greater frequency of revelations coming to the prophets of both Islam and Mormonism when those movements were under fire, is well known.

It is interesting to remember that Plutarch, a priest of Apollo at Delphi, referred in several places to statues speaking and moving. (De Pythiae Oraculis, 8, 397E–398C, *Camillus*, 6, *De Fortuna Romanorum*, 5, 319A, *Coriolanus*, 38, 4). Although the institution he served was not a prophetic one, it was certainly dying: he wrote a long essay (*De Pythiae Oraculis*) to explain why the oracle no longer spoke in verse, and Plutarch was apparently supplying, in the passages cited, an apologetic for carefully stated speeches by the temple statuary.

We are further reminded of Mme. Blavatsky's various hoaxes to provide sensory percepts of supernatural apparitions for the edification of important converts to Theosophy, whose faith was weak. Cf. Williams, Gertrude Marvin, *Priestess Of The Occult, passim.*

deal with them, it now seeks to bring forward problems which it *can* solve, whether actually or ostensibly. While these may not be the problems felt by the clientele, at least they do give the impression that the institution is concerned with the welfare of the rank and file, and their reputed solution keeps the institution going for a while longer.

a. Problems of Nature Brought Back
Problems of nature are brought back. Although problems of nature are the first to gain solubility with the advance of science, and so migrate out of the religious category, they are easy to bring back: and miracles of healing and resuscitation appear, some based on unexplored psychic phenomena, and others on pure imposture. Any natural occurrence of a favorable character will be cited as evidence of divine favor, institutionally procured, and conversely, any natural disaster will be characterized as an expression of divine anger against whatever adversaries the institution may have.

b. Shift to a Metaphysical Emphasis
At the same time, the institution through its leaders, does everyting possible to inculcate the idea that supernatural, metaphysical, or post-mortem problems and rewards are the only significant ones. Here we find the stress upon original sin as an inherited taint that must be institutionally expunged, together with the explicit doctrine that designated ritual performances have a calculable effect upon the subject's status after death; here the insistence that some state of sinlessness can be attained within measurable time that will be valid for eternity, whether by making pilgrimage to Mecca, accumulating or eliminating Karma, or being baptized by the Holy Ghost; and here the doctrine that some paranormal state, such as glossalalia, is both psychically beneficial and cosmically meritorious. Underlying all these individual dogmas, of course, is the implicit premise that the only valid concern of any sensible person is his post-mortem status, as defined by the institution itself: and entailed by this assumption is the explicit teaching

that nothing could possibly be as important as having a numinous experience.

c. Negative Morality Stressed

Negative morality now receives its greatest emphasis, and indeed requires this context to make it fully comprehensible. What began as a shortcut to unusual merit for the enthusiastic, is now imposed upon the entire clientele. Its employment has a two-fold basis: to facilitate the production of guilt, and to perpetuate or create religious problems.

i. To Produce Guilt *The production of guilt* which the institution can then absolve is the ultimate motivation for many taboos of food, dress and custom. The prohibition of pork (Judaism, Islam), beef (Hinduism), drinking alcoholic beverages (Islam, Protestant fundamentalism), and kindred taboos may all have had some rational origin, but they end as part of a ritual system involving some form of confession and absolution, which gives the institution power over the individual.

Of course the production of guilt is not limited to the items mentioned. All aspects of negative morality are utilized in the effort to convince the religious subject of a desperate need for the institution's services. Indeed, *not* feeling a religious problem is often held up as evidence of religious insensitivity, and a condition of spiritual peril: and failing to feel sufficient religious ecstasy is similarly cited as a basis for guilt.

ii. To Perpetuate Problems *Perpetuation of problems* that should have migrated out of the religious realm is clearly the motive for other items of negative morality. Thus, early opposition to anaesthetics made illness and injury more fearsome and Heaven brighter: vaccination was opposed for the same reason, although in both cases the opposition was cloaked in rhetoric having to do with the temerity of tampering with divine decrees. The Jehovah's Witnesses oppose blood transfusions on theological grounds ("eating" blood is forbidden) that end in the same area, while Catholic opposition to contraception and that of Protestant fundamentalists to abortion keep the lower classes impoverished, despairing and devout.

iii. To Preclude Non-Religious Solutions   The precluding of non-religious solutions is the motive for a third area of negative morality. Thus, the *prohibition of learning* is a widespread technique for binding members to a meaningless institution. The Muslim burning of the library at Alexandria was encouraged to eliminate non-Koranic ideation. The use of the abacus was restricted to the clergy in Europe for some three hundred years, (1000–1300 A.D.), thereby making them a necessary part of every important business transaction, to say nothing of admitting them to fullest information about it. Hence it is not surprising to find that when the Arabs brought the zero, or cipher, to Europe from the Hindus in 1200 A.D., and so completed the "Arabic" systems of number notation, which was speedily replacing the Roman use of letters for this purpose, its use was immediately forbidden. Its general introduction would obviously have made the proprietors of the abacus less necessary; and so the use of this most essential of numerals was ecclesiastically proscribed for another three centures (1200–1500 A.D.), making its use clandestine, and giving rise to the meaning of "cipher" as "secret code."[31]

The *Index Librorum Prohibitorum* is intended to prevent the spread of ideas considered dangerous by the Catholic Church. The diehard opposition of this body in the recent past to the study of symbolic logic is matched by the intransigence of Protestant fundamentalists in rejecting evolution and depth psychology, and the Amish denial of formal education to their youth beyond the elementary grades is well-known. Less well-known, but even more directly illustrative of our point are the activities of the Publications Committee of the Christian Science Church, of which the stated duty is to keep out of circulation any literature whatever that takes an unfavorable position toward Christian Science.

[31] Fuller, Buckminster, *Nine Chains To the Moon* 2ed, Carbondale, Ill., Arcturus Press, 1966, pp. 138–140.

d. Archaic Cosmology Made Official

Insisting upon the acceptance of an archaic cosmology is a fourth way in which religious problems are manipulated by a dying institution. This strategy is adopted in an obvious attempt to discredit the progress of science, which is making traditional problems migrate out of the religious realm, and so rendering the institution obsolete. Moreover, if the mythos has become literalized, it may contain references and provisos which are nonsensical outside of an archaic context. Thus the rejection of Copernican astronomy and Darwinian evolution, and the long retention of Aristotelian cosmology all fall into place.

3. Effort to Control All Thought

As a logical extension of the last two items, as also of the effort to monitor numinosity, we find the dying institution going to extreme lengths to *control thought* in all its dimensions, although the effort is naturally focused on religious matters. The techniques of inquisition are familiar; employment of the confessional to ferret out ideas that have been pronounced heretical, and the declaration that spiritual deviancy is a civil crime, with consequent punishment by the secular authorities.

Another technique in the process of thought control is excommunication. Not only is this a denial of immortality to the one subjected to it, but since the sacred and the secular are so closely intertwined, it makes physical survival problematical, as all members of the society are forbidden to have any transactions with one who is under this ban.

A further aspect of thought control by a dying institution is denial of exit. Apostasy has always been institutionally viewed as the supreme spiritual transgression, and when an institution becomes convinced of its own deterioration, every effort will be made to prevent its happening at all. One might suppose that a thoroughly disenchanted subject might simply move out of an institution that he disliked, and that disapproved of him: but fear of the new institution into which he will no doubt move impels the rejected group to insist that he remain, and indeed to prevent his departure by physical means, even when this involves him in horrendous persecution. The result is a clientele of stoic and inarticulate unbelievers, whose only experience of the institution is that of a massive force for repression and fear, communicating at most a negative numinosity, and whose deities are now felt as problem gods. We see this mechanism illustrated in the flight of excommunicated persons into the witch cults of medieval Europe, and in the Church's determined efforts to bring them back for prosecution, as well as in the desperate efforts of dissidents to escape from the Communist regime in Russia today.

4. Incorporation of Successful Competitors

The next response to recognized obsolescence that we shall note is the effort of a declining institution to incorporate contemporary movements that are successful.

Plutarch of Chaeronaea (46–120 A.D.) was a priest of Apollo at Delphi throughout his career. His essay *Concerning Isis and Osiris* is a systematically conceived attempt to identify the Egyptian cult of these two deities with the religion of Dionysus, which had been made a part of the Delphic establishment a thousand years earlier, in order to quiet the maenadic excitement with which it was inflaming the country at that time. Since the Delphic oracle was steadily losing influence at the end of the first century A.D., while the Isis cult was spreading uncontrollably, the elaborate apologetic that Plutarch gives to the Egyptian religion, elsewhere officially deplored, becomes understandable.

In our own time we see the Methodist Church improbably giving countenance to Oral Roberts, while the Catholics make room for various "charismatic" sects, and the Episcopalians try to learn faith healing.

5. Claim of Being the Ideal Society

The final reaction to institutional obsolescence which requires notice is the institution's own representation of itself as the Ideal Society. As the environing secular society becomes increasingly chaotic by reason of the weakening of its religious structure, the institution, which formerly supplied the entire social complex with an authentic pattern of sacredness, is now reduced to the claim that it contains within itself all the values that were at first expected to redeem humanity: so that, instead of being the custodian of their archetypal source, it now purports to be the repository of everything that originally gave symbolic impact to that figure.

Indeed, in certain frames of reference, and for persons of unquestioning mind, it may even seem to be so. Order and mutual supportiveness are supposedly found within its confines, and the aesthetic appeal of its rituals stands in pleasant contrast to the stridencies of the society it has ceased to influence; while its claim of being the only valid channel to immortality makes it the antechamber of paradise for those who still accept its pretensions.

However, these claims are only believed by a small minority of the society; and while the thought control which the still powerful—but no longer religious—institution is able to exercise, precludes their overt denial, yet they are so patently exaggerated, even when made by implication alone, that by this posture the institution takes on an intra-mural quality which contradicts its true nature, reducing it to particularity, and making it merely a center for the certification of respectability.

F. At the Nadir

1. Recapitulation

We have already pointed out that the demise of a religious institution is never complete: it may mediate sacredness in unpredictable ways. However, when such decline is as complete as it can become, so that the institution purveys virtually no sense of numinosity, makes no conversions, can no longer inspire prayer with faith, produces no solutions, and when the archetype it enshrines structures no activity and releases no energy, the point is reached where its rituals are either ridiculous or repugnant, and its doctrines are entirely without credibility.

In this state of affairs, when what amounts to a vacuum has come to obtain in the religious realm, the environing society, deprived of its structuring authority, becomes fragmented and even atomized. Apparently it is a law of sociology that any vital society requires a powerful archetypal figure as its focal point.

Although this entire study might well be considered an exposition of the Archetypal Figure, let us review in this context the manner of its functioning, whereby its vitality is so essential to a society.

It is a personification of the values upon which society is based. When universally accepted, understood and revered,

—it guarantees the efficacy of a living morality;
—it dynamizes and inspires intense effort, for any valid achievement;
—it provides an alluring ideal;
—it permits no deviation from its moral tenets, and this by inherent imperative, rather than by any external coercion; like gravity, or the need to breathe;
—it provides an unalterable plan for life;
—it is the definition of sanity and health: and
—it is affirmed as the portrayal of true sacredness.

This archetypal ultimate is, in the nature of things, beyond any systematic proof, yet does not require it, being self-evident and psychically autonomous. It requires a genius of particular type to reveal it, flourishes best among and within a limited group of seekers or *appreciators*, whose problem it has solved, and requires an institution to represent it adequately.

However, when the custodial institution has frittered it away by endless reinterpretation, the society it has structured is left with no inner authority. Lacking authentication for its values, it becomes an arena where all value systems compete. Other exploiters now do everything they can to accentuate this situation, in the interest of keeping the people from having any firm convictions that might enable them to resist fraudulent presentations, and political enemies seek to discredit all firm dedication to anything that would make for social cohesiveness, or justify resolute social action. This chaotic lack of religiously authenticated values in the society is reflected in the moral vacillation of individuals, rising out of their total confusion of priorities.

2. Popular Superstitions

When this point is reached, the yearning for sacredness is displayed in the acceptance of popular superstitions by increasing numbers of people, including some members of the educated classes.

Perplexing as this seems at first, it is apparent upon reflection that many of them are seeking solutions for religious problems which are always a part of the human condition. Rumors of miraculous solutions filter upward from the lower ranks of society, and lacking any authenticating alternative, those in religious extremity turn to various preposterous beliefs that have been present all along, but have hitherto been regarded as beneath notice. Thus, flying saucers, ouija boards, astrology, poltergeists, mediums, ESP, and all manner of paranormal psychic experiences, to say nothing of drug-induced revelations, attain disproportionate prominence in the popular mind.

Nor are those in religious extremity the only ones who embrace these popular superstitions; there are, of course, those who are titillated by the mysterious, and are looking for a cheap thrill: but beyond both of these are many who are searching for some supreme value upon which to bestow their total commitment, but who confuse importance and worth with the merely supernatural.

3. Cultic Religion

Along with heightened acceptance of these random superstitions, and indeed overlapping them,[32] is membership in cults. Such membership flourishes when archetypal authority

---

[32] Such systems as Rosicrucianism and Psychiana do (or formerly *did*) a mail-order business, and have no group meetings.

declines, being inversely proportional to the vitality of what-ever religious institution is central to the culture.

The importance of cultic religion in the cycle of institutional evolution is so great as to require a section of its own.

G. What The Nadir Is: The Cultic Phenomenon

1. Introductory

Cultic religion is truly the nadir of the religious cycle, and of social evolution as well; for here, in the midst of the greatest technological accomplishments and humanitarian advances, we find masses of people so throughly out of touch with the world of scientific achievement, and even with the religion which (a) has structured its social applications, and (b) is supposed to offer compensation for its failures, that they can be manipulated by some present day medicine man, operating with exactly the same techniques of chicanery and imposture as were employed by his counterpart in primitive society.

Cults are extremely difficult to discuss, inasmuch as they exhibit many similarities to other religious institutions on the surface, yet differ radically from them in their outcome. Fur-thermore, distinctions that will identify cultic religion must often be made by value judgments. Fortunately, such judg-ments are so obvious in most cases as to produce immediate agreement. Moreover, all investigation of religious experience involves the analysis of subjective states, either reported by the subject who experiences them, or deduced by the investigator's interpretation: and this analysis depends upon some decision as to whether such states have or have not been of benefit to the subject.

Let us, then, attempt to bring the defining characteristics of cultic religion into review.

2. Defining Characteristics of Cultic Religion

a. An Insincere Founder

The most radically interpretative and illuminating statement that can be made about a cult is that it has an insincere founder.

The insincerity is thrown into high relief once we become fully aware of the complete variance between the founder's attitude toward the institution he has created, and that of its members. The latter view it as the veritable home of their souls, and the vehicle of their salvation, and make all manner of sacrifices to fulfill its declared purposes. The leader, on the other hand, no matter what the piety of his utterance, or the manner of his rationalization, obviously views it as the agency whereby the members can be most efficiently exploited, along whatever lines he may choose. He is the one who demands the sacrifices, whereby he is able to support an opulent life style, and indulge whatever drive for power he may have.

In many cases, and those the most typical, the promoters have no numinous experience at all until the movement clicks, at which time they are numinously affected by its success, and begin to take their own pronouncements seriously.

In other cases, e.g., the Jehovah's Witnesses, the promoter may indeed have had a numinous experience, or at least an idealistic orientation at the outset, but at some point along the way he has yielded to the allurements of power and gain that have opened before him, so that his ethicality at the time of the cult's success is altogether negative. Of course, the truth of such a claim of numinous revelation would be interesting to check, but it is frequently impossible to do this, although in certain instances, e.g., Mormonism and Christian Science, it has been done. We should note that the presence of some elaborate literary record of the alleged revelation does not in any way guarantee its archetypal status, or for that matter, even its occurrence.

By accepting the need to evaluate the founder's motives, often clearly stated in some obscure source, unacknowledged or repudiated by the movement in its efflorescence, we are enabled to distinguish cultic groups from the multitude of weird and misguided prophetic movements that have led their adherents into purposeless or detrimental activities, but are in fact based upon the genuinely numinous revelations of ignorant or psychotic founders.

b. A New Revelation

The second characteristic of cultic religion is *a new revelation*. This differentiates it from that of the sects, which are schismatic groups within an existing tradition. The content of such a revelation may be anything at all, and attempts to generalize in this area are ill advised. However, a few observations can validly be made.

i. The "revelation" offered by a cult leader will contain the purported solution to whatever problem is central to the clientele he wishes to approach.

ii. It will represent that solution as inhering in, stemming from, or being purveyed by, the leader himself, with his divine authority either explicitly proclaimed or carefully hinted at. By this device, the founder is able to represent himself as being either divine in his own right, as having had contact with divinity, i.e., as being a true revelator, or as possessing divine powers, however obtained.

iii. Although cultic "revelations" that promise some future advantage are not wanting, the prototypical solution is for the leader to offer an immediately present benefit, supposedly miraculous, that is made available by the application of some little known or generally unexplored scientific technique, principally from the areas of psychology (healings, self-development, ESP, supposed contact with the dead) and sociology (material support, social resonance, or political power in a commune). The type of benefit offered, always with an aura of the miraculous, will naturally depend on the ability and experience of the promoter, as well as upon the needs of the clientele.

iv. When the "revelation" does predict some cosmic event, whether for good or ill, it is likely to be proclaimed as near at hand, thereby gaining immediate attention, and rousing definite fear or hope among the credulous, which the cult is of course programmed to allay or exploit, as the case may be. If the predicted cataclysm does not occur, the cult can either take credit for averting it, or rationalize its failure through the familiar channels of theology.

Moreover, such predictive revelations, whether cosmic or personal, are typically the hollowest of promises: transcendent powers, supernatural insight, vast wealth, the restoration of health, or a new social order, are blandly guaranteed, with no expectation of fulfillment. Some escape clause will be provided to give theology a basis for its inevitable apologetic: your faith was insufficient, greater contributions are necessary, political conditions elsewhere make it impractical now, or, simplest and most irrefutable of all, the Hidden Masters changed their minds, or the powers of evil are too strong as yet . . .

c. The Abandonment of Selfhood

The third characteristic of cultic religion is *the abandonment of selfhood*. Now although exhaustion of the ego is a feature of any conversion experience, and although mergence *per se* has been defined as the state in which a religious subject is not aware of any difference between his own will and that imputed to the personification he has made, yet in Prophetic religions both of these experiences terminate in a new dimension of selfhood, in which the subject is not only able to structure his activity with rational purpose, but is free to do so, commonly on a higher and more effective level than before.

However, in cultic religion, the mergence is with the cult leader; and while he may have some archetypal force for the individual member, his motives and abilities fall far short of the archetypal level. Also, he is totally committed to the promotion of his own advantage, however this may be defined or implemented. The result is that the cult member, in return for the solution of his religious problem, is deliberately reduced to a selfless puppet, required to undertake anything the leader demands, *and this upon the pulse of his own religious commitment*.

This paralysis of selfhood is accentuated by the frequent cultic requirement that all vital affect must be directed to the cult leader alone, so that close fellowship with other members is largely inhibited (Father Divine) or even systematically discouraged, when it is discovered (Jim Jones). Thus the beginnings of a personal initiative which might be generated by communication and cooperation are effectively precluded.

The obliteration of selfhood that is so commonly found among cult members is the more pronounced because they are characterized by ego weakness prior to their involvement with the cult, being people who have been, for whatever reason, unable to manage their own lives.

d. An Intramural Society

The fourth characteristic of cultic religion is that it manifests itself in *an intramural society*. In this respect it shows a marked resemblance to Ethnic religion, and we have elsewhere referred to it as the New Ethnos. However, in an Old Ethnic religion, the ethnos is the total society, and fully recognized as such, with all human groupings outside its confines being regarded as somehow deficient in reality, as "lesser breeds without the law"; whereas in a cult, the intramural group is self-consciously withdrawn from a larger total society, acknowledged as entirely real, but felt as either insensitive or hostile.

This intramural aspect may be quite informal, and altogether *de facto*, by reason of the eccentricity of some cultic belief (spiritualism, Theosophy) or practice (Hare Krishna): it may rise from the cultic headquarters constituting a refuge or welfare center for helpless people (Father Divine, Maharaj Ji): or it may be the result of overt restraint, so that escape is impossible (Moonies, Jonestown, the Berlin Wall, early Mormonism).

In any event, the intramural aspect of cultic religion serves a number of purposes, all advantageous to the leader.

It provides the most favorable conditions for the cultic solution to work. Indeed, in cults where the solution is not countenanced by the larger society (free love, polygamy, communism) the intramural group affords the *only* environment where the solution can be implemented.

It provides the ideal setting in which the leader can propagandize his "revelation" and present additions to it.

It removes the members from contact with hostile comments and criticisms of the cult, and at the same time generates a social resonance that is favorable. In this connection, we may note that in those cults where overt brainwashing is practiced, the intramural society provides the location where this is possible.

It creates an economic and political power structure which the leader can throw into action at any time.

It facilitates exploitation: and with this observation we move to our final point.

e. Exploitation

The final characteristic of cultic religion that we shall note, and the most important one, is *exploitation*. In certain circumstances, this is altogether obvious. Credulous and suggestible people are overpersuaded to give money they cannot afford to Oral Roberts on the promise of future prosperity to be gained thereby; or to Kathryn Kuhlman, out of fear that by failure to do so, they may "lose their healing." Early converts to Mormonism were required to donate their property to the movement; all of them labored relentlessly, with heavy tithes demanded at every turn. The women were kept busy breeding, as well, right up to the biological possible, and the Danites rode them down and shot them when they tried to escape. The Moonies beg in the streets, and are not allowed to go home. In Jonestown, the members not only had to contribute such property as they had, but their social security cards as well, and were then required to die, to keep the intramural system intact. The list goes on and on.

Yet the writer has often been asked how cult practices can be called exploitative, when the members affirm them so completely, or when they convey obvious benefits. How, for instance, is an adherent of Father Divine exploited by being given food, shelter, and clothing in return for his labor, when this is more than he or she was ever able to manage before? Or how is some abandoned drughead exploited when Maharaj Ji takes him off the habit, even at the price of his affluent allowance? Or, going a step farther, how is a wealthy adherent of Meher Baba exploited, even at the price of very large sums of money, when she is given a feeling of cosmic significance, and is heartily in favor of her situation?

First of all, there are definite considerations of morality that utterly proscribe taking advantage of another person's credulity for one's own gain, and this is what the cult leader does. The eventual end of delusion must come to the cultic adherent, and with it a sense of betrayal and tragedy that no one should be forced to undergo, least of all in the name of religion: but this does not answer all the questions.

Such indubitable benefits as the cults purvey to their adherents are indeed beneficial, and this is not to be disputed. However, *these benefits are conferred at the price of keeping the adherent fixated in the situation where he needs them.* In short, *the religious problem is not allowed to migrate.* This is the core of religious exploitation, and it is the central fact of cultic religion.

3. Institutional vs. Functional Cultism

In just this connection, a cautionary note is needed. Numbers of exploitative enclaves are to be found within the ranks of traditional religion, promoted by charismatic leaders, and displaying all the characteristics of cults except the new revelation.

Thus, the healing cults of Oral Roberts and Kathryn Kuhlman were ostensibly Christian. The Children of God, which began as a Jesus movement, is perhaps the outstanding example of such an affiliation. Other groups, epitomized by that of Marjoe Gortner, claiming no unique revelation, and offering no special benefit other than a perfervid salvationism, yet exploiting their adherents shamelessly, are always awaiting discovery by the persistent investigator.

These groups typically feature some sectarian emphasis, given by the promoter, whereby orthodoxy is reinterpreted to his own advantage. This replaces the new revelation *per se*, but otherwise they display all the characteristics of cults.

As cults, such groups are *institutionally* atypical: having more the formal appearance of sects; yet their cultic impact is undeniable. In the discussion that follows, whenever general references are made to cults, it is our intention to include such groups as these.

Having thus presented the defining characteristics of cultic religion, it becomes our task to consider its impact upon the individuals who are swept in such numbers into the groups thus characterized.

Religious experience *per se* has already been analyzed in depth: hence we shall examine its cultic manifestations from the converging perspectives of the people who are attracted to such groups, the nature of their problems, the personality of the cult leader, and the characteristics of cultic institutions; and attempt to show how each of these is related to the solutions which give the cults their dynamic.

4. Characteristics of Adherents

a. Religious Alienation

The initial characteristic of cultic adherents to claim our attention is their alienation from the background religion. Whether they have themselves rejected that institution, and left it voluntarily, or whether the institution has rejected them, it is axiomatic that they have received no solutions for their problems there, but that the problems remain insistently present. Furthermore, all are at last rejected by the institution, despite their clear and present need for its services.

The first group to be noted as having turned away from the Pseudo-Ethnic religious structure on their own initiative is that of the highly intelligent who see its weaknesses clearly, and in depth. Although we do not ordinarily think of intelligent people as being cult members, a surprising number are to be found there, and we must remind ourselves that no one ever becomes so intellectualized as to be immune to religious problems or to numinous experience: Swedenborg, Arthur Conan Doyle, Stewart Edward White and C. D. Broad are names that come readily to mind as illustrating this point. A sincere commitment to their own numinous experience, which found no acknowledgement in the traditional churches drove these men into spiritualistic involvement; and Theosophy, Ba Haiism, New Thought and the Meher Baba group all have adherents who are truly intellectual.

At the opposite end of the intellectual spectrum are the deeply ignorant, who abandon the traditional churches because they simply cannot grasp their complex and often abstruse theology, which may have, despite its intricacies, a good deal of validity.

Moreover, they cannot grasp the religious directives for scientific and social measures that might well enable them to solve their own problems, and so provide them with a truly valid religious solution. Their neurotic indecision, combined with their religious conditioning, is such that nothing short of a literal miracle can break them out of their psychic apathy. Thus their religious alienation extends out into the society which the religion has structured, and in which other people get along quite acceptably. This is why those who are too ignorant to participate in such values as the Pseudo-Ethnic society does indeed make available, also feel the typical cultic hostility toward its religion, which will be discussed in due course.

However: without trying to classify them further at this point, we return to the undoubted fact that cultic adherents are originally individuals for whom the traditional institutions have failed to provide needed solutions to religious problems.

Nor is this the whole story of religious alienation. While certain groups may reject the Pseudo-Ethnic religious structure, at last it rejects them, and others along with them, who may need its services even more. In one way or another, all who presume to differ with the religious power structure in any way are branded as unworthy, by this self-constituted arbiter of moral values. This may be quite explicit, as with the intellectuals, whose criticisms are most trenchant, or less so, in the case of the ignorant, but all who are less than enthusiastic in affirming the religious institution are given some label, subtly or otherwise, which is indicative of negative value.

Furthermore, the criteria of affirmation are very stringent: the officially recognized problems are held to be the only ones properly within the range of religious consideration, and secondly, the numinosity of the power structure, i.e., the religious institution itself, must be fully accepted and enthusiastically acclaimed. Conformity or rejection are the only alternatives offered, whatever be the magnitude of institutional deficiency.

Moreover, many people are to be found within the cults who never wanted to abandon the background religion, but who have been rejected by it nonetheless. One such group is made up of *those who are clearly guilty of some overt moral fault.* Whereas the obvious function of an Old Ethnic religion is to weed out and reject those who are unacceptable in terms of the ritual morality, that of a Prophetic religion is to redeem and rehabilitate those who have fallen into error: to impart the Prophetic morality to any who have forgotten it, and to educate them in its practice. However, at the Pseudo-Ethnic stage of the religious cycle, we have the Prophetic theory, but the Old Ethnic practice; instead of redeeming the wayward, they are completely rejected, except in the rarest of cases. Hence we have the clear-cut and overt criminal, of the type represented by Malcolm X, who was completely untouched by any orthodox religion, but who responded to the organized hostility of the Black Muslims, and became an effective personality within that group.

Also in this category are those who are obviously immoral, although not always criminal: the violators of the sex mores, the dishonest and the irresponsible. Such persons are virtually out of touch with organized religion, although some of them find their moral confusion a religious problem; yet as Pseudo-Ethnic usage goes, they are religious rejects.

Then too, we have the enormous numbers of those who have become addicted to alcohol or drugs and so find themselves totally outside the pale of religious respectability. Yet all of these find acceptance, and some degree of rehabilitation in the cults, whatever be the price they pay for it.

b. Inability to Qualify

All kinds of people are to be found in the cults, and they bring all kinds of problems with them; yet some of these problems are centrally characteristic; so much so, that cult members can, in large part, be described, if not completely identified by the problems that they have. Despite the wide range of personality types represented, and the great veriation in social backgrounds displayed, it is an obvious fact that the most typical cult members come from the lower classes; and this remains true, even when we take account of the great numbers of middle class youth who are to be found in the cults today. However, if we revise this generalization, and speak instead of *an inability to qualify in some area that is important to them*, we shall be more accurate. This inability can be observed in several areas.

i. Economically Pursuant to what was just said about their coming from the lower classes, we note that the outstanding area where cultic adherents have been unable to qualify is the economic. With all due allowance for wealthy adherents in such groups as Christian Science, Theosophy, Spiritualism, and the Eastern cults, their total numbers can only be a fraction of those who have followed various miracle mongers in the hope of obtaining either immediate assistance or eventual improvement in the economic area, as witness the followers of Father Divine, Jim Jones, Prophet Jones, or the Black Muslims, not to mention Aimee McPherson and the Jehovah's Witnesses. But simple enumeration aside, certainly the economically disabled are a prominent factor in the total cult movement.

Unemployables for whatever reason—illiteracy, a physical or a language handicap, low intelligence, a criminal record, or membership in an unpopular minority—all are accepted in cult groups, and such abilities as they do have are utilized somehow, always to the advantage of the cult leader. The temporarily or technologically unemployed, who are disgruntled and desperate, are represented proportionately. Victims of prejudice or circumstance are of course part of the list: but suffice it to say, that without listing the reasons in greater detail, cultic adherents are strongly characterized by the inability to qualify in the economic area.

ii. Physically It is an obvious generalization about cultic adherents that they suffer from problems of nature. Along with unemployability, with its economic problems, and of course as an aspect of this, is the incidence of outright physical handicaps among them. The healing cults are among the more prominent cultic manifestations, comparable to those providing economic maintenance: Oral Roberts, Kathryn Kuhlman and Mary Baker Eddy are names that occur immediately to any student of cults, and the self-evident field for their activities is found among people with physical defects, although their successes naturally stem from treating ailments with a psychic origin. The lame, the halt, the blind, the overtly afflicted and the chronically ill: the aging, and persons who have or fear they have, some incurable malady, are the natural clientele for any miracle monger. Beyond the reach of science, they are yet adjured to find their help there; and outside of this uncaring advice, their problems are almost totally ignored by the decadent institutions of mainline religion.

iii. Intellectually Although cultic adherents are not universally ignorant, certainly the inability to qualify on intellectual grounds, in whatever area the disqualification takes place, would characterize many of them. There are the technologically inadequate, whether uneducated or ineducable, for whom competition in a mechanized economy is out of the question; there are those whose religious alienation is the result of their inability to comprehend theological presentations which are found lucid and convincing by others who hear them; and there are those who are simply baffled by the world they live in. The claims which the cults make of being able to impart cosmic insight (Theosophy, The Great I Am, Psychiana, Rosicrucianism) are indicative of a widespread feeling of insecurity at this point. Even if a person is employed, is not economically dependent, and has a standard of living not conspicuously inferior to that of his neighbors, the inability to evaluate, or even to comprehend the implications of, social and scientific advances which others *seem* to understand, may leave him baffled and uneasy, with an intense longing for certainty to which the cults are quite ready to pander. Thus, although he is still entirely unable to participate in any part of the scientific enterprise, he is made to feel that he is a part of great things when some magic formula is made available to him.

Along with those who are aware of their intellectual shortcomings, we must take account of those who have lived by intellectual pretense. The pseudo-intellectuals in any society constitute a group illustrating with peculiar clarity the inability to gain acceptance at the level desired. The partly educated, the *soi-disant* poet or critic of society, all persons with enough insight to appreciate intellectual prestige, but not enough to understand intellectual effort—such individuals may attain a considerable degree of local recognition, but not the acceptance of the real intellectuals, with whom they wish to be associated. Thus they profess interest in fields of knowledge that are increasingly esoteric, moving from psychology to ESP, and on into the occult, and finally joining a cult wherein physical science is subordinated to correspondence-course "metaphysics", all as a result of their desire to feel themselves included in the company of the community's most advanced thinkers.

iv. Personally Another area in which cultic adherents have been unable to qualify is the personal. Although some of them have found acceptance in groups, they have been unable to form satisfying personal relationships, and have remained essentially friendless, because of traits that make them personally unlikeable. They may be socially unskilled, ignorant, or

neurotic to such an extent that they make others uncomfort-
able, or they may be avoided simply because they are incapable
of communication in emotional areas.

Indeed, it is characteristic of cultic adherents in general that
they have had so many disappointments in this area that they
no longer believe in their own ability to find any satisfying
personal intimacy, nor even in the possibility that relationships
involving such intimacy can exist at all.

v. Socially For anyone familiar with cults, it goes without
saying that their adherents have been unable to qualify *socially*.
Reasons for such failure naturally vary from person to person,
and are as numerous as the people involved; but in addition to
the disqualifications we have already considered, which, of
course, show up in terms of social non-acceptance, there are
two other contributing factors which must be mentioned;
minority status, and non-cooperation.

(a) Minority Status The fact of social rejection on account of
racial or national origin is so familiar as to need only the barest
mention to include it as a characteristic of the cultic personality.
However, other minority groups, less obviously constituted
and even more definitely rejected are to be found. Thus, the
excessively prosperous may, by some failure of public relations, have every advantage purchasable, but not the goodwill
of the populace which they desire and may conceivably merit,
at least on certain grounds. Again, members of certain occupations not admired by the respectable will be socially handi-
capped, and this not always rationally: for along with the
prostitute, the gambler and the racketeer, whose activities are
socially deleterious, we see that fullest social acceptance may be
denied to the junk dealer and the horse trainer, whose activities
are in no way harmful. Although these people may enjoy a
considerable level of prosperity, they experience a social exclusion almost as complete as that met by the scrubwoman and the
shine boy, whose occupations are similarly innocuous, but
whose poverty is all too apparent.

(b) Non-Cooperation   One of the amazing phenomena of our century is the presence of great numbers of middle-class youth in cult movements whose professed goals and day-to-day activities are entirely at variance with the backgrounds and prospects these young people have known.

Even when we have taken account of every cultic technique of entrapment and restraint, there remains a substantial number of such young people, who have chosen to abandon their selfhood in these movements.

The reasons for their voluntary immolation are only partly understood, but it is clear that they reach very deeply into the culture of the moment. William J. Peterson, in an otherwise shallow book, *Those Curious New Cults,*[33] lists nine causes of cultic involvement by American youth: (1) Disillusionment with America, (2) Dehumanization by science, (3) Advent of the drug culture, (4) Future fright, (5) Breakdown of the family, (6) Popular culture, rock music and cynical literature, (7) Psychology and the occult, (8) Decline of the Church and (9) The ecology crisis.

While all of these doubtless play some part in the pathetic and gullible quest of these young people for redemption, it is obvious that some of them are a good deal more salient than others. Thus, disillusionment with America on various grounds, but principally by reason of the Vietnam War, is clearly a factor: so is the drug culture. What the connection between these may be cannot be adjudicated here. The breakdown of the family is surely a factor in the disorientation of today's youth, and so is the decline of the Church. Preoccupation with the occult is probably an aspect of this decline, since archetypal experience is bound to increase as the sense of crisis grows, while at the same time, the institutional defenses against such imagery are diminished. But whatever the causes of their disaffection, they have focussed their resentments on the political entity *per se*, and have carried their protests to lengths that are completely unacceptable—promiscuity, homo-

---

[33] Keats Publishing Co., New Canaan, Conn., 1973, pp. 4–10.

sexuality, uncleanliness, drug addiction, and the refusal to work. This total withholding of cooperation with the elementary obligations of social participation has, in turn, brought about their social rejection to such a degree that efforts of reform on their part are given no credence, and attempts to reenter the mainstream of society are effectively blocked, even when such efforts are made.

Finding one's place in society is never easy, even when every effort is made to meet its requirements. It is still more difficult to become socially rooted on some basis that makes room for personal preferences, desires and uniqueness. Hence when deliberate attempts are made to flaunt a counter-cultural pattern of existence, the result is predictable—a disqualification from the mainline society that is virtually complete, even when the mood of protest is over, and efforts are made to demonstrate a return to responsibility.

Nor is this exclusion simply prejudicial; the youth who have been exploring the by-ways of counter-culture may be diseased, addicted to drugs or alcohol, in flight from some criminal charge, or simply burned out by a habit they claim to have overcome. Even if none of these disabilities apply, they still need to internalize the basic requirements of life in society: this always requires practice, often take time, and proof of it is universally demanded.

So it is that they find their way into the cults, where acceptance is immediate, guidance and direction are detailed, and demands upon the ego much less. The function of such membership on the road back to respectability has been widely recognized: the Jesus movements, the Meher Baba cult, and the Divine Light cult of Maharaj Ji have served this end. However, for some of the members, whose disillusionment with the tensions of industrial society is more complete, the cults simply provide an opportunity to drop out, by offering a radically different life-style: this seems to be a part of the attraction of the Moonies, and certainly of the Hare Krishna cult, recently joined by Henry Ford III.

One thing should be definitely noted. Although frustrations, tensions and perplexities confront all of today's youth, and although cultic involvement, with or without a counter-cultural preamble, is only one form of the maladjustments into which they can fall (e.g., crime), yet a solid and reassuring majority of today's youth manage to mature with nothing worse happening to them than the usual readjustments of the moral code which are made by every new generation. They get into the same scrapes their parents did, albeit with greater complexities, and get out the same way—with belated chagrin, some parental help, and a few scars.

In short, the ones who find their way into the cults exemplify the generalization we are presently making: an inability to qualify, in the social dimension.

c. Hostility

Another notable characteristic of cultic adherents is their pervasive *hostility*. Since they have been unable to qualify socially, and have then been rejected by the religious institution which might have been expected to help them, this negative attitude is not hard to understand. Let us look at it a little more closely.

i. Background Religion Seen as an Obstacle   The background religion is seen by the cultic adherent as itself problematic—an obstacle. Since hostility is essentially obstacle-removing behavior, its appearance in the present situation is implicit. As the voice of society, which offers the false alternative of conformity or rejection, the religious institution is *feared*, and it is a psychological commonplace that what is feared is hated.

ii. Expression of Hostility Forbidden   The expression of hostility is forbidden by the power structure, which is what the Pseudo-Ethnic religious institution has become. We are all familiar with the relative immunity to criticism that religious institutions enjoy, even at the present time. When we add to this, the insistence often expressed through institutional channels, and echoed by persons of religious sincerity, that any attitude toward an enemy except love is wrong, that only as we learn to appreciate those whose interests are in conflict with our own are we dealing with them on a "mature" basis, etc., we have a situation which is extremely protective of the status quo in general, and the religious institution in particular. Obviously, this increases the frustration and hostility of anyone who has been unable to qualify in the society, and is alienated from its religion.

iii. Unexpressed Hostility Inhibits When not expressible as obstacle removing behavior, hostility becomes an inner-psychic problem, in that it *inhibits the ability to love*, since the Eros cannot flow until environmental obstacles have been removed. The congruence of this fact with the failure of cultic adherents to make good personal relationships, noted earlier, is thus seen to be more than coincidental. Moreover, this characteristic hostility will necessarily be repressed, prior to the entry of the religious subject into a cult.

iv. Cults are Vehicles of Social Protest The ubiquitous hostility which characterizes cult members is reflected in the ritual expressions of the cultic institution. These reveal the cult as a vehicle of social protest, whether such protest is directed against the existing political entity *simpliciter*, or against the religion that structures it.

v. Cultic Rituals Perpetuate Hostility As these rituals are celebrated, the repressed hostility of the adherent is restored to consciousness. The resultant catharsis might be expected to free him of the hostility by which he is dominated, but in the cultic situation it frequently has the opposite effect, so that he may never again relinquish his hostility to everything outside the cult. That is: although he finds emotional clarity in the cultic rituals, and although his repressed frustrations, by being restored to consciousness, are given access to the ego, and thus should be able to find appropriate expression in its adaptive behavior, yet the rituals offer so much support for his hostility that instead of letting go of it, he finds it religiously sanctioned, and clings to it. If the religious problem were allowed to migrate, such a subject would stand a chance of becoming able to structure his adaptive behavior in ways that might eventually circumvent whatever obstacles, institutional or otherwise, had brought him to this pass, until finally he became able to embrace the environment, i.e., to love. However, by both ritual and doctrine his cultic exploiters make certain that he remains fixated in the recitation of his problems, and thus continues to need the cultic solution.

d. They Find Selfhood Burdensome

Another important characteristic of cult members is their insistent sense of their own selfhood as burdensome. As already noted, one of the defining characteristics of cultic religion *per se* is the abandonment of selfhood by its members. The present observation is of course related to this earlier one, although not entailed by it.

As we note the willingness of cultic adherents to resign from the effort to create and employ an ego-structure, i.e., to organize their personalities along lines of practicality, the reader is referred to earlier discussions of this phenomenon, in connection with inner-psychic problems, in Part Three, III, C, 4, c, (pp. 168–186), and in Part Four, II, C, 3, (pp. 234–235, supra), in the consideration of the personality types of those who accept institutional conversion. The phenomena there described are met to an even more pronounced degree among persons who join the cults.

At the risk of some repetition, let us review the aetiology of this characteristic, all but universal among cult members, noting as we do so, that all reasons advanced are rooted to some extent in the nature of the Pseudo-Ethnic religious complex.

i. Lack of Meaningful Religious Experience   Being filled with hostility which they are not permitted to discharge, cultic adherents, (or those who are about to become so), are *ipso facto* unable to behave lovingly, and their hostility is repressed, so that their instinctual forces are locked within the id, and they are able to produce only a minimal amount of "drive" or personal energy. The lack of this in a severely competitive society is obviously a severe handicap. Moreover, its relation to their religious alienation is implicit, since they have been unable to obtain the kind of religious experience that would relieve this psychic stasis.

When the undifferentiated energy of the organism enters awareness as discernible instinctuality, we have the primordial appearance of love and hate. Their structured expression, it will be remembered, is to be understood as either environment embracing, or obstacle removing behavior. Until the obstacles are removed, however, or the subject's attitude toward them revised, the more profound structuring of his energy as love cannot take place, for he will not embrace an environment that is vitiated by obstacles. The enormous importance of valid religious experience in releasing psychic energy becomes evident at this point, since the central fact of such experience is the appearance of an Archetypal personification, who shows the subject how to deal with his problem; either by removing the obstacle, or by ceasing to regard it as such.

Both aspects of the id are thus unlocked: the obstacle removing behavior is either structured or rendered unnecessary, and the environment embracing behavior is made available. But both of these turn out at last to be, quite simply, constructive, thoughtful *work*: for it is thus that obstacles are removed, and thus that the environment is embraced! The tremendous dynamic of religious symbolism in making this possible can hardly be exaggerated.

The cult member, however, has missed this, for reasons under discussion, and so remains immured in whatever his religious problem is.

ii. Native Inferiority   We have already noted certain areas in which cult members are unable to quality. Many of them have less than average ability, which is certainly pertinent to their feeling of selfhood as burdensome. They are basically deficient in finding socially acceptable ways of channelling their id drives into motor expression. Phrased another way, they lack, or at least fail to demonstrate, the intelligent originality which makes consciously directed action effectual, even when they have any energy that might be available for goal-seeking behavior. They have weak ego structures; possibly because they have never had an adequate ego to lean on. Moreover, such people are at a still greater disadvantage in a society where science is glorified to the extent that it is in the Pseudo-Ethnic situation, since scientific pursuits presuppose both personal energy and its organized application. The demands which all of them must nonetheless meet in the world as it is, force the awareness of their own deficiencies upon them, and intensify their sense of independent selfhood as burdensome. The making of decisions, the structuring of their energies, the putting forth of consistent effort for the attainment of definite goals—these are acts to which they are enjoined, but of which they are for the most part incapable—and of which the cult leaders are waiting to relieve them.

iii. Institutionally Related Guilt In addition to the anxiety they feel by reason of their various incapacities, cult members in general are suffused with guilt: and not merely on account of the routine peccadilloes that maladjusted people are prone to commit. Some of them are conscious of failure because an ideal selfhood which they are still able to conceive is no longer available to them. Others, by reason of their neurotic conditioning, become guilty whenever they initiate any purposive activity at all. Most impressive, however, in the guilt patterns of cultic adherents, are two related facts, with which we are already familiar: (1) They have called into question the massive authority of the whole Pseudo-Ethnos, by the very fact of their presuming to insist that they do, in reality, have problems with which the prevailing religion is unfitted to cope; the problematic quality of which it may deny; or the solution to which it may even forbid. Not unnaturally, the institutional response is one of unmistakable censure. (2) As we have repeatedly pointed out, they have been, *de facto*, rejected by that religion, in varying degrees of official pronouncement. And guilt as a psychic symptom follows social rejection just as surely as rejection follows guilt.[34]

The lack of meaningful religious solutions, discussed a couple of sections earlier, is of course clarified by these observations.

When the above characteristics are viewed cumulatively, the statement that cult members find selfhood burdensome is seen to emerge as their summary, and to be largely explanatory of the irrational eagerness with which such people abandon their critical faculties in acts and programs of literally "selfless" immolation, within the cults.

iv. Neurosis Neurosis as a factor inhibiting purposeful activity has been discussed already. It has its rise in repressed fear of irrational disapproval of whatever activity the subject wants most to undertake, coming from some important authority in his environment; it eventuates in a pervasive anxiety which makes effective goal-seeking impossible for him, and it is to be finally understood as a rigid attitude of emotional defensiveness. This attitude is, of course, invalid for the most part, depending on individual circumstance, but it is nonetheless extremely difficult to eradicate, since the subject clings to it unyieldingly, even in deep therapy.

In the present context, it becomes apparent that this pattern of symptoms, which is routinely observable among cult members, is largely instrumental in producing the sense of selfhood as burdensome, which leads to its widespread abandonment in the cults.

As long as they are permitted to retain the neurotic personality structure which has been their lifelong defense against the contradictions in the reality they have had to face, they will merge unprotestingly with the cult leader, who plans all their activities for them, and supplies them with some prestigious

[34] Cf. *Supra*, Part Three, III, C, 4, c, i, p. 171.

sounding "miraculous" solution, *without any self-directive effort of their own.* They will do this, even though required to accept heavy exploitation in other areas of life. The general set of symptoms which bears the name neurosis is thus seen to be intimately related to the abandonment of selfhood in cultic religion, by its contribution to the sense of selfhood as burdensome.

Furthermore, it is the collapse of critical judgment which accompanies their resignation from personal responsibility that makes it possible for cult members to be led to the acceptance of the allegedly paranormal solutions that are a part of every cultic revelation. As the cult leader claims that the benefit he offers is supernatural, whatever it may be—healing, supernatural insight, communication with the dead, life on a plane higher than human, fellowship with a new god, or whatever— their neurotic willingness to take shortcuts, added to the intensity of their need, dynamizes their experience of this promoter as an archetypal figure, and makes their mergence with him even more complete.

At the same time, the allegedly "miraculous" quality of the solution is itself seen to have a part in bringing about the typical cultic abandonment of selfhood, quite apart from mergence with the leader. The problem that the cult member has been unable to solve may be so commonplace that people all around him are managing it routinely; and the cult member will accept the ready-made solution with an even more uncritical alacrity *if he is told that it is miraculous,* or if it openly appears to be so: for in this way, the problem he could not solve is made to seem worthier of consideration, and his overt dependency in accepting the solution on the terms given is correspondingly dignified.

However, the abandonment of selfhood to which all of this leads is the major cultic solution offered, and the most welcome. Far from being a desperate price exacted for some other benignity, this is the central dynamic of cultic membership, and the deepest craving to which it panders.

5. Characteristics of Problems Observable in Cults

As we turn to the consideration of the problems which characterize cultic religion, there is always the possibility that we may reiterate material that has been considered in the preceding section. If such be the case, at least the present treatment will have the advantage of continuing the discussion from a new perspective. Similarly, we may anticipate matters to be covered later, in connection with the structure of the cultic institution, but with equally small harm.

a. All Types Are Represented

All types of religious problems are to be met with in the cults. Whereas Old Ethnic religions are focused principally upon problems of nature, and Prophetic religions are directed to solving problems of society, Cultic religions address both of these, and also inner psychic problems, as well as those of prior formulation.

The latter two are for the most part institutionally caused: inner-psychic problems indirectly, and those of prior formulation directly.

Problems of nature are dealt with only secondarily in Prophetic religion, although the Ideal Society is not without its economic aspects. Also, and more importantly, Prophetic religions *have no social metaphysic for the present*, being solely concerned with the Ideal Society that is to come. As these religions decline, their Pseudo-Ethnic successor either ignores this situation, or tries to take advantage of it by defining social status in terms of institutional conformity, thus giving rise to various formulations which are immediately problematical. Again, as described elsewhere, its failure to deal with problems in other areas, permits the inner-psychic problems of fear, hate and guilt to grow to the religious dimension for numbers of people.

Within this religious vacuum, problems at every level are standing unmet, which the cult leaders manipulate to their own advantage. Problems of nature are the first to attract the investigator's attention; since they are prominent among the cultic adherents we have described, and since they are addressed by the more typical cultic techniques, it would be easy to assign them a more exclusive role than they deserve. Healings are the most obvious, but we must remember that in pushing his "Blessing Pact," Oral Roberts promised an overall material prosperity in return for generous contributions,[35] as did Frank B. Robinson, the promoter of the mail-order Psychiana religion,[36] and even Charles Filmore, in his semi-respectable Unity tracts.[37]

Social inferiority has always plagued the Jehovah's Witnesses: H. H. Stroup called them "the cult of the consciously inferior," and they are still looking forward to Armageddon, when all non-Witnesses will be exterminated, and they will gain ascendency. Sex and marriage are problematical to the Moonie adherents, as evidenced by their willingness to let the cult leader arrange these deeply personal matters for them. Interracial acceptance was undoubtedly one of the central dynamics that made some of its members willing to die for the Peoples' Temple.

Turning to inner-psychic problems, guilt over sexual involvement with the leader himself was also a dynamic within the last mentioned group, as well as among the Children of God, and in the Love Israel cult. The deliberate excitement of unendurable guilt, which the subject depends upon the leader to absolve, is common to many groups. Personal failures as well as guilts, unassuaged in the mainline churches, find a specifically tailored alibi in the doctrines of Karma that are integral to the Eastern religions.

Curiosity about previously formulated doctrines of life after death, and a strongly continuing fear of hell, along with inability to cope with bereavement, are religious problems which appear in both Spiritualism and Theosophy.

---

[35] Jacobs, Hayes B., *Oral Roberts, High Priest of Healing.* Harpers, February, 1962, p. 43.

[36] Braden, Charles S. *These Also Believe*, N.Y., Macmillan, 1949, pages 98 and 103.

[37] *Op. Cit.*, p. 171.

Of all the problems addressed, an inner-psychic one is probably the most important for the understanding of cultic religious experience; it is also largely unconscious. We refer, of course, to the burdensome quality of selfhood, already discussed in some detail.[38]

The notion of individual responsibility, apart from institutional direction, makes its appearance with the rise of Prophetic religion, and in this context, individual persons develop the ego-structure that permits decision making.[39] However, as the Prophetic hope declines, with the accompanying decay of its morality, and the Pseudo-Ethnic religious institution progressively gains power, individuals are systematically discouraged from making their own decisions, and are urged instead to let the institution assume the ego function, as was the case in the Old Ethnos. Their resultant confusion is characterized as neurotic.

The emotional distress which accompanies the introjection of this stultifying requirement is so severe that it is for the most part repressed; yet whatever be the other problems for which people gain solution in the cults, they all but universally abandon their selfhood at the same time, although their compelling need to do this does not appear in consciousness.

b. They Are Without Social Resonance

The problems characterizing cultic adherents are not universal to the society, and indeed are not acknowledged by its Pseudo-Ethnic religious institution to be suitable objects for its official concern.[40] However, religious problems are no longer experienced unanimously in Pseudo-Ethnic societies, so this is no distinction, which is rather to be found in the fact that persons having problems that drive them to the cults *are ashamed that they have them*, or sensitive about them in some unusual and humiliating way. For example: a bereaved person

[38] Cf. *Supra*, pp. 292–295.
[39] Cf. Appendix, p. 355.
[40] That is: their solutions are not interpretable in the "ultimate frame of reference" which characterizes the religious realm.

will hurry to the neighbors to report his loss, and be greeted with every consideration that sympathetic understanding can provide: whereas one who has been imprisoned for child molestation will not be extended any similar compassion, although his trouble is far deeper. Again, a person with a broken leg will receive every commiseration (although this is hardly a religious problem . . .); while the same person with a venereal disease will not, although he has a far worse handicap.

These introductory examples are drawn from problems brought into being by sexual transgressions. Although we shall turn to other types in a moment, we may well pursue this line of thought a little farther, in the interest of making our meaning fully plain. A problem of truly religious proportions to many people is sexual unattractiveness, and yet none of the traditional religions do anything about it. Again, sexual inabilities—frigidity and impotence, although attacked in part by the counseling programs of some forward-looking churches, are not by any means the matter of public prayer in routinely held meetings. Sexual deviance, although currently publicized in certain quarters as merely "an alternative life-style," is still kept from public notice whenever possible; and it is certainly not among the problems addressed by the rituals of any official religion. Finally, lack of control in the sexual sphere constitutes a definite problem: multiple bastardy, rape, exhibitionism, promiscuity, and even inconveniently rapid breeding, are dealt with along recognized lines, by sociological and legal agencies, but not by those of religion outside of the cults, although they have the religious dimension for many people.

Again, disfiguring physical deformities can constitute embarrassing and demoralizing religious problems, impelling those afflicted by them to seek relief in the healing cults. How many victims of harelip, cleft palate, unsightly birthmarks, and spinal curvature are to be found in a Kathryn Kuhlman or an Oral Roberts meeting? Certainly more than the average of the population, and certainly very many more than will be found in a comparable meeting at one of the orthodox churches.

Another group wherein problems unacknowledged by the generality of society are to be found is that of the permanently unemployable. Whether non-achievement through the neurotic introjection of social censure be the cause, whether it be simply a degree of inferiority that puts them below the commonly accepted level of social usefulness, or whether we must consider persons who, by the loss of reputation, previous criminal activity, or defective socialization, have lost their employability, we have here a group who must be heavily traumatized, and yet who are completely outside the interest of most ecclesiastical "programs." It is thus no coincidence when we discover them associated in considerable numbers with cultic religion.

Hostility, particularly when its expression is officially forbidden, has already been discussed in connection with the cultic adherents who are incapacitated by it. Hence we need only point out here that this problem—being choked anger which the subjects dare not express—shares in the characteristic we are now delineating.

This characteristic, in slightly different wording, may be summarized by saying that the problems to which cultic religion is addressed *are without social resonance*; and in a frame of reference only a little more extensive, we may say that such problems are among the symptoms of social rejection.

c. They Are Homogenous in Each Group

Another characteristic of the problems to which cultic religion is addressed is that they are relatively homogenous within each group. In this respect a cult illustrates its aspect of being a New Ethnos, since this is a characteristic of Old Ethnic religion as well: the high level of agreement as to what the religious problems are, and the thorough commitment of each religious complex to the solution of just those problems which are its peculiar concern.

As regards the cults, this hardly need be elaborated. The healing cults heal, and do little else; each of the cargo cults has a constellation of problems which is uniquely its own. Inability to cope with bereavement characterizes spiritualism, and racial discrimination is the only religious issue in which the Black Muslims are really interested; the same statement holds, with regards to the Father Divine cult. The unfortunate adherents of the People's Temple found numinosity in Jim Jones' purported relief of their economic and social futility, while the Jehovah's Witnesses are loaded with resentment at the areas of society in which they have failed to qualify, so that they look forward to Armageddon, when these (to them) Satanic forces will be liquidated.

Of course, a cult may be dynamized by not one, but by a closely related group of problems, as Theosophy in its heyday was dynamized by the desire for "spiritual" prestige, rising out of incomplete social acceptance, combined with the fear of death, and with an accompanying curiosity about an after-life. Yet whatever the syndrome, and whatever the astuteness necessary to identify it, it will be shared to a remarkable degree by all members of the cult to which it appertains.

d. They Are Presently Without Religious Solution

The fourth generalization that can be made about the problems which impel the cults is that they are *religiously* insoluble, in terms of anything the existing society has to offer. The importance of having a religious solution available, both for the individual with a problem of this magnitude, and for the society of which he is a part, has been pointed out repeatedly. Such a solution provides energy release, whether by imparting hope, consolation, a new perspective, or an actual correction of the difficulty, and in its most valid manifestation makes the subject able to solve his own problem, thus restoring him to usefulness in the society. However, no religious solutions are obtainable for the problems by which cults are characterized.

i. They Are Defined Out of Existence　The dominant religious institution of a Pseudo-Ethnic culture acknowledges *as religious*, only those problems with which it is specifically equipped to deal; and thus nearly everything that troubles the characteristic adherent of the cults is defined out of the area. Then too, while some cultic problems are outside the range of institutional competence, others are regarded as too trivial for religious consideration. Nor is this unnatural; religious problems are those which are insoluble by science or morality as these are available to the subject: and this area of insolubility is much larger for the inadequate, the disaffiliated and the neurotic than for the normally well-adjusted members of society, for whom many problems have been removed from the religious category by the natural process of migration: but this leaves the truly religious problems of a hard core of people with a complete denial of institutional recognition.

ii. They Are Caused By the Institution   As we have seen, many problems found among cultic adherents are directly *caused* by the Pseudo-Ethnic institution, which is, of course, the problem *de facto* for them, whether or not it is recognized as such. Prior formulations create the problems here: promises that have failed, doctrines that have become irrelevant or repugnant, such as infant damnation, and specific moral *dicta* of such negative quality that they impair the individual's welfare, to the obvious advantage of the ecclesiastical structure. The plight of a reproductively exploited woman who is denied contraceptive information, and the Negro complaint, so often met in Black Muslim literature, that while others were told of freedom, they were enjoined to obedience, are instances in point. The constant and increasingly ingenious employment of guilt as a technique of religious pressure is from this perspective seen as *the* religious problem of those who are victimized by it. Under circumstances such as these, to expect a religious subject to obtain the solution for his problem from its very source is obviously expecting the impossible.

iii. No Protest is Tolerated   In the third place, we note once more that obstacle-removing behavior—hostility—toward the background religion is out of the question. Indeed, any expression of hostility is likely to be regarded, or at least spoken of, as immature, naive, or religiously incomplete; and any reasoned criticism of the power structure is frowned upon, let alone any systematic efforts to modify or remove it. Since it, the religious institution, *is* the problem afflicting the subject, he is not only unable to find a solution within it, but he is unable to *seek* a solution concerning it, and his religious impoverishment is virtually complete.

iv. Their Disclosure Brings Institutional Rejection   Despite the small likelihood of their obtaining any solace or assistance from the Pseudo-Ethnic institution, some of the people with problems that will eventually drive them into the cults, still turn to it for help, since none is available elsewhere. They have been trained to expect a religious solution within the institutional complex; but as they turn to it for whatever Archetypal Contact is still available, *the institution rejects them, simply because they have the problems we have been characterizing.* Whether or not valid and autonomous archetypal experience might come to them later we cannot say; for in the meantime they become involved with the institutional solution offered by one or another of the cults, and their individuation is aborted.

e. They Inhibit Adaptive Behavior
   Our final observation is that cultic problems inhibit adequate ego activity. Let us review the evidence.
   The ego is the totality of adaptive behavior, and the range of its activity is set by the resultant of forces between the super-ego and the id. Thus the removal of obstacles, and the affirmative engagement of the organism with all relevant aspects of the environment are both a part of its function. Both entail the flow of energy; the difference is in the emotional tone of its expenditure.
   We have seen that the subject who is impelled into a cult by one of the characteristic problems is ashamed that he has it; that its problematic nature is religiously unrecognized, and that it produces institutional rejection if admitted at all, even though the subject is seeking a religious solution at the time. It

is institutionally caused, but he must not engage in any obstacle removing behavior concerning it, for such activity would be hostile to the power structure. Indeed, this prohibition is introjected completely. Yet the institution, by any approach whatever, is an important part of his problem (direct cause, failure to solve, rejecting agency), and until the obstacles have been removed, the eros cannot flow, and he cannot love, i.e., embrace his environment. The introjection of this taboo against making any protest, (i.e., engaging in any obstacle removing behavior) against the massive authority of the background religion thus makes him virtually unable either to do constructive work, or to initiate warm personal relationships, for he certainly cannot embrace *this* environment! Constructive ego activity is accordingly made all but impossible for the cultic subject, and the "weak ego structure" or "neurotic temperament" of cultic adherents is accounted for very satisfactorily in terms of the dynamics of the available religious institution(s). These constitute the value structure of the society in which he lives; and when the value structure is not only insensitive to his problems, and even inimical to his interests, but is also identical with the power structure, it is obvious that the Archetypal Contact which alone might enable him to marshal his efforts along remedial lines, is unavailable to him.

There remains only a Magic Formula, which will take the problem entirely out of his hands, and solve it for him, thereby making radical departure from the whole Prophetic tradition, and going all the way back to the Ethnic situation.

6. The Cult Leader

As our exploration of religious experience moves from the examination of cult members and their problems to that of solutions offered in such institutions, the first object of our consideration is the cult leader, since much of the format of any given cult is imparted to it by the organizer. Indeed, this quality of being the extension of the leader's personality is one of the first differentia to impress itself upon the observer of cultic groups.

Three generalizations are to be made concerning cult leaders: (a) They inhibit ego activity. (b) They are, or at some time have been, severely alienated from the mainstream of their society, particularly its religious institutions. (c) Once the cult is under way as an institution, the leader's inordinate industry in keeping it going, as a standard phenomenon.

a. His Radical Insincerity

The basic, and most penetrating of these generalizations is, that from whatever perspective a cult leader is investigated, the ensuing inquiry becomes a study of (and frequently a debate concerning), the degree and flagrancy of his religious cynicism and exploitative intent. The writer is well aware that value judgments are involved in making such estimates, and that being subjective, they may be charged with invalidity; but the total impact of a cultic promoter's career is typically such that ordinary common sense will corroborate this conclusion. Moreover, precise and binding facts supportive of this position have a way of turning up in surprising places as various cult leaders are investigated. Of course the utterances of a cult leader will be framed in religious terms, and will necessarily be capable of an idealistic interpretation by members of his clientele, but their exploitative intent will nonetheless be transparently evident to the objective investigator. Also, when the opulent circumstances of a cult leader are pointed out, attention is bound to be called to the obvious comfort in which ranking officials of the religious establishment live. Even so, there is an enormous difference between the legitimate practitioner of religion whose professional competence enables him to live well, and the cult leader who relentlessly amasses great wealth by the exploitation of his adherents.

This observation as to the radical insincerity of the cult leader simplifies our discussion greatly, since promoters who have clearly had some numinous experience, and who have believed in the truth of their own revelations are thereby eliminated from the cultic classification, however preposterous their doctrines may have been, and however they may have led their followers astray.

This is, of course, the final and definitive difference between the cult leader and the prophet: for however misguided the latter may be, and to whatever tragic fate he may lead his disciples, his motivation is solely the quest for their ultimate good, without regard for his own condition, except as he seeks to remain true to whatever personification is the source of his message. Indeed, it is to the archetypal insights of the pro-founder members of this class that a significant part of human progress is to be traced.

The cult leader, on the other hand, seeks nothing but his own advantage. Instead of unfolding his most sacred insights for the welfare of his followers, he directs whatever solution he is able to purvey, to their immediate exploitation, and applies all of his ingenuity to this undertaking. This is perhaps the central characteristic of cultic religion: that whereas the adherents view the leader religiously, by reason of whatever benefits he has presently supplied or numinously promised, the leader himself views his constituents altogether instrumentally, and solely in terms of their potential advantage to himself. This will be found consistently true, in spite of explicit claims to the contrary which cult leaders or their official spokesmen (often a generation later) are wont to make.

In the light of these considerations, we can readily discern the non-cultic character of some of the more eccentric religious promoters, as well as the movements they founded. Thus, Joanna Southcott (1750–1815), who not only believed that she was, at the age of sixty-three, about to become the mother of a new Messiah, to be named "Shiloh," but managed to convince a small yet persistent following that this improbable state of affairs was true, must surely be classified here. Interestingly, she died before her prophecy could be disproven!

Similarly, William Miller, the commonly acknowledged "founder" of the group bearing his name, after prolonged Bible study, came to the numinous belief that the world would end in 1843; which date was presently "corrected" to the tenth day of the seventh month in 1844: and although forced to watch his followers thrown into all sorts of distressing embarrassments when the prophecy failed, he held this conviction to the end of his life, postponing the date from year to year. Hence there is no way that he can be called a cult leader. However, one Joshua V. Himes, a Boston clergyman with a sadistic penchant for producing religious emotion, seems to have been the moving force in obtaining the wide hearing that "Prophet" Miller received, and in bringing about the tragic frenzy into which believers in the world's end were thrown as the date approached—and passed . . . The extent to which he profited in other ways by the excitement which the movement engendered is unclear, as is the cultic status of the Millerite movement, after he became involved in it.

Turning, then, to movements that definitely *are* cultic, we note that there are two levels into which their leaders can be classified, in just this connection: (1) those who were originally sincere, but subsequently yielded to the power-gain-prestige syndrome, and (2) those who were imposters from the outset. While the typical pattern of a cult leader is to have no numinous experience until the movement succeeds, at which time he begins to find it sacred, we do not, of course, exclude the possibility of even a thoroughgoing imposter having twinges of numinosity along the way. We are merely describing the careers of a preponderant number of the organizers who seek to profit from the religious exploitation of a following.[41]

[41] It should be noted, however, that a cult leader may be quite sincere, even numinously so, in developing some aspect of the movement that permits the further exploitation of the adherents, particularly if this involves pandering to some abnormal facet of his own personality. Thus, Paul Erdman, promoter of The Church of Armageddon, who calls himself Love Israel, is obviously expressing some inner compulsion in his *macho* insistence on keeping the women of the Love Family socially inferior and reproductively active. By the same token, Eleanor Daries, Pastor of the Faith Tabernacle, apparently hates men, and will go to any length to prevent the marriage of a female member. Her sincerity in such opposition is unfeigned, and is surely more than organizational. Cf. Enroth, Ronald, *Lure of the Cults*, pp. 60–61.

i. Originally Sincere but Drawn into Cult Activity The first class of cult leader, i.e., originally sincere, but subsequently drawn into cultic activity, is well illustrated by Charles Taze Russell, the initial promulgator of what became the Jehovah's Witnesses. Despite the difficulty of winnowing facts, it would seem reliably true that he started with certain formulations of his own, critical of the fundamentalism of his day, and numinously arrived at, and that he later exploited these cultically, once he realized their commercial possibilities as required reading for the Zion's Watch Tower Society, as the first organization was called. There can be no doubt of the cultic status of the movement in Russell's later years,[42] and of course it became notorious after "Judge" Rutherford assumed control of it in 1916.

Whether or not the founder of Psychiana ever had a thoroughly numinous moment is impossible to prove, but his advertising repeatedly said that he did. ("I TALKED WITH GOD! I REALLY DID!") Assuming the truth of this claim, Frank B. Robinson certainly made the most of whatever advice he received, when he began making his insights available to the perplexed on a mail order basis.

Oral Roberts claims numinous experience on at least seven occasions, including the first one, when he was healed of stuttering and tuberculosis.[43] Again, assuming the veracity of the claim, Roberts has since unquestionably become a cultic operator.

However, it is in no sense our purpose to enumerate all the cult leaders who turned originally numinous experience into the basis for exploitative profit seeking, but rather to provide solid evidence that such a classification must be taken account of.

[42] Cf. Braden, Chas. S., *These Also Believe*. N.Y.: Macmillan, 1939, pp. 358–361.

[43] Jacobs, Hayes B., art., *Oral Roberts, High Priest of Faith Healing*. Harpers, Feb., 1962, pp. 37–43.

ii. Outright Imposters   The second, and far more numerous class of cult leaders is that made up of outright imposters, which is to say, persons who have had no revelatory experience, however strongly they may claim it, but who simply apply whatever promotional abilities they have to creating an organization which will yield them a personal profit.

Let us look at some representative instances of such imposture.

According to the official version, Joseph Smith, Junior, the founder of Mormonism, had certain golden plates revealed to him by an angel; the story is familiar. However, William Linn quotes affidavits from persons to whom Smith confided that this was a hoax from first to last, and that it had its beginning when he brought home a quantity of sand wrapped in his coat, and told the trumped up story of the plates to his credulous family. Their response was so immediate and so numinous, as was that of others who presently heard the yarn, that he never did abandon the imposture.[44]

The likelihood that his further propagation of this hoax was made possible by Sidney Rigdon, who supplied him with the manuscript of a pseudo-historical romance by one Solomon Spalding, which Smith then "translated" from his non-existent plates as a new religious revelation[45] is a view that is widely held, although still surrounded by controversy even at the present time.[46] It is, of course, denied by the Mormon Church. If this sequence of events, of admittedly high probability, is ever conclusively proven, it will substantiate beyond any question the complete fraudulence of Smith's primary "revelation."

That he produced later "revelations" as needed, in order to pull himself out of dubious situations, even doing this at the

[44] Linn, Wm. A., *The Story of Mormonism*. N.Y.: Macmillan, 1902, p. 25.

[45] Cf. Arbaugh, Geo., *Revelation in Mormonism*, Chicago University Press, 1932, *passim*.

[46] Cf. Davis, Howard A., Scales, Donald R. and Cowdrey, Wayne, *Who Really Wrote the Book of Mormon?* Santa Ana, Calif.: Vision House Publishers, 1977. The authors claim to have discovered new evidence.

suggestion, and upon the advice of, his confederates, is shown in the depositions cited by Fawn M. Brodie,[47] as well as by the circumstantiality of the "revelations" themselves.[48] No further proof of his basic insincerity should be necessary.

The approach of Father Divine to his organizational beginnings shows a marked parallel to that of Joseph Smith. When George Baker got off the chain gang in Georgia, he started North, working his way as best he could, and associating himself with a series of religious pretenders in the cities through which he passed. From each he picked up whatever of the man's technique was most successful; an appealing phrase, a dynamic idea, or a sure fire promotional device, and presently incorporated them into his own structure. By the same token, he was careful to avoid pitfalls, legal or psychological, into which other organizers had fallen. At no time, however, do we discover him undergoing any profoundly numinous experience; his procedures and policies have rather been dictated at every turning solely by considerations of practicality, that is to say, by their efficiency in promoting his own ends, principally those of power, gain, or prestige.[49]

Dakin, Milmine and Bates-Dittemore are at one in their portrayal of Mary Baker Eddy's promotional techniques as showing this same characteristic.[50] From her pitiful beginnings with parlor spiritualism and private readings of Phineas P. Quimby's views on healing by suggestion, she went on to compile her own volume, and to found her own economic establishment on exactly the same principle as was followed by the two cult leaders already cited: namely, that of accepting any

[47] Brodie, F. M., *No Man Knows My History*. N.Y.: Knopf, 1957, *passim*.
[48] Cf. *Doctrines and Covenants*, throughout.
[49] Cf. Parker, Robert Allerton, *The Incredible Messiah*, and Harris, Sara, *Father Divine, Holy Husband*.
[50] Cf. Dakin, E. F., *Mrs. Eddy: The Biography of a Virginal Mind*. N.Y.: Scribners, 1929; Milmine, Josephine, *The Life of Mary Baker Eddy and the History of Christian Science*, London: Hodder and Stoughton, 1909; and Bates, E. F., and Dittemore, John V., *Mary Baker Eddy, The Truth and The Tradition*. London: Geo. Routledge & Sons, 1933.

doctrine and admitting any practice that she thought would be instrumental to her own advantage, in the way of attracting adherents and obtaining access to their money. Thus, she was always careful to avoid the role of a healer; rather, she wrote and sold a book which contained doctrines about being healed; operated a "Metaphysical College", where she taught the techniques of healing; she tried to pledge her students to pay her a percentage of whatever they earned in their subsequent healing practice,[51] and finally she created a church, within which she was honored as a revelator. Each of these moves was dictated by motives of the coolest prudence, if not by outright necessity, which she was always able to apprehend well in advance of anyone else.

But what of the official claim that Mrs. Eddy was numinously motivated in all this, particularly in the revelatory "discovery" of the principles of Christian Science, in connection with her supposedly miraculous recovery from crippling spinal injuries received in her famous fall on the ice, on February 1, 1866?

Dakin cites evidence showing conclusively that her attending physician, Dr. Alvin M. Cushing, did not believe the injuries sustained on that occasion to have been anywhere nearly as severe as Mrs. Eddy (then Mrs. Patterson) later insisted that they had been;[52] and various authors have concluded after a study of the sources, that the material embodied in *Science and Health*, and claimed as her own, supposedly attained or received numinously, upon the occasion of the alleged injury and its miraculous cure in 1866, was really the work of Phineas P. Quimby, from whose manuscript *The Science of Man*, Mrs. Eddy had been lecturing and copying since 1864, and with which she had been familiar since 1862.[53]

The thesis we are advancing about cult leaders in general was stated regarding Mrs. Eddy, in 1910 by Frederick W. Peabody,

[51] Dakin, *Op. Cit.*, pp. 87 and 138.

[52] Dakin, *Op. Cit.*, p. 62.

[53] Peabody, Frederick W., *The Religio-Medical Masquerade*, Boston: The Hancock Press, 1910, pp. 92 *et seq*.: Dresser, Horation W., *The Quimby Manuscripts*, Thos. Crowell, 1921; Cf. Dakin, *Op. Cit.*, pp. 37–64.

an attorney; who had, just prior to that time been instrumental in collecting much of the source material upon which our present understanding of Mrs. Eddy rests. Here is his statement:

> In the course of the preparation for the trial of this case . . . all of Mrs. Eddy's published utterances from the beginning down to that time, including every edition of her book, "Science and Health," and every number of the *Christian Science Journal* were turned over to me by my client and studied with most thorough and painstaking care. Then it was I learned that Christian Science was a deliberate fraud foisted upon mankind by Mrs. Eddy in the name of religion for the mere purpose of extorting money from credulous people.[54]

Indeed, if one wished to dispute the present thesis, it would be far easier to do so by citing "Dr." Quimby's strong emotional influence upon the impressionable Mrs. Patterson in the early days of their association, as evidence of some numinous experience on her part:[55] and yet she has gone to every possible length to deny that any influence existed at all from that quarter.

Another cult of which the leader exhibits every characteristic of unalloyed imposture is Theosophy.

Whatever radical cynicism is shown by the foregoing cult leaders is equally observable in the approach of Mme. Helena P. Blavatsky to the founding of this movement. After initial forays into Spiritualistic territory, which, in their turn, had represented her attempts to make a better living than she could achieve in the sweatshop which was her first place of employment upon coming to New York, she looked about for something that would provide her with basic security. A "Miracle

---

[54] Peabody, *Op. Cit.*, pp. 13–14. The lawsuit mentioned is the notorious Woodbury case. Mrs. Woodbury, an influential Christian Science healer, citing Mrs. Eddy's (well authenticated) teachings, claimed that a child she bore was conceived by mental means alone! Mrs. Eddy expelled her from her Church with violent contumely, upon which Mrs. Woodbury sued for libel, but lost the case.

[55] Dakin, *Op., Cit.*, pp. 37–52.

Club" was founded, but, despite its elaborately occult format, it aroused little interest outside of a very small circle, and certainly was not meeting the purpose for which HPB had brought it into being, namely to make money. It was during this time, early in 1875, that she voiced her motivation with the utmost candor, in a letter to A. N. Aksakov:[56]

> Here you see is my trouble, tomorrow there will be nothing to eat. Something quite out of the way must be invented. It is doubtful if Olcott's Miracle Club will help . . . I am ready to sell my soul for spiritualism but nobody will buy it, and I am living from hand to mouth and working for ten or fifteen dollars when necessity comes.[57]

Under the pressure of this bitter necessity, she acted promptly. She had had extensive experience in Spiritualism, so that she was familiar with the notion of "spirit controls," or particular inhabitants of the "spirit world" who would communicate with mediums, and provide such persons with information about other members of the spirit realm. Furthermore, she had, in company with A. L. Rawson of Vermont, and at his expense, put in some time in Cairo, during the winter of 1851–52, studying magic from one Paulos Metamon, who was apparently well qualified to give such instruction. So it is that we find these two skills combining in a series of letters, of supposedly supernatural origin, that began coming to a certain Col. Henry Steele Olcott, with whom she had had some spiritualistic dabblings, and whose credulity she was well able to discern. These letters, purportedly written by certain "Mahatmas," belonging to a "Brotherhood of Luxor," directed him to form an organization for the further investigation of occult phenomena. This organization did indeed materialize, and became the Theosophical Society, the history of which reads like some contrived comedy, involving a series of transparent

---

[56] Aksakov was Imperial Privy Counsellor in Petrograd, and an enthusiastic spiritualist. Since she had never met him, her desperation is reflected in the fact of her writing him at all.

[57] Letter quoted in Solovyov, V. S., *A Modern Priestess of Isis*, p. 253. Cited by Gertrude M. Williams in *Priestess of the Occult*, p. 83.

impostures[58] arranged for the beguilement of credulous seekers after esoteric phenomena who presently joined it. Indeed, Mme. Blavatsky has herself revealed the attitude she held toward the cult she founded. In an 1883 conversation with Moncure Conway, a Unitarian clergyman who was visiting her at Adyar, she said, with an unusual burst of candor, "It is all glamour. People think they see what they do not see. That is the whole of it."[59]

It is not our purpose to catalog the religious insincerities of all the cult leaders presently or recently operating. The representative illustrations just cited should be sufficient to establish our point. Nonetheless, additional evidence of this salient aspect of cultism is cumulative. Thus: Bhagwan Sri Rajneesh, who has taken over the town of Antelope, Oregon, now (1982) has twenty-two Rolls-Royce automobiles. The discovery, made in the early seventies, that Maharaj Ji, supposedly only fifteen years old at the time, was well past thirty, was widely publicized. "Rev." Sun Myung Moon admits having thirteen million dollars in his own name, beside the various corporately held properties where he lives. One of the writer's students reported having seen Father Divine stage the pretended resurrection of an adherent. Another student was intimately acquainted with a banker of normal business instincts who was moved to moral outrage by his professional observation of Kathryn Kuhlman's practice of stripping aged people of their property by playing upon their religious emotions. The list goes on and on . . .

b. His Social Alienation

Our second observation regarding cult leaders is that they are, or at some time have been, socially alienated. This statement is, of course, made generally, not universally, and we are well aware that differences of opinion may obtrude, as to what alienation really is, and to what degree it is felt by the cultist under investigation: yet the observation is nonetheless mean-

[58] Cf. *Priestess of the Occult*, Chapters XII to XV.
[59] *Op. Cit.*, 212.

ingful, and sheds much light on the indubitably counter-cultural atmosphere of so many cults, as well as upon the exploitative intent of their founders.

As in the matter of their insincerity, the examples illustrating the alienation of cult leaders are intended to be representative rather than exhaustive.

Thus, Father Divine, as George Baker, was a Georgia Negro who did time on the chain gang for impersonating Jesus Christ . . . Joseph Smith, Jr. had practically no gainful employment as a young man, except a series of fraudulent searches for buried treasure, which he claimed the ability to find by looking into a "peepstone." On one occasion he was convicted of fraud in connection with such an enterprise . . . Mme. Blavatsky was a *declassé* noblewoman who spent ten lost years beating about the Near east with various *pro tempore* companions, and who, according to Gertrude Marvin Williams, bore a child to one of them, somewhere in the Caucasus.[60] Mary Baker Eddy was, from childhood, out of step with her social milieu, and from 1864 to 1879 was hard pressed to meet the expenses of board and lodging. After being befriended by a family named Wentworth for more than a year, she attempted to burn the house as she was leaving, being piqued at Horace Wentworth's refusal to subsidize the printing of her book . . . [61] Kathryn Kuhlman was married to another evangelist named Burroughs Waltrip in Mason City, Iowa, on October 19, 1938, the marriage being recorded in Swaledale, Iowa. It lasted just one night. Moreover, in 1953, a completely reputable acquaintance insisted to the writer that he had first-hand knowledge of a man in a nearby state, whose wife had been seduced by this evangelist . . . Sun Myung Moon was in prison in Korea for four years, prior to his coming to the States: whether this was for political activity or sexual irregularities is a question that is answered according to the perspective of the respondent . . . He has recently served a prison term in this country, for tax fraud. Jim

[60] *Priestess of the Occult*, pp. 45–48.
[61] Dakin, *Op. Cit.*, pp. 76–78.

Jones exhibited paranoid tendencies from childhood, and was socialistically inclined for years before he moved to Guyana . . . The reader can make his own investigation of other cult leaders, but it seems a valid hypothesis that their willingness to exploit has at least some connection with their own social and religious alienation, and that whatever else may be said, they are at some point entirely out of sympathy with the society in which they are operating.

c. His Charisma and Industry

In order to found a cult, the leader must be able to detect a generally felt religious need, and to purvey a solution to it. The sole requirement of such a solution is that it affect the followers numinously; i.e., with supreme valuation and mystery. It may be an insight, a little known scientific technique, a skill, a particular ability, a world view, or a promise that matches the problem felt; but whatever its nature, it must be presented as miraculous, or as having an aura of the supernatural, or at least being paranormal.

The next step is the development of an inner circle of lieutenants who will, with unswerving loyalty, assist the leader in promulgating whatever idea is central to the cult. Whether these inside confederates are numinously affected by the leader's message, or whether they are as exploitative as he is, is difficult to determine, and will vary with the particular situation. However, an obvious characteristic of this group of confederates is that they stand to profit substantially, if and when the cultic institution succeeds.

To accomplish all this, and to keep it going, requires an incredible expenditure of energy, even though the undertaking is streamlined by the absolute simplicity of its motive, which is the personal advantage of the promoter. Other personal characteristics of the cult leader may vary greatly, but all of them share two abilities; a phenomenal gift of plausible persuasiveness, and an infinite capacity for hard work. This persuasiveness is commonly spoken of as "charisma", and consists, as

Randall H. Alfred has pointed out,[62] of the ability to make his followers accept a definition of reality that will permit his predictions to come true, and his magical claims to be seen as successful. This usually involves the presentation and very possibly the construction of a cosmology different from that ordinarily accepted by normal people. Thus David "Mo" Berg, promoter of the Children of God, presents a well-known theology of millenialism, but backs it by the threat of a massive landslip, soon to occur along the California coast. Jim Jones had his followers convinced, both in Los Angeles and Guyana, that the United States was in momentary danger of nuclear attack. Oriental promoters are at pains to present all aspects of the theology underlying the Hindu doctrine of Karma, which provides the perfect apologetic for any kind of personal inferiority; and Mme. Blavatsky wrote *Isis Unveiled* to structure the cosmology which made her Ascended Masters theoretically possible. Whatever he may have been before the cultic venture, the leader now works harder than would seem humanly possible, and, of course, the charismatic effort is the most laborious thing he does.

Once a formal organization has been established, he must not only keep the miracles coming, i.e., perform healings, promote free food, make the new world plausible, or whatever, but he must function administratively at a peak level. He must clarify policy for his lieutenants, in addition to keeping them inspired; he must write propaganda for the movement; constantly formulate the new policies that growth makes necessary; provide a supernatural apologetic for earlier mistakes of policy and personnel, to say nothing of making ceremonial appearances, and most importantly of all, creating the overall metaphysical framework that an emergent movement requires. Thus we see Blavatsky, Moon, Joseph Smith, Ron L. Hubbard and others, all producing massive amounts of literary material,

[62] Art. "The Church of Satan" in Glock and Bellah, *The New Religious Consciousness*, pp. 191–192.

all of it irrational in content, yet capable of being given a pseudo-rational interpretation to a growing clientele.

7. *The Cultic Institution*

a. *Its Rise: The Terminal Phase of the Theological Continuum*

The cultic institution *per se* is the end point of a continuum that begins when the original prophetic revelation is solidified into institutional form. This has been described earlier, in Section III, D of Part Three, and the process of religious deterioration has been referred to throughout the preceding sections of the present examination of institutional religion in Part Four.

Let us recapitulate this development briefly.

The migration of religious issues decreases the appeal of religious formulations and of the institutions which embody them, in that various problems which they formerly solved are removed from the religious category, as scientific solutions are found for them. The more intelligent segments of a population thus come to be less religious, simply because they have fewer problems. At the same time, and by the same token, the *less* able and less intelligent elements of society may well be developing extremely acute religious problems, as the society becomes too complex for them to deal with. A lower class of uneducated, unthoughtful and largely helpless people is an inevitable part of any technological society, and these people are as receptive to religious claims as any primitive group ever was.[63] Moreover, they are neurotically prone to seek the emotional shortcuts that the cults provide.

Interestingly, the lowest classes of the population, at the present time, are to be found in the cult-*like* sectarian groups of which we spoke earlier, rather than in the fully typical cultic institutions. Apparently the old fashioned salvationism, with Heaven as its hope and a Messianic apocalypticism as its dynamic, is still deeply appealing. At the same time, however,

---

[63] Of course, archetypal experience is not limited to the uneducated: nobody ever gets so sophisticated that he may not have a nightmare.

the youth of the upper and middle classes have become attracted in large numbers to the full-scale cultic groups, seemingly drawn by an atavistic desire for valid archetypal contact.

Again, we have seen the reinterpretations of theology transforming the prophetic dream of an Ideal Society into a supernaturally grounded power structure, which simply duplicates other political entities, as ambitious members advance their own doctrinal intereepretations in whatever ways will shape the institution to their personal advantage. Also, and most crucially of all, we have observed those same leaders making every effort to *produce* numinous experience *for its own sake*, forgetting the basic psychological fact that numinosity is a concomitant emotion, attendant upon the release of unconscious energy into consciousness, at moments of supreme need or supreme value.

In the light of these considerations, we see that the cultic phenomenon is itself the terminal expression of the same theological activity which first molded the original revelation into institutional form, and then brought about its decay. The moment when cultic institutions become possible comes at the absolute nadir of a religious cycle, when the prophetic religion which has structured an entire society, has fallen into such complete decay that its mission is unremembered and its worst abuses are made central and sacred.

At the same time, the scientific advance has been introducing new problems, and making old solutions meaningless, so that social change is inevitable. This is the moment when social ferment and religious impoverishment intersect; and the cult leader manipulates the ensuing chaos to his own advantage by the agency of the cultic institution.

Such an institution can only arise out of the Pseudo-Ethnos, for the cult is in actuality a new version of the Ethnic situation, and the Pseudo-Ethnos is a necessary preliminary to it. The theological enterprise, which brought the Pseudo-Ethnos into being in the attempt to give the obsolescent Prophetic movement the appearance of Ethnic autonomy and inevitability, is now taken over by the cult leader, who, in seeking to produce effects that can be claimed as supernatural, resorts to all the worst elements of primitivism, where chicanery is axiomatic, the medicine man determines what aspects of science shall become official, and where the individual does not exist.

b. The Impact of the Institution: Cultic Religious Experience
The cultic institution is essentially a New Ethnos, being similar to the Old Ethnic situation at a number of points, although not identical with it. We shall try to present these similarities, listing them in their order of importance as far as possible, and then point out the crucial differences between the two.

i. The Cult as the New Ethnos: Its Ethnic Similarities
(a) The Magic Formula Insofar as any real problem-solving goes on in the cultic institution, it takes place by the operation of a Magic Formula. The central importance of ritual acts in making the Formula work is to be noted in both the Old Ethnos and the New. Everyone is familiar with the notion of rain following a ritual of rain-making: and a similar pattern is seen in the supposed ability of Synanon members to stop using drugs following their sessions of criticism, and in the avowals of Transcendental Meditators that repetition of a mantra produces psychic benefits. Similarly, members of the Sokka Gokkai believe that by chanting toward a *Gohonzon*, or cardboard wall-shrine, they can change the world.[64] The bliss resulting from chanting the Hare Krishna formula is constantly asserted within that group.

However, in the cults the desired results are brought about by the direct agency of the cult leader to a greater extent than by the medicine man in primitive religion, who is more closely bound by the ritual traditions. This is particularly so in the healing and social-welfare cults, although by no means limited to them. Thus, whether by direct statement (Jim Jones), indi-

[64] This ritual has a peculiarly magical quality, since the great majority of those who practice it have no idea what they are saying.

rect implication (Father Divine), or coy disavowal (Oral Roberts and Kathryn Kuhlman), the idea is clearly advanced that whatever benefits accrue to the adherent have been produced by the immediate exercise of the leader's supernatural power.

(b) Living in the Presence of the Supernatural Thus the cultic religious experience is essentially one of living in the presence of the supernatural: the importance of this fact is beyond exaggeration. The institutional proximity of a leader with a plausible claim to divinity gives the adherents hope that their lives need no longer be defined by the humiliating failures they have so often met. Confident of his acceptance, their resulting feelings of significance and belonging intensify the numinosity which the leader inspires. The insistence with which his divinity is asserted, and the tenacity with which that belief is held, are indicative of the sense of powerlessness for which it brings relief.

Such a leader may be regarded as divine in his own right (Jim Jones, Father Divine, Bhagwan Shri Rajneesh), as the avatar of an earlier divinity (Meher Baba) or may be one who, as a mystic, has transcended the ordinary barriers of human capability by the originality or perseverance of his discipline (Maharishi Mahesh Yoga, Mme. Blavatsky, Mary Baker Eddy). Again, he may be one who has himself received a direct revelation (Joseph Smith, Jr., Sun Myung Moon). But whatever be the nuances of the role that the leader is thought to play, being close to such a source of supernatural power, and having some access to it, colors every aspect of institutional life with an aura of numinosity for the adherent. It is indeed the central dynamic of cultic religious experience.

Naturally enough, the cult leaders have always been ready to exploit it to the utmost. Thus, when the judge who had sentenced Father Divine to jail suddenly died of a heart attack, Divine said in effect, "I hate to do these things, but perhaps it will be a lesson." His staging of a faked "resurrection" has been referred to earlier (P. 315). Mme. Blavatsky had a large effigy, of vague outline, that could be carried on a person's shoulders, which she would cause to be paraded past the windows of new or doubtful converts, to convince them of the "materialization" of some deceased person: and of course all of her "Mahatma" letters were purportedly sent from a supernatural source. Jim Jones would exhibit chicken livers as evidence of cancers that had been passed from the bodies of those "cured" in his meetings, and hardcore members were routinely sent out to sleuth the dwellings, and even inspect the garbage of persons thought to be likely prospects, so that Jones could state intimate facts about their lives in what were called "services of discernment."[65]

Promoters of Oriental cults have been equally extravagant in their claims, and if anything, even more successful. Western scholarship has traditionally paid great deference to the supposedly total integrity of Hindu holy men; and the consequence has been that almost any Bhagwan, guru or swami who would show up in America, propounding the metaphysical efficacy of his own brand of meditation, would find his words and person alike taken, in effect, as those of a divine being, and his techniques accepted as going beyond the paranormal to the truly miraculous. A. C. Bhaktivedanta of the Hare Krishnas, Maharishi Mahesh Yoga, Meher Baba, Maharaj Ji and the Bhagwan Shri Rajneesh are all cases in point, and the followers of each one bask in his supposedly supernatural quality.

Moreover, the actual effects of the meditation, chanting or other ritual practice may indeed contribute to this impression, as the emptying of the mind, or its cancellation by constant auto-suggestion brings relief from conflict, a sense of peace, or even the cessation of physical symptoms, all of which are accepted as evidence of whatever bliss the guru has promised. Thus: protracted suggestion has brought certain Scientologists to the conviction that they can remember many previous existences, back through vistas of astronomical time, and that they have sub-microscopic vision.[66]

Again, the claims of the cult leader to supernatural status are

---

[65] Reiterman, Tim, *Raven*, E. P. Dutton, N. Y., 1982, pp. 138 and 165.
[66] Conway and Siegleman, *Snapping*, p. 164.

enhanced, on the grounds of moral ultimacy, when arduous duties are assigned to his adherents, instead of being diminished, as one would expect, in a consciousness of exploitation. Apparently a vast longing for some commitment, is abroad among the youth of the middle classes, so that the leader's "revelation" of a new age soon to be ushered in, is all that is needed to evoke their complete dedication. Indeed, the very extremity of his demands seems to impart a sense of his supernatural stature: the reaction of his adherents seems to be "None but a god could require this."

Finally, excessive fatigue from long hours of enforced activity, whether devotional or economic, combined with inadequate diet, and isolation from all familiar social facts, may well produce a feeling of unreality, which it is easy for the pressured subject to translate into a belief that he is having supernatural contact, as the Secondary Process at last gives way.

(c) Total Mergence: The Abandonment of Selfhood The total mergence of all the adherents with the leader, which is the result of their acceptance of his claims to divine status, eventuates in a collective unity which is very similar to that of the Old Ethnos. Abandonment of selfhood has been mentioned repeatedly: it takes place, most logically, by way of this mergence with the divine figure.

Cultic adherents have been seeking an opportunity to abandon selfhood, i.e., to escape the need for using their egoes, and this is their excuse: for who would be so froward as to oppose his personal preference to the will of a divine being? Thus, whether we call it the dominance of the super-ego, control by an external ego, abandonment of selfhood, or simply surrender to the collectivity, the result is the same: the end of the subject's effort to structure selfhood, and organize his existence according to the necessary dictates of the Secondary Process.

Whether cult membership merely involves the acceptance of some preposterous belief, such as the impending arrival of flying saucers to transport the members to other planets, or whether it involves organizational commitment, beginning with the sacrifice of all one's property, and including sadistic sessions of criticism, degrading sexual abuse, long hours of forced labor, or even mass suicide, a common characteristic of all such membership is that the subject has abjured the use of his ego, and cancelled out the Secondary Process, whether in its function of rationality, or that of practicality, or both. He will accept beliefs that are demonstrably false (quite apart from metaphysical generalities located in the future, or in some spiritual dimension, equally impossible to verify . . .) and will submit to the most humiliating forms of exploitation, with obvious patience and apparent goodwill.

There are several observations to be made about this situation.

(1) Cultic adherents may have little or no ego in the first place, being drifters, uneducated, or of low intelligence. Numbers of Father Divine's members, as well as those of Jim Jones, were of this type. Thus, when they turned themselves over to the cult leader, they had little selfhood to abandon, and all they lost was the opportunity for growth.

(2) Some cultic adherents may have a self that they don't want. Being "born again" is an honored Christian tenet, and getting a "new heart" is a part of this experience. Drugheads obtain some kind of transformation in Synanon, as well as with Meher Baba and Maharaj Ji. The Black Muslims make a central issue of obtaining a new identity upon joining that movement, and of course, leaving the old one behind.

(3) We have seen in several frames of reference how neurotics cling to their neuroses, which are, after all, their basic defense against the contradictory demands of their existence. The cultic freedom from decision-making fits them perfectly, and is authenticated by the supernatural claims of the leader.

(4) The youth of the upper and middle classes, who have joined the heavily exploitative cults of the late twentieth century in such numbers, may not be lacking in ego structure, or at least the potential for it, but they have come to regard its exercise, in any kind of competitive activity as repugnant, be it economic, athletic, or sexual. While it is true that some of these

young people may have undeveloped ego structures, by reason of over-indulgence, too easy economic circumstances, and too little valid parental example, for the majority of them, cult membership involves a true abandonment of selfhood.

The idyllic, dreamlike "rightness" of the Ethnic situation, the *pax deorum* of Roman religion, has been well described in its present-day Indian manifestation, by V. S. Naipaul, in his book *India: A Wounded Civilization.*[67] The Ethnic state of mind is there called *dharma*, and this author, himself of Indian birth, regards it as the greatest impediment to progress in the entire Indian culture. This *dharma*, usually translated "law," must be defined at last as loyalty to one's caste duties: here are Naipaul's comments on its outworkings:

> But *dharma* . . . can also be used to reconcile men to servitude and make them find in paralyzing obedience, the highest spiritual good.[68]

And again, still speaking of *dharma*,

> The blight of caste is not only untouchability and the consequent deification in India of filth; the blight, in an India that tries to grow, is also the over-all obedience it imposes, its ready-made satisfactions, the diminishing of adventurousness, *the pushing away from men of individuality and the possibility of excellence.*[69]

This Ethnic feeling of primitive "rightness," of being in harmony with, and in submission to, forces that are at once benign and inescapable, is what the cultic adherent achieves. It is, of course, a delusion, which may have been protective at the primitive level, but is unreal and delusory now. It is a return to childhood; it is a surrender to all the forces that make for neurosis by forbidding purposeful effort; it represents the death of the Reality Principle, as the dictates of the leader are introjected, and all efforts to structure the personality come to a slumbrous end.

[67] Alfred A. Knopf, N. Y., 1977.
[68] *Op. Cit.*, p. 186.
[69] *Op. Cit.*, p. 187. Italics added.

ii. Differences From the Old Ethnos
(a) The Problems Are Diverse This characteristic of cultic religion was discussed earlier, as we considered the problems of cultic adherents. Present reference to it is made for the sake of distinguishing adequately between the New Ethnos, as it appears in the cultic institution, and its older prototype in primitive religion.

The problems dealt with in Old Ethnic religions are always at bottom those of nature: social status is determined by the individual's ritual proximity to the Magic Formula, but the latter is clearly primary. Inner-psychic problems are not recognized in the Old Ethnos, and those of prior formulation are simply not tolerated. However, in cultic institutions, while problems of nature are undeniably prominent, and in some instances predominant, solutions to the entire range of religious problems are presented, although it must be remembered that each group will be focussed on its own distinctive area.

It is worthy of note that explicit expressions of longing for valid religious experience keep appearing among adherents of all cultic groups—obviously an inner-phychic problem. This yearning for Archetypal Contact is, of course, the symbolic expression of a desire for immediate value experience as it may relate to whatever need the subject has. It contributes directly to the personification of the cult leader as a solution god, and is at the same time a problem of prior formulation, to the extent that the doctrines of the background religion have failed to make satisfying connection with the problems of the laity.

So it is that along with healings of the body, and survival maintenance, social problems are solved within the cults either by the intra-mural society, or the proclamation of a new world soon to arrive. Inner-psychic problems are dissolved in the abandonment of selfhood which is structural to the cultic format, through mergence with the archetypal figure. Should they not disappear in the surrender which this entails, a program of devotional exercises will be imposed, that is designed to empty the mind altogether. Finally, problems of prior formulation are burned away by the incandescence of the new revelation, and the bliss of being able to enjoy the living presence of an archetypal figure; for a new age is soon to be ushered in, and the cult leader is the one who has promised to bring it.

(b) *Mergence Is With the Leader, Not the Group*   In the Old Ethnos, each member of the group is totally secure in his relationship to all the others. He belongs to his sept or gens, and its status within the total tribe, its ritual duties and economic functions, are all supernaturally established and guaranteed. The tribe is explicitly regarded as the total society, and his metaphysical rootage in it has a cosmic dimension.[70] The individual is totally merged with *the group*, and the sense of belongingness that he enjoys is never again equalled.

It is this relief from competition, and this kind of blissful membership in what amounts to an extended family, that the convert to a cult is seeking. Thus, the "love bombing" that is practiced by various cultic groups, in which the prospect is overwhelmed with expression of affection and esteem, both verbal and physical, has been enormously successful, as numbers of converts have testified. Probably the extreme instance of this is the "flirty fishing" by female members of the Children of God, who are explicitly urged by "Mo" Berg, the leader, to practice seduction in the quest for more members.

Also, in a less specific way, a sort of easy acceptance, characterized by a feeling of having chanced upon a group of kindred spirits, is an experience common to many of those entering cults. An appeal to supposedly mutual ideals will go along with this; and when we remember how many cultic converts have made their entry as the final phase of the "hippie" syndrome, having run through the drug-and-sex culture, and emerged unwanted at its latter end, the appeal and effectiveness of these tactics are seen even more plainly.

However, this interval of seemingly universal affection is strictly temporary. The new member is shortly assigned to

[70] Cf. Appendix, p. 355f, *infra*, s.v. The Social Metaphysic.

duties that tax his physical endurance to the utmost: i.e., begging in the streets, or selling literature for eighteen or more hours a day: he is required to undertake devotional procedures of meditating, chanting, praying, or memorizing, that empty his mind, and may affect it for a long time if not permanently: he is given a low protein diet that does not contribute to any attitude of resolution, and in all of this, his principal emotional solace is his awareness of the cult leader as a supernatural figure, to whom reverence is due, and to whom these sacrifices are rightfully owed.

Moreover, he is rendered powerless by the early demand that he turn over all his personal possessions and property to the cult, so that any decision to withdraw, should he get so far as to make it, would be extremely difficult to implement.

Most pertinent to our present purpose, however, is the fact, attested by members of various cultic groups, that should he turn to any other member to question any of these exploitative tactics, he will be at once reported, and subjected to highly pressureful and probably guilt producing reproaches, recriminations, and possibly punishments: and should his intended confidant prove sympathetic, he too will be penalized, and effective steps taken to prohibit, or at least minimize, any further contact between the two.

All cult members are explicitly taught to be informers, and each new member will have an older one attached to him as a sort of chaperone or mystagogue, from whom the neophyte cannot separate himself for more than a moment; who keeps up an incessant barrage of doctrinal propaganda, and from whom escape is all but impossible, whether physical or psychic. This surveillance will be continued until the convert gives evidence of his total introjection of the cultic doctrines and practices. The moment when this takes place is the experience that Conway and Siegelman have termed "snapping."[71]

In short, far from being a member of a glowingly affective family of appreciative friends, with whom high level commu-

---

[71] This is the title of their excellent book. N. Y.: Dell Publishing Co., 1979.

nication is available at all times, and whose emotional support is axiomatic, the confirmed cult member is lonely and sick, with total obedience to the whims of the leader his only emotional solace.

(c) A Solution God, Not a Cause-Cure   A third difference between the cultic institution and the Old Ethnos is seen in the character of the deity. The cult leader is essentially a solution god, whereas all deities of the Old Ethnos are of the cause-cure variety.

Even when the problems are those of nature, the cult leader typically personifies their solution, rather than their matrix in the cosmic order, as would be the case with a cause-cure god. This remains true despite whatever protestations he makes as to his merely instrumental status, *vis-a-vis* some larger deity: for the cult leader is viewed as an archetypal figure, and to the extent that this is true, it is as the personification of the solution to the problem with which he and the cult are dealing.

In its role as an intramural society, the cultic institution solves the social and inner-psychic problems of its clientele, and it is an extension of the leader's personality to a greater extent than anywhere else in organized religion, with the possible exception of the earliest stages of a prophetic movement. Moreover, the leader, as repeatedly shown, is viewed by the group as its archetypal head, thereby placing him squarely in the role we are describing.

Finally, problems of prior formulation are either solved in the same way, i.e., in and through the cultic institution, or else reduced to insignificance by the new revelation. Since this is issued by the cult leader, we see that in this capacity he personifies religious solution from yet another perspective.

(d) The Cultic Institution Is Not The Total Society   A fourth difference between the cultic institution and the Old Ethnos, and the final one to which we shall call attention, is so obvious that its mention may seem redundant: viz., the fact that whereas the Old Ethnos is regarded as the totality of the social world by its members, the cult is recognized as a haven of retreat from a larger society: an intra-mural collective, in which

persons of a unique orientation can put their faith into action. Briefly stated, the Old Ethnos is an unchallenged majority that is viewed as a totality, and the cultic institution is a self-conscious minority.

This cultic institution as an intramural society has been carefully described in the context of its being a defining characteristic of religions of this type, and we shall return to it presently, to consider this aspect of cultic religion as an instrument of policy. Suffice it then to say, that while the cultic institution is indubitably a New Ethnos, in the sense of being a return to the primitive, it can only achieve this on the limited basis of an enclave, wherein its adherents gather in some form of protest against a larger, total society, of which they disapprove, but which is nonetheless regarded as altogether real.

c. The Operation of the Institution: Cultic Policy

i. Forced Abandonment of Selfhood   The abandonment of selfhood is not only an inner tendency of the cultic adherent, but an instrument of policy consciously employed by those who operate such institutions, and a requirement relentlessly imposed on all who enter them. It is from this latter perspective that the present discussion proceeds.

The kind of abandonment of selfhood that the adherent has been seeking is for the most part a simple escape from responsibility: he wants "to get out of the rat race." In some cases he is trying to find a form of neurotic non-achievement that is socially acceptable: in others, to find a haven where survival, rehabilitation and acceptance of what he has become are available. Along with the obvious yearning for belongingness and love, there may be a drive to satisfy some urge to idealism, e.g., to withhold cooperation from a society deemed militaristic or exploitative. In each of these situations there is an implied willingness to accept the ego structure of anyone who will provide the thing desired, or, for that matter, the ego-structure itself. In briefer statement, what the prospective adherent desires, is to abandon the practicality function of the ego.

However, the extent of the ego resignation demanded by the cult leader is much more extensive than this, for he demands the abandonment of the basic reality function, which is at the heart of the Secondary Process. He requires the cultic subject to abjure not merely some practicality, but all rationality as well.

These generalizations apply to all cults. Only the techniques of producing this abandonment of critical judgment will vary; the end is the same in all of them: namely, to make the adherent totally amenable to the will of the leader, so that he can be exploited to the latter's advantage. This is plainly seen in the operative procedures of Christian Science and Theosophy. Although the external appearance of these nineteenth century cults is obviously much different from that of the Hare Krishnas, the Moonies, or the Children of God, since in the earlier groups the adherents were free to come and go at their own discretion, and recruiting was in a much lower key than that practiced today, yet the imperative to abandon selfhood was essentially the same, for in order to obtain what the cult purported to supply, i.e., healing in the one, and supernatural insight in the other, rationality certainly had to be abandoned. Any fully committed member was brought to the unquestioning acceptance of doctrines that were completely at variance with those of common sense and science, in the hope of gaining the promised benefits.

The pivotal point in thus gaining control of the prospect's mind is to get him into a state of mergence with the promoter: for in mergence the subject by definition is conscious of no distinction between his own volitions and those of the one with whom he is merged. This obviously constitutes the abandonment of selfhood, and puts him directly into the leader's power.

Now in what we might call legitimate religious experience, such mergence would typically come about by the subject's having had a problem solved: e.g., the restoration of hope through the cosmic promise, a physical healing, the experience of compassion, an extraordinary deliverance from danger, or some massive guilt release. Following such an experience, the subject will typically identify with his benefactor and introject his every wish.

At this point we must remind ourselves that mergence with a validly archetypal figure is not the abandonment of selfhood, but its origination: for such a figure, i.e., a solution god,[72] is at once a symbol of selfhood[73] and of the morality, i.e., the social program, *that such a personification always announces*, whether directly or by implication. Thus the introjection of these elements, otherwise describable as the formation of relationship that follows personification in the basic religious mechanism, is a true energy release, and the restoration if not the actual attainment, of the interpersonal techniques that make up a valid personality structure. It is the enhancement of personality at the very least, and may be its veritable creation.

This is still true when the archetypal figure is a human one, such as Moses, Zoroaster, Gotama, or Jesus: these men were committed to wisdom and liberation, and introjection of their programs could only be the enhancement of selfhood. Each of them had profound communication with the dynamics of his collective unconscious, and their insights were truly symbolic and liberative.

However, mergence with the leader of a cult is an altogether different matter, since he is not the *valid* revelator of any archetypal insight, but is committed rather to deceit and exploitation: a total imposter. Nonetheless, the religious solution is his stock in trade, and with a seeming concern for the religious problem(s) of the prospect, he produces all the numinosity he can, but always in a non-liberative way.

So it is that he begins with the prospect's desire to escape responsibility, and inveigles him into the institution: the tactics employed have been described a few pages earlier. There the

---

[72] Mergence does not occur with the other types of personifications, i.e., problem- and cause-cure gods.

[73] Cf. Edinger, Edw. F., *Ego and Archetype*; N. Y.: Pelican Books, 1973, Pages 64, 65, 70 and 78.

new adherent is not only permitted to retain his neurotic structure, but is affirmed in his effort to do so, by the repudiation of the society outside, where effortful achievement is necessary. Indeed, the neurotic's predilection for shortcuts is another open avenue to the numbing of the subject's judgment of reality; for he is beguiled by the cultic promise of a miracle, contingent only upon the proper mental approach. Finally, he is accorded full acceptance just as he is, without being condemned for present addictions or past failures.

All of these have been religious problems, and their alleviation may well result in the abandonment of selfhood that the leader is seeking to effect, i.e., the convert's mergence with himself. There are, however, further inducements to the same end that can be applied. The prospect may be exposed to a vast religious promise: a new world order to be awaited or worked for, an impending crisis to be averted, a superior status in an after-life to be attained, or the supernatural destruction of his enemies. . . .

The final step in his abandonment of rationality is to accept the cult leader as having some supernatural status. Such a claim may be advanced in various ways: a preferred one is to have one of the hard-core members present it, so that the leader can disclaim it with becoming modesty if this seems advisable. He may, however, proclaim it boldly, as the central fact of his message.

At this point we should note that the conversion experience is always characterized by that of mergence, and that the two become complete at the same moment, since mergence is the relationship the convert forms with a solution god, and is in fact the solution that he attains. However, the two are not identical, inasmuch as mergence also characterizes mystic experience as well as institutional membership, so long as the latter remains vital.

Conversion *per se* is also clearly identical with the experience that Conway and Siegelman have termed "snapping," and have described so well in their excellent book by that name. This experience has been previously described and analyzed in depth by William Sargant in two books: *The Battle for the Mind*, 1957, and *The Mind Possessed*, 1973. In these books, Sargant shows that under the pressure of intense suggestion, torture, group enthusiasm, or other reiterated pressure, there is a moment when the mind reverses itself, or at least surrenders its defenses, so that unbelief gives way to belief, and introjection takes place. This is what Conroy and Siegelman speak of as "snapping": and it is of course the moment of conversion, long since observed in that context. It is also the occasion of complete mergence, and in a cultic setting the subject is subsequently under the power of the organizer.

Once into the institution, and once committed to the idea of the leader's supernatural status, it is the institution's task to solidify and perpetuate these attitudes. It must never be forgotten that the ultimate and irreducible function of a religious institution is the *maintenance of relationship*. So it is that the new convert will presently be subjected to prolonged sessions of orientation, forced to listen constantly to recorded propaganda, to undergo extended periods of "meditation" or chanting, and to endure long sessions of religious excitement, prayer, or some other form of mental pressure designed to immerse him still more deeply into the cultic world view.

Furthermore, he will be subjected to the artificial creation of new religious problems: he may be required to undertake some contrived form of pseudo-therapy aimed at convincing him that he is sexually perverse; and extended sessions of forced confession may instill the belief that he is doctrinally obtuse or deficient in loyalty, all to the end that he can be impelled to labor with piteous intensity, in order to demonstrate his worthiness to be a member of the cult.

In short, from whatever perspective we observe the cultic phenomenon, this cancellation of the adherents' rational judgment is seen as a central instrument of policy.

ii. An Intramural Society As we turn to the intra-mural society as a feature of cultic policy, we again find ourselves in the awkward position of seeming to recapitulate material that has already been covered, and of anticipating material that will be discussed later. Nonetheless, there is a clear distinction in our perspective, as will be apparent.

Also, we might seem to be making statements that are without any foundation in reality, in even talking about the cultic institution as an intra-mural society: for while some groups maintain (or have maintained) enclaves from which escape is at best difficult, (Mormonism, the Moonies, the Children of God, and Love Israel) others have no residential requirements at all (Christian Science, Theosophy) and still others operate on a mail-order basis (Psychiana, Rosicrucianism), with at least some precautions taken by the organizer to keep the members from learning each other's identities. How can they be said to be characterized by an intra-mural society?

Let us address this question first.

The intra-mural society is indeed a fact, even though it may be only a matter of eccentricity of belief or practice. The binding force of a delusive idea, pursued in the hope of relief from some intolerable situation, is incalculably great. People will associate together for the social resonance they afford each other in such expectations as promised healings, communication with the dead, the end of the world, paranormal psychic powers, the advent of a better society, or the assurance of life after death.

Also, people who have made really large contributions to an organization have a vital interest in what goes on in the movement they have subsidized. To the extent that such sacrifices have embarrassed or crippled them financially, their absorption in the movement will be correspondingly more complete.

Then too, as their interest in the cult becomes more intense, their withdrawal of interest from the world outside becomes more pronounced, and their *de facto* membership in an intra-mural society is progressively more apparent. Thus we see that whether the membership of a cult is a tightly regimented strategic force, or simply a fellowship of commitment to the preposterous, its character as an intra-mural society is beyond dispute.

This intra-mural society is an *agency*. When examined as an instrument of cultic policy, it is immediately apparent that the institution has a totally different meaning for the cult leader than it has for the adherent, particularly at the moment when he joins. The latter thinks of it as a utopian retreat, an end in itself, a *desideratum*; but the leader has put it together for its instrumental usefulness to him: initially it facilitates bringing the prospect into mergence with the leader himself, in its beatific nature: subsequently, however, it is the agency of exploitation.

Both of these functions have been outlined already, in one frame of reference or another, hence our recapitulation will be brief.

For the adherent, it both establishes his mergence with the leader, and maintains it. The things it does to accomplish both of these ends are exactly the factors that make up the cultic religious experience: it gives him an environment where he can abandon selfhood and still receive maintenance; it not only accepts him as he is, but gives him a sense of significance, and above all else, it makes available the symbolic impact of association with the leader, who is credited with providing all the other benefits.

The essential function of any religious institution is the maintenance of relationship with the religious symbol, and this the ritual structure of the cult accomplishes by way of all the mind emptying exercises that can be generally subsumed by the word "meditation." And since mergence is accepting the will of the symbolic figure as one's own, the relationship being maintained is willingness to be exploited!

The leader, however, views the intra-mural society from the opposite perspective: for him it is the vehicle of the exploitation which the enamored member has accepted. Thus we see that the religious experiences that the cult supplies are in their inner nature contrived and delusory; and it is the intra-mural society that makes this deception possible, as we have already pointed out.

The institution provides the locale for all else that goes on.

Not only is it an environment where the religious solution can take place, but one where the revelation can be propagated, developed, and improved upon; where the brainwashing of new members can be carried on; where they can be shielded from adverse comments, and their favorable experiences can have resonance. Finally, the intra-mural society constitutes a power structure for the leader, both economic and political, that can be thrown into action at any time.

In those cults which have residential facilities, the exploitation is most complete, for here the New Ethnos is a deployment center, from whence the members can be dispatched on all sorts of tasks: gainful labor, for which the cult collects the (frequently sub-standard) payment; distributing or selling literature, or begging in the streets.

Those who remain at home can be employed at organizational tasks, and all of them can be maintained on a low protein diet, which is not only extremely cheap, but contributes to the collective lethargy and irresolution of the clientele, so that the perpetuation of their religious problems, and consequently their cultic commitment, is practically guaranteed.

d. The Telos of the Institution: Cultic Exploitation

By now the exploitative intent of cultic religion should have been made fully apparent. In what follows we shall try to etch the outlines of its implementation as indelibly as possible.

In the nineteenth century cults, exploitation was for the most part limited to the unethical solicitation of funds, generally under the guise of promoting the movement in which the adherent had become interested. Thus, although Augusta Stetson managed to collect a sizeable fortune in personal gifts, and Mary Baker Eddy used to run elaborate post-Christmas acknowledgements of gratitude in her *Christian Science Journal* for gifts that had never been received at all, thus stimulating a fine flow of charity the following year, it might still be argued that such contributions were nothing more than an index of what the movement had been worth to the contributors. The same judgment can be made of Mme. Blavatsky's tactics, despite her shameless exploitation of human credulity: indeed, once she got to India, the impact of her organization upon that society was probably benign.

However, as we turn to the later cult movements, there is far more to be said. If, as reports have it, Oral Roberts charged three hundred dollars simply for a place in the healing line at his meetings, this is surely preying upon the desperation of some piteous incurable to an unwarranted extent: and when Kathryn Kuhlman strips the indigent aged of their property under the threat of "losing their healings," this is certainly what anyone would mean by exploitation: yet even these practices are innocuous when compared to the sophisticated chicancery of other twentieth century cults.

Missionary activity is one thing, and persuasion to modify belief is a constitutional right; but seductively luring troubled youths into the Moonies from the fringes of counselling centers, chaplains offices and bus stations, with "love bombing" and deceptive promises is something else . . . Female members of the Children of God are overtly urged by Mo Berg to practice actual sexual seduction as a technique for gaining new members; they call it "flirty fishing." An attractive and appealing program is all very well, but systematically engineered conversions are intolerable, no matter who engineers them. Emotional stress, manipulative social arrangements, deception, and actual physical restraint are all documentably included in the list of unethical techniques that present day cults employ to gain converts.

Yet this is only the beginning. Once the conversion is an actuality, there are two goals of cultic policy: first, to make the new member as economically productive as is humanly possible, and second, to keep him from leaving.

In pursuing the first of these objectives, the convert's labor is commandeered to an incredible degree. Whether it be kitchen work, secretarial effort, farm labor, industrial employment, selling literature or other cult produced articles, or simply begging in the streets and around public buildings, they are kept at it for fantastically long hours, and the records of their productivity are startling. Bromley and Shupe estimate that the Moonies average $100 a day on a ten hour basis, begging in airports. In addition to their own experience, which heightens their efficiency as they become streetwise, they are given systematic instruction in the technique of this activity, including an elaborate theological rationale for engaging in it. Such public solicitation has been calculated to bring in twenty-five million dollars a year for the organization.[74]

Nor is public solicitation the only way in which the economic productivity of cult members is exploited; in the early days of his movement, Father Divine would send truckloads of his people out to do stoop labor, and simply collect their wages. The workers received only maintenance, whether their labor was on the cult's own farms, in its restaurants, or in the open market. Admittedly, a cooperative plan of part-time paid labor was introduced for some of the members as the depression wound down. Be this as it may, the Love Israel cult pays its members nothing for kitchen work, and the Moonies pay extremely low wages to the workers in their fish canneries. Sri Rajneesh gives only maintenance to those who work in his various enterprises: the Jehovah's Witnesses are expected to live out of the proceeds of the literature they sell, which is forced onto them on a quota basis, and those who work in the Witnesses' printing plant receive only a pittance above their board and room. The colonists in Jonestown worked twelve hour days, in addition to attending indoctrination sessions at night. *Und so weiter.* . . .

And, of course, the labor of the members is actually the *second line* of their exploitation, although obviously the major one in most cases. The first is their property, which they are persuaded to donate to the cult immediately upon their entry, though it be only a used car and their personal luggage. However, when one adds to this their Social Security cards, savings accounts, insurance policies that can be cashed, and the amounts obtained from an occasional really wealthy client,

---

[74] Bromley and Shupe, *Strange Gods*, 164–72. Cf. also JSSR, Vol. 19:227–233.

Helena Rubenstein in the Meher Baba cult, or Henry Ford III in the Hare Krishnas, the financial dimensions of cultic exploitation begin to appear in their staggering immensity.

However they may pose as world changing movements, centers of deepening spirituality, of some revitalizing trend in society, or some technique for the increase of personal efficiency and power, the fact remains that the cults are the most ruthlessly exploitative of any noncriminal segment of our society.

As we saw in the section on the defining characteristics of cults, the essence of exploitation is the refusal to let the religious issue migrate. Let us look at this again, as it is embodied in the second of the cultic objectives.

During the heyday of a new member's enthusiasm, every effort will be made to get him to make commitments and to become involved in situations that will irrevocably prevent his returning to the social habitat that would have been natural for him. For example, in addition to giving up all his money, he may be influenced to contract a polygamous marriage, as in the Love Israel cult, or to accept an interracial one, arranged by Sun Myung Moon. A female member may be prevailed upon to conceive a child by the cult leader. Overt and explicitly stated rejection of family ties is commonly a prerequisite.

We have seen that those attracted to cultic religion are likely to be persons with weak egos, who are looking for a place where they can stop taking responsibility, but that, upon joining, a total resignation from rationality is demanded of them. This is enforced and brought about by protracted mind bending exercises, which, over and beyond the fixation of their social status at the cultic level, may preclude their ever regaining the normal use of their minds.

This brings us to what may well be the most pernicious of all cultic practices: the brainwashing by which these movements seek to ensure the permanence of their adherents' commitment. However indignantly this term is repudiated by those who favor cultism for one reason or another, it has been shown by Conway and Siegelman, in their book called *Snapping*, and in various articles, that the new cult member is subjected to prolonged sessions of forced indoctrination, sadistic confessional sessions, and a bombardment of misleading or untrue information, such as, Your parents are your enemies, Your mind is your betrayer, The intellect is a bar, or, Ninety percent of those who leave the cult commit suicide. These pressureful techniques of indoctrination are followed by auto-suggestive practices that are mandatory: meditation, chanting, prayer and exercises of concentrating on a picture of the cult leader, some aspect of his teaching, or other mind emptying activities. The result is, as William Sargant has previously shown,[75] and as these authors describe, that the subject sooner or later undergoes an instantaneous "snapping," or personality change, in which he agrees totally with all that has been pushed at him, and which he finds himself unable to discard or surmount, even in the unlikely event of his leaving the cult.

Deprogramming, along psychiatric lines, can restore him to a tentative normalcy upon which he can rebuild his life, but without it, he will slip back into the negation of mental activity, and begin to meditate again, whenever he tries to think, for as long as two or three years after separation from the cultic environment. Along with this inability to think purposefully and with clarity, ex-cultists are troubled by hallucinations, nightmares and a persistent sense of unreality, for months after they have left the cult. Disturbances of perception, memory failures, and periods of depression are also common. Conway and Siegelman refer to this pattern of symptoms as "information disease" and point out that it is caused by the cultic disarrangement of the normal flow of information into the member's mind.[76] Again, these symptoms can be alleviated to some extent by psychotherapy.

We would insist on the legitimacy of the term "brainwashing" as descriptive of these altogether typical practices of cultic orientation. Such usage has been disputed on two

---

[75] *The Mind Possessed*, Penguin Books, 1974, pp. 9–12, *et passim*.
[76] Cf. *Snapping*, p. 164, and *Science Digest*, Jan., 1983, p. 33.

grounds: (1) "Brainwashing" is a pejorative term, and should not be exclusively applied to the conversion-orientation techniques of the newer religions, which admittedly have certain parallels among the more conventional religious organizations; and (2) As used in describing the treatment of Communist prisoners, where the term originated, it connotes prolonged physical abuse, which the subjects cannot escape, until they accede to the doctrines thus presented.

With regard to the first of these objections, it should be plain to anyone that the involuntary imposition of beliefs and attitudes is at best ethically questionable,[77] however, subtly undertaken; and when it is carried on for the benefit of an institution or its promoters, at the expense of the individual member's rational judgment, it is totally repugnant to the moral sense, no matter what the institution is.

As to the second objection, while cult members are not ordinarily subjected to physical coercion, the emotional and social pressures under which they are placed are almost as tangible as though they were: and even physical restraint and abuse are not unknown in the cults. Thus, not only Jim Jones but Mo Berg and Sri Rajneesh have been known to require a recalcitrant member to enter into an unequally arranged "boxing match" covered by some thin pretense of physical education, whereby such a member is beaten into a state of agreement deemed acceptable. So it is that the incessant barrage of propaganda to which the convert must listen is finally introjected: this is our understanding of "snapping"; and when this has taken place, the thinking processes of the subject are influenced almost ineradicably. The term "brainwashing" is thus abundantly justified.

Other exploitative practices only await the investigator's patience to become apparent. Some have already come to our notice. Confessional sessions, aimed at intensifying guilt rather than absolving it; systematic undermining of the member's

---

[77] A possible exception may be made in the case of military training and orientation.

confidence, in order to convince him that he could not survive outside the cult; the instilling of a bizarre and completely aberrant cosmology into ignorant or credulous minds, so as to convince them of the necessity of cultic practices; appeals to neurotic cupidity in selling one series of "lessons" after another, upon the promise of supernatural benefits to be gained; and following this, the false persuasion that such paranormal abilities have in fact been imparted; the limitation of members to a low protein diet that reduces their capacity for any resolute action—all these devices for exploitation are a part of the record.

While it is true that a certain number of those whom the cult tries to convert manage to resist the overtures and get out, yet the ones having the characteristics we have described as typical of the cultic mentality are unlikely ever to leave the movement at all, once they have been given the treatment. Our major contention is thus plainly authenticated: namely, that the entire program of cultic religion is pointed toward exploitation, and that this consists at last in the refusal to let the religious issue migrate, as the problem is solved.

IV. Prospice

Religious experience and religious institutions are thus seen to structure each other. The personifying experience of a revelator is found numinous by a circle of believers, and the institution enshrines and perpetuates the archetypal figure thus revealed, maintaining the relationship of the worshippers with this figure by ritual, myth and morality. As the institution provides this continuing renewal of their contact with the deity, it purveys a certain amount of valid numinosity in its own right. But when orthodox institutions have squandered their numinous potential, and the cults offer nothing but chicanery and deceit, it becomes pertinent to ask, Where do we go from here?

Of course, any answer that we give is speculative, but

speculare means "to see into," and it is possible to give certain *pro forma* suggestions that are not sheer guesswork.

How long existing institutions will last, and in what form, it is certainly impossible to say: but probably longer than we think, although with greatly altered impact. All of the mainline religious institutions in America have gone through the cycle of decay described above. The areas of its manifestations may differ, but the institutional decadence is the same.

The Roman Catholic church continues as a viable economic operation, despite severe losses of its "religious" personnel. It displays many cult-like characteristics, and despite its occasional involvement in economic reform, its commitment to positions that have made the reforms necessary, and to the deployment of power that makes those positions possible, remains unchanged.

A suddenly discovered concern for the lower classes has characterized most of the traditional Protestant denominations throughout the past decade, and their fumbling efforts in this direction, commendable in themselves, have succeeded in alienating numbers of their formerly loyal members about as often as they have either solved religious problems for the underprivileged, or produced statistical gains for the organizations making the effort.

The Episcopal Church has lost itself in trying to incorporate an aura of modernity into its structure without fully understanding why. Methodism is falling apart at the seams. It lost 1,030,128 members in the ten years between 1970 and 1980,[78] and the end is not yet. Exhibiting virtually all the characteristics of decay to which attention has been called in this chapter, it nevertheless remains a formidable power structure, although the constituency it represents has changed. The Presbyterian denomination has embraced an economic radicalism so shrill as to proclaim its sales orientation to anyone with ears to hear. All have fallen into the error of either neglecting or offending their members of long standing, in a belated effort to appeal to the

[78] *United Methodist Reporter*, Dec. 2, 1983.

lower classes. The reforming concerns that they are presently trying to implement cannot be neglected, but to the investigator of numinosity it is clearly apparent that being well adjusted in economic and social areas, as many of the existing members are, is no guarantee that they are without religious problems of their own, occuring at more sophisticated levels, with greater complexity, and felt more keenly than those of people lacking their lifelong commitment to the tradition. The failure to recognize this has been a serious tactical error, for which the mainline churches are paying dearly.

As to the cults, their future is even harder to predict: it is logical to expect that more and more of them will appear, as religious problems proliferate. Currently, the cult-*like* sectarian groups of ultra conservative Christianity are having the strongest success. Some of the cults have died out, quite unnoticed: who hears of Psychiana, the I Am movement, or Daddy Grace today? Probably more will disappear, as their religious issues migrate. Transcendental Meditation is beginning to be a joke, with initiates whimsically citing their utterly secret and supposedly incommunicable mantras at meetings and in print.

On the other hand, some have gone legitimate. Despite the known fact that the movement has a polygamous wing, and considerable evidence that violence has again been employed to gain control of a recently discovered document discrediting its original revelation,[79] Mormonism has become almost respectable, with its exploitative practices only noticed by a few dissidents who have been hurt by them.[80] In the same frame of reference, we see that newspaper references to Christian Science carry the same tone of respect that is accorded the Southern Baptists.

Then too, there is a kind of weary tolerance extended to all the cults, accompanied by a certain tendency to apologize for them. This is evidenced by James Richardson's article pub-

[79] Warren, Ohio, *Tribune-Chronicle*, Oct. 20, 1985, p. 24: Youngstown, Ohio, *Vindicator*, Oct. 21, 1985, p. 15, quoting from the Salt Lake *Tribune*. Cf. *Time*, Nov. 18, 1985, p. 85.
[80] C. B. S. "Sixty Minutes," Dec. 9, 1969.

lished in the *Journal For The Scientific Study Of Religion*, which attempted to draw sharp distinction between the People's Temple and other "new religions."[81] While it goes without saying that no other cult has produced nine hundred suicides, yet in this writer's judgment, the differences between the Jim Jones cult and all the others are entirely quantitative. Be this as it may, the Jehovah's Witnesses are now regarded as merely an excusable nuisance; Spiritualism as an amiable eccentricity, and the Moonies are referred to as a "church," which received harsh treatment when "Rev." Moon was convicted of income tax fraud.

In short, there seems to be a general decay of valid idealism, or perhaps of the ability to discern its source; and in this moral twilight, the cults are given a kind of acceptance, as though the public was afraid it might overlook some source of benefit.

But what of numinosity in all this? All we can say is, that as, if and when some widespread religious problem arises, it is psychologically sound to expect that another new revelation will appear, which will once more gain wide acceptance. Of course, this too will cycle out as others have before it, in the sequence we have described in the foregoing pages. Who will convey the revelation, and what will be its content are alike impossible to predict, although we can outline the prophetic personality to some extent: viz., a member of the upper classes, who is thus able to see what a good society should be, and what is wrong with the present one; a man of religious life, and one who has had prolonged adversity. But who he will be, what the distress to which he will speak, and what the content of his revelation, are equally unknowable.

However, the release of energy that comes when a subject personifies the solution to a religious problem, and then forms the appropriate relationship with the archetypal figure thus made conscious is an ineradicable human mechanism. The personification is of course autistic and involuntary, and the

[81] "People's Temple And Jonestown," *Journal For The Scientific Study Of Religion*, Sept. 1980, (vol. 19:3) pp. 239–255.

energy enters consciousness, along with the archetypal figure that structures it, on a tide of numinosity.

Such is religious revelation, and there is no reason to suppose that it will not occur again and again, as often as humanity requires it, *per saecula saeculorum.*

December 6, 1983

Appendix

As we have come to understand it, there are exactly four types of religious institutions. These we have termed the Ethnic, Prophetic, Pseudo-Ethnic, and Cultic. A fifth variety, the Sectarian, is actually a sub-varient of the Prophetic.

I. Ethnic Religions

Ethnic religions comprise those groups which are commonly spoken of as primitive, and, as the term suggests, they are typically *tribal* religions. Their outstanding characteristics we have termed the *Magic Formula* and the *Social Metaphysic*. We must explain these terms.

The *Magic Formula* consists of the totality of rituals by which the religious establishment deals with whatever problems are central to the tribe. These problems pertain in general to nature: such problems include the assurance of a food supply, those of health or survival, and war. Thus the ritual will deal with bringing rain, making sure game returns, or that the grain sprouts: with fertility of man and beast, and with healings and the aversion of disease. Problems not occurring in the environment are not reflected in the rituals, and no provision is made for sporadic or occasional disasters—earthquakes, tornadoes, and tidal waves. The number of problems to which a single ethnic religion is addressed is always very limited.

War, when it occurs involuntarily, is met exactly like any other problem of nature. When it is voluntarily undertaken, it is a matter of practicality, and has the same status religiously that the planting of a crop would have, so that the rituals attending its beginning simply deal with the margins of luck, as do those of planting, or of launching a boat.

It is commonly understood within the Ethnic milieu that when these rituals are performed correctly, their efficacy is automatic, and that they are able to deal magically with the problem to which they are addressd—to ensure adequate rainfall, to make certain that the buffalo will come back; to heal the sick, to ward off plagues, or to bring either victory or peace out of warfare. Thus we speak of the ritual structure in its entirety as the Magic Formula. However, despite the mechanistic efficacy of the Magic Formula, which is popularly accepted throughout the tribe, the rituals comprising it are dynamized by a precatory core. The highest ranking members of the ritual group involved will be in retreat while the ceremonies are going on, unfeignedly imploring the gods to make this ritual work!

Curiously, a Magic Formula can be relatively ineffective without being discredited. However, if it fails totally, i.e., if the natural forces upon which life depends, and which it purports to control, become completely hostile, the tribe will become extinct.

The Social Metaphysic is the ranking of prestige within an Ethnic social complex, in terms of the importance of each member's ritual function, within the Magic Formula, *or* in terms of his ease of access to persons having such essential functions. This calculation of social importance in terms of ritual centrality is a vital aspect of theology in an Ethnic society. The referent of this system of ranking is the total society, and it should go without saying that the social positions thus assigned are regarded as supernaturally authenticated. Also, keeping track of all the gradations of social prestige by which its members are affected makes an Ethnic society socially erudite, and more socially sensitive than it will ever be again.

Thus: Have you had an unusually lucky hunt, so that you can make gifts which will elevate you into an honor society? Has your daughter married a grandson of the *pekwin* (the sun priest, in Zuni . . .)? Or is your father near death, making it obligatory for you to become a rain priest? The subject's social status is open to notable change in every case mentioned, and he knows exactly what it will be, following each possible alteration.

Ethnic religions reflect the basic mechanisms of religion with little modification; they do not have personal founders, although they frequently incorporate major insights that have been numinously received by trusted members. Speculation as to origin is always hazardous, but Ethnic systems seem to represent the compilation of all the random religious impressions that have appeared among the clientele: assembled, and to some extent systematized, by whatever personality has assumed responsibility for the ritual, at some hypothetical beginning of things.[1]

The problems of nature with which Ethnic religions are concerned are socially approached, i.e., by the ritual activity of the entire group, with due allowance for necessary specialization. Also, they are problems which affect the entire tribe: the individual *per se* has only a rudimentary existence in the Ethnic situation, although opportunities for obtaining personal distinction are by no means lacking. What we mean is, that the individual is unable to think of himself in any frame of reference other than his membership in the group.

Apparent exceptions to the above statement are to be found in certain healing rituals, notably among the Zuni. However, the healing function there is carried on by "curing societies," each society in charge of a definite group of maladies, and it is unclear whether the rituals of such a group may not be addressed as much to expelling a single instance of evil from the tribe, as to curing a single member. The Eskimo rituals of healing by forced confession are well-known, as reported by Rasmussen, and here the entire tribe takes part, albeit in the interest of a single individual.

Nonetheless, our generalization can stand: that the problems

[1] Cf. Radin, Paul, chapter on "The Role of the Formulator," in his *Primitive Religion*.

of nature with which Ethnic religions are concerned, are in the main social in their scope, and are dealt with by action of the entire society. This statement will serve any investigator as a useful point of departure.

Since all problems of vital concern to the tribe are dealt with by the Magic Formula, a group dominated by an Ethnic religious institution is *scientifically static*, although not absolutely so, since new techniques, valuable to the survival process, can eventually find their way into use by becoming part of the ritual structure.

Members of an Ethnic complex are for the most part born into it. The notion of conversion is somehow inapplicable to religions of this type, although they may be entered by initiation. This gives access both to the social life of the group and to its gods, which are definitely limited to the group itself. However, full participation in an Ethnic complex is like residency in a small town: one may own property there, pay taxes on it, and sleep there every night, but he doesn't really *belong* until it makes him cry inside to read the names on the war monument.

The gods of an Ethnic religion are for the most part cause-cure deities, with a few residual problem gods lurking about as devils, or, what is more likely, as demons. Thus the relationship sought with them is commonly the arrangement of a satisfactory bargain: sacrifice is accordingly very prominent at this stage of religious development. Such problem gods as remain are, of course, dealt with apotropaically by rituals developed for the purpose.

Mergence is prominent in the Ethnic situation, and might indeed be termed its most outstanding feature: but it is not with the gods. Rather, the social group is the entity into which the individual is immersed, with a mergence that can only be likened to the union of an exploratory mystic with the Reality which at last engulfs him. If the reader wishes to argue that mergence with the gods of an Ethnic group does indeed occur, but indirectly, we shall not dispute him.

The morality of an Ethnic group is completely included in its rituals. If the various ritual occasions are observed, and their requirements met, there is no moral remainder, for nothing outside of this all-inclusive structure is a moral issue. Not only is this ritual morality prescriptive, but the ritual duties prescribed are, of course, social, to be undertaken for social ends, i.e., ends beneficial to the entire tribe.

The ritual group, i.e., the group involved in the performance of these ceremonies, includes the total society, since sooner or later all members of the complex participate in them.

It is possible for an Ethnic religion to grow to enormous size by the same process which was cited as bringing it to discernible existence in the first place—namely, the assimilation into itself of whatever generally related religious material comes into contact with it. This necessarily involves a complexity which need puzzle the investigator only in the matter of definition, inasmuch as the expanded complex now deals with a great number of problems, instead of the one or two that are prototypical, and may come to reach international size, instead of being merely tribal. Nonetheless, if we examine the local manifestations of such a religion at any place where it is found, we will discover the two essential characteristics which identify it as Ethnic—a Magic Formula and a Social Metaphysic.

Hinduism is a case in point. Although it is so vast, and so diverse that it hardly fits many of the statements we have made about Ethnic religion, its primary problems are those of nature, and it is held together and given unity by its Social Metaphysic, which is the Caste system. The philosophical overtones by which it is haunted represent either the theological exposition of this social doctrine, and of the notion of Karma, by which it is backed, or the efforts of later thinkers to circumvent the effects of this same Karma, by somehow taking thought.[2]

II. Prophetic Religions

Although Prophetic religions may come into existence at any time, the typical moment of their origin is when an Ethnic religion has collapsed. This occurs when the Social Metaphysic

---

[2] The natural dread of the multiplicity of existences which are produced by Karma is a prime illustration of a problem of prior formulation, as discussed in Part One, V, B, 4, page 23f, and Part Three, III, C, 4, d, pages 186–200.

has either become too strong, permitting abuses to creep in, on the part of those who administer it, or too weak, so that it is no longer meaningful. The first situation is illustrated by the rise of Buddhism, as a protest against the spread of Brahmanism, and the second by the appearance of the Ghost Dance, at a time when the religions of several Plains Indian tribes had all failed at once.

Prophetic religions rise out of the revelatory experience of *personal founders*, and are primarily concerned with *social problems*. The gods worshipped are *solution gods*, personifying the answer or solution to the problem of social chaos out of which the prophet rises, and to which he speaks.[3] Such an archetypal figure will either be entirely new, or, if the modification of an earlier deity, will exhibit radically new and original features.

Members of a Prophetic religion become such by *joining* it. In the early stages of a Prophetic movement, before the group has been institutionally structured, this may be an informal event, but is always a significant one, because (1) the Prophetic message is inevitably subversive of the background religion, and (2) nothing less than complete acceptance of the Solution-god and his message, as presented by the prophet, will suffice for entrance. Indeed, no one *could* want to join the forlorn and often persecuted minority that comprises such a religion at its outset, apart from a total conversion experience, in which the archetypal figure assumes personal reality for him. However, the symbolic impact of such a figure is so great, by reason of what he promises, and his ability to promise it, that converts abound.

The conversion experience itself merits a brief review here. In it, the religious subject finds the solution to his own problem in the Archetypal figure that the prophet proclaims. This takes place with such immediacy and vividness (symbolic impact) as to trigger the basic religious mechanism of personification-and-relationship; which is to say that the subject finds the Archetypal figure *personally* real, and, without reserve, seeks the

[3] The terms Prophet and Originative Mystic are synonymous.

appropriate relationship with what is now Him instead of "it." Since the solution is the aspect of the problem personified, the ensuing relationship is *mergence*, and as he enters it, his religious problem is completely solved. All of this process has been considered at length, in the appropriate sections above.

The revelation that the prophet receives and proclaims may vary in its details according to time and place, but it always is structured around two elements—the promise of an Ideal Society, presently to be supernaturally established on earth by the Solution-god, and a New Morality, which is immediately enjoined upon those to whom the revelation comes, which will be the rule of life in the Ideal Society, and is indeed its definition.

This morality is altogether individual, and is a matter over and beyond such ritual requirements as the new religion may include. Even in the very early Prophetic religions, their moral codes reveal ethical insights that are surprisingly lofty, and the reference is always to the responsibilities of the individual, although its ends are socially oriented, i.e., altruistic, with a commitment to mutual aid. Its basic thrust is always an attack upon problems that are felt throughout the society, and are of the religious dimension: hitherto insoluble, of vital importance, and so intense as to be intolerable. This applicability, combined with the arresting originality of its insights, ensures its ready acceptance.

Moreover, the coming of the Ideal Society is always related in some way to the sincerity with which the New Morality is undertaken, or to the extent of its adoption. Its practice is thus a negative condition of the Ideal Society, for until it is generally put into effect, the new world will not come. We might put it into a formula by saying, "In a Prophetic religion, the world is not saved *for* you, but *by* you."

Other than this one condition, however, the arrival of the Ideal Society is strictly at the will of the deity, and its prediction is always against all probability. In this respect Prophetic religion differs diametrically from the Ethnic type, which is always careful to make no claim that it has not already proven able to deliver. Yet this radical promise of a better world, proclaimed in the face of all likelihood, and contrary to every rational indication, is what the converts find most appealing.

These two features—a Cosmic Promise and a New Morality—will be found to characterize all Prophetic religions. While it may be necessary to look closely to find them, and they may appear in strange guises, they are always present.

The foregoing discussion of the individual quality of its morality leads us naturally to another outstanding characteristic of Prophetic religion, namely the prominence of personal individuality among the members of such institutions. Indeed, a strong case can be made for arguing that Prophetic religion is the creator of this highly important psychic phenomenon.

There are three factors contributing to this situation.

1. In order to join the Prophetic group, the religious subject must, of necessity, break free of the Old Ethnos, or what remains of it. This is a serious, and indeed, a desperate move; for although the Ethnic religion is now moribund, it is still the matrix of the individual's life, and more than that, of his most sacred values. Nothing short of the tremendous archetypal attraction of the new revelation could impel him to make this move, which apart from mere nostalgia, is bound to leave him exposed to superstitious terrors at which we can only guess. However, once he has taken such a step, he is unlikely ever again to fear standing alone on any issue, or to hesitate at making a painful decision.

2. Nor is this all. Having accepted the Solution-god, he completes the religious mechanism by moving into the relationship of mergence with him, which is, by all reports, blissful. Furthermore, beyond euphoria, he now views the world from the point of view of the god, with whom he feels himself at one, so that his psychic independence is guaranteed by a sense of divine upholding, and his traumatic separation from the past is again beatified by this new certainty.

3. The new individuality which the subject has gained by leaving an old (Ethnic) and embracing a new (Prophetic)

religion, and experiencing the swing from panic to rapture that goes with it, does not end in a mere gush of emotion. Merged as he is with the god, he is at one with the divine imperative to practice the morality. This involves incessant decision-making of the most difficult kind; and as he implements this inner drive for subjective perfection and fraternal compassion, the capacities of the human personality for individually motivated action are revealed with a clarity unknown in any other situation.

An interesting facet of Prophetic religion is the absence of any Social Metaphysic for the present world. We do not expect a Magic Formula, since the problems dealt with are different (society instead of nature), but it is with a sense of bemused acknowledgement that we realize that the only order of prestige Prophetic religions are interested in is that pertaining to the Ideal Society. It is a *future* Metaphysic, outlining the positions members will occupy there, and it is determined altogether by the faithfulness with which each one has observed the New Morality.

The *ritual group* of a Prophetic religion includes the entire collectivity. This does not mean the total society, as the membership is limited to the number of converts who have separated themselves from society at large, to await the coming of the Ideal Society.

As we have already indicated in various contexts, *mergence* in a Prophetic religion is with the Solution-god. While the fellowship of believers is very close, and is characterized by a deep mutual affection that approximates mergence, nonetheless, this is secondary to the mergence of the converts with the Archetypal figure who personifies it all.

III. Pseudo-Ethnic Religion

A Pseudo-Ethnic religion is essentially a Prophetic religion that has had wide success, and then fallen into obsolescence. The form such decadence takes is the Pseudo-Ethnic situation. Its process and the factors leading to it have been discussed in

Section III of Part Four. In what follows, we seek to outline the characteristics of what we have come to understand as a definite stage of institutional development, evident in many places, but generally unremarked.

As our term indicates, a Pseudo-Ethnic religion is one that has assumed, however spuriously, certain characteristics of the Ethnic situation. This may well begin when, in the furore of great success, the Prophetic religion assumes temporal authority, which is inevitably accompanied by a social metaphysic; but the referent of such an ordering of society is neither the supposed social importance of benefits generated by the individual's ritual function, as in the original Ethnic situation, nor his faithfulness to the morality of mutual aid, with reference to a future Ideal Society, as in Prophetic religion, but rather, the extent of his institutional involvement as being the key to his respectability in the here and now.

This however, convinces very few people apart from a small cadre of those who stand to profit from institutional success, and the society as a whole is left without any conclusive pronouncement regarding the social importance of individual members.

As we have shown in Part Four, the Prophetic institution is largely the product of promoters who manage to derive the authority for their organizational strategies from the mythos, by giving it their own interpretation, and by expanding it, which is, of course, the theological enterprise. This succeeds until the institution gains acceptance throughout the total society.

However, the hope of the coming of the Ideal Society has meanwhile dwindled to little more than rhetoric, and the institution accordingly finds itself in a position of tremendous social power, but with no real religious dynamic, which is to say, no valid authentication. Pseudo-Ethnic religion can be understood as the reaction of the once-Prophetic institution to this situation.

Before going farther, one clarification must be made. The parallels which we point out between religious institutions at this stage of decay, and those of primitive societies, are in no way consciously sought, but are rather symptomatic of the persistence of unconscious mechanisms, and the universal human gravitation toward archetypal patterns.

Of course, the various strategies which the institution adopts in its struggle for survival, and which we have described, are indeed undertaken by its leadership in fullest consciousness, as supposedly effective promotional techniques, but not as parallels to some primitive type of religion.

The most salient feature of the Pseudo-Ethnic situation is the institution's claim that it *is* the Ideal Society. This gives some authenticity to its attempt to assign social importance, as the religious institution does in the Old Ethnos. Again, it shows similarity to the original Ethnic situation, in that the institution *no longer has to be joined by conversion*: members are to all intents *born into it*, and are given some simple rite of initiation at the appropriate time.

However, the parallel breaks off abruptly, for *there is no mergence with the institution* in the Pseudo-Ethnic situation. Indeed, there is no mergence at all at this stage, for the (formerly) Archetypal figure has lost all symbolic impact, and outside of the institution's own rituals, is hardly mentioned except on ceremonial occasions. The individual is free to take the institution seriously or not; and while its power to control his destiny may be considerable, he frequently has small respect for it.

This is true because it solves no religious problems except a very few of its own choosing: notably, the foregiveness of hypothetical "sins," particularly the removal of some supposititious metaphysical taint held to be innate, so that the individual is enabled to embark upon the quest for immortality, which is held to be his only true and proper destiny. Since interest in these matters is limited at best to persons of a certain type, the institution is frequently without any real function. More than this, it is itself felt as a problem, by reason of its stress upon a negative or artificial morality, and an archaic cosmology.

It is thus entirely logical that numbers of people find selfhood burdensome under these conditions, and are ready to abandon it in the cults.

For all these reasons, the Pseudo-Ethnic institution tries hard to *produce* numinous experience, and in this effort slips back into an involvement with problems of nature, beginning with healings, and going on to the pretended control of nature in other areas. These problems, traditionally the province of Old Ethnic religions, have all but migrated off the religious stage by this time, as the advance of science brings more and more areas under control. However, despite the attraction which institutions of this type feel for problems of nature, Pseudo-Ethnic religions have no Magic Formula.

In addition to this contrived and anomalous interest in problems of nature, Pseudo-Ethnic religion will be seen to do anything possible to prevent religious issues from migrating, so that the institution can continue to "solve" them in traditional ways. Also, leaders of such an institution will deliberately make the members guilty, so that the institution can gain function by absolving them, or, even more deplorably, by manipulating their behavior in this way, in default of more obvious and physical methods of coercion. In short, whatever be the institutional attempts to gain function, our earlier statement stands: that apart from these ruses and pretexts, Pseudo-Ethnic religion solves few real problems.

The morality of a Pseudo-Ethnic religion resembles that of its primitive prototype in that it is almost prescriptive. However, its basic thrust is institutional conformity, and its professed goal is to prepare the individual for entry into an after-life; whereas that of Old Ethnic religions is to maintain adjustment to the order of nature. Also, it may be characterized as individual, for individual ends, and is thus seen to contrast sharply with that of the Old Ethnos, which is social, for social ends. Prophetic morality can be described as individual, for social ends. Then too, Pseudo-Ethnic morality may have a negative dimension, forbidding constructive activities such as contraception, the killing of vermin, or the acceptance of blood transfusions, and requiring acts or practices that are valueless or inimical to the individuals, viz., eccentricities of diet and dress, or physical mutilations.

Although Pseudo-Ethnic religion is actually a general state of religious obsolescence, it is still best understood as the shape a declining Prophetic religion takes as its leaders try to make it appear sociologically autonomous, psychologically inevitable, and metaphysically structural.

IV. Cultic Religion

Since cultic religion is fully discussed in Section III.G. of Part Four, we shall make our outline of it here as brief as possible.

Religions of this type come into being in the religious vacuum of the Pseudo-Ethnic situation. Their defining characteristics are, (1) An insincere founder, who views the organization from a completely different perspective from that of the members; (2) A new "revelation," propounded by this founder, which purports to make available some supernatural solution to problems common to the membership; (3) An intra-mural society; (4) Abandonment of selfhood on the part of the clientele; and (5) a telos of exploitation, defined as the refusal to let religious issues migrate, but exemplified in all possible ways.

All types of problems are dealt with in the cults, although any given group will address its efforts to solving a single one, or a very limited number. Problems of nature are prominent. Mergence is with the cult leader, who is regarded as a solution god, and the order of social importance within each group is judged by the member's closeness to him.

Each cult is a New Ethnos: it will have some kind of Magic Formula, which, administered by the leader, imparts a sense of being in the presence of a supernatural force or forces. The similarity of cultic religion to Ethnic is heightened by the intra-mural aspect of its organization, but is limited, in turn, by the fact that the cultic group is in no sense the total society.

Robertson, Robin

C.G. JUNG AND THE ARCHETYPES OF THE COLLECTIVE UNCONSCIOUS

New York, Berne, Frankfurt/M., 1987. XXII, 250 pp.
American University Studies: Series 8, Psychology. Vol. 7
ISBN 0-8204-0395-4   hardback $ 30.50/sFr. 46.–

The author presents a stimulating panorama of Jung's psychology, and shows how accurately it corresponds to the strange world described by twentieth-century scientists in fields other than psychology. He traces the development of the concept of the archetypes of the collective unconscious from the dawn of the scientific method in the Renaissance to twentieth-century mathematician Kurt Gödel's proof of the limits of science. Robertson's presentation of Jung's psychology is the most complete to date, treating it as a connected whole, from the early experimental studies to the final work using alchemy as a model of posychological dynamics.

Contents: A panorama of Jung's psychology, tracing a history of ideas from the Renaissance to 20th century mathematics – For both the intelligent general reader and the specialist on Jung.

 PETER LANG PUBLISHING, INC.
62 West 45th Street
USA – New York, NY 10036

Damico, Linda Hope

THE ANARCHIST DIMENSION OF LIBERATION THEOLOGY

New York, Berne, Frankfurt/M., 1987. XII, 213 pp.
American University Studies: Series 7, Theology and Religion. Vol. 28
ISBN 0-8204-0443-8   hardback $ 32.50/sFr. 49.–

While other studies of liberation theology have shown a close connection to Marxism, none have probed its anarchist dimension. This original study reveals that in many of the most prominent themes of Latin American liberation theology there are close parallels to the ideas found in nineteenth-century European anarchism. These themes include an ethical concern with freedom, justice, equality and love; a denunciation of political and economic structures of domination; an emphasis on action; a championing of all oppressed people; a realistic consideration of the issue of violence; and the vision of a future free from servitude. These common concerns, along with historical connections to both religious and secular anarchist sources, show a revolutionary theology deeply indebted to its anarchist roots.

Contents: This is an original work showing parallel themes in Latin American liberation theology and nineteenth-century European anarchism – While many works have focused on the Marxist aspect of liberation theology, this is the first work to show that liberation theology also has a significant anarchist dimension – Academic level – college and university, graduate and undergraduate.

 PETER LANG PUBLISHING, INC.
62 West 45th Street
USA – New York, NY 10036

Mitchell, Lynn E., Jr.

THE VISION OF THE NEW COMMUNITY
Public Ethics in the Light of Christian Eschatology

New York, Berne, Frankfurt/M., Paris, 1988. 213 pp.
American University Studies: Series 7, Theology and Religion. Vol. 29
ISBN 0-8204-0450-0   hardback $ 37.–/sFr. 50.–

A major concern for Christian theology is the tension created by the «already» and «not yet» aspects of Christian eschatology. This study seeks to characterize the nature of that tension as it has been interpreted in the Biblical materials and in selected representatives of the history of Christian theology. The study then suggests the implications of eschatological tension for a Christian approach to a public ethic; i.e., an ethic for a pluralistic, natural community.

Contents: Analysis of the problem of eschatological dualism in the New Testament and in selected post-Biblical representatives – Implications for development of a public ethic.

«...Professor Mitchell's study, in my opinion, is carefully crafted, original in construction, and suggestive for future study of the perennial problem of the conflict between theological vision and mundane reality.» (James Sellers, David Rice Professor of Ethics, Rice University)

«...Dr. Mitchell's writing illumines the theme of eschatology in a manysided way while giving it contemporary relevance. He offers a significant thesis in his description of two communities rather than two kingdoms, appropriating materials from Karl Barth, for example in a very balanced and critical manner.» (Niels C. Nielsen, Jr., Rayzor Professor of Philosophy and Religious Thougt, Rice University)

 PETER LANG PUBLISHING, INC.
62 West 45th Street
USA – New York, NY 10036

DATE DUE

JUN 28 1997			
DEC 29 2000			